Carlson's Raid

Carlson's Raid

The Daring Marine Assault on Makin

George W. Smith

PRESIDIO

To my girls: Mary Ellen, who never doubted my abilities,
and Anna, a computer whiz who made the task so much easier

Published by Presidio Press, Inc.
505 B San Marin Drive, Suite 160
Novato, CA 94945-1340

ISBN 0-89141-744-3

Printed in the United States of America

Contents

Rank has no privileges, only responsibilities
—Evans Fordyce Carlson

Preface

On the morning of December 7, 1941, the United States was dealt a swift and staggering sucker punch at Pearl Harbor in Hawaii, one that catapulted a reluctant and ill-prepared nation into total war against the Empire of Japan.

The Japanese also launched air assaults that same Sunday morning at Midway, Wake Island, Guam, and the Philippines, but it was the devastating sneak attack at Pearl Harbor and the 3,500 Americans killed and wounded that enraged the nation and caused a near panic in Hawaii and on the west coast of the mainland.

The Japanese achieved complete surprise at Pearl Harbor, launching a total of 350 warplanes in two waves from six carriers stationed just over two hundred miles to the northwest of Oahu. The first wave swept in from the west over the jewel-green checkerboard of Oahu's cane fields and pineapple plantations and then turned along the southern edge of the island over Pearl Harbor shortly before 8:00 A.M. The first flight consisted of 51 dive bombers, 43 Zero fighters, 40 torpedo planes, and 49 high-level bombers. A second wave, which also struck other airfields and port facilities on Oahu, consisted of 78 dive bombers, 35 fighters, and 54 high-level bombers. That wave swept over the island an hour and forty-five minutes later.

When the smoke cleared and all the shooting had stopped, a total of eighteen U.S. warships had been sunk or seriously damaged, including all eight battleships anchored at Pearl Harbor. The *Arizona* suffered a fatal blow, the *Oklahoma* was capsized, her twisted superstructure lying on the harbor bottom. The *California* was ablaze and listing to port, the *West Virginia* was struck by two torpedoes and had settled into shallow water at her mooring, and the *Nevada*, at the rear of Battleship Row, had struggled to get under way only to be run aground to keep her from sinking and blocking the shallow waters of the harbor. The *Pennsylvania, Maryland,* and *Tennessee* suffered lesser damage and were eventually repaired.

At Wheeler Field, explosions and strafing runs tore apart the rows of parked fighters. On Ford Island, bombs plastered the flying-boat slips. Along Battleship Row, the forenoon watch had just been piped to breakfast. Smartly drilled color parties were lined up on the fantails awaiting the bugler to signal the hour to break out ensigns. But the calls were abruptly drowned by the rattle of machine-gun fire, the whistle of falling bombs, and the sickening "crump" of torpedo explosions.

The *Arizona* erupted in a volcanic sheet of flame. It was a total loss. A "lucky" Japanese bomb had found its way to the boiler room, setting off a vast amount of gunpowder stored in the forward magazine. The ship, which had its spine broken, foundered in nine minutes and burned for two and a half days. A total of 1,177 men perished aboard the *Arizona,* including thirty-six sets of brothers and one father-and-son tandem. It could have been worse. Four of the sets of brothers had a third brother aboard who survived the attack.

"It was a dead sound, like a big swish of wind going through foliage," one witness said of the destruction of the *Arizona.* The heat from the burning ship was so intense that the crew of the *Nevada,* who were frantically trying to guide their vessel through the harbor, had to shield their stores of ammunition with their bodies until they had passed her. As the *Arizona* settled into its watery grave, it came to rest directly atop the main that supplied Ford Island with fresh water, severing the pipes.

Six torpedoes below the waterline had ripped open *Oklahoma*'s port side. She turned turtle within minutes, entombing more than four hundred crew members.

A rescue party was put aboard the *Oklahoma* within minutes of the attack, but there was little they could do.

"I was terribly afraid," seaman Joseph Hydurskia told a reporter. "We were cutting through with acetylene torches. First we found six naked men waist deep in water. They didn't know how long they had been down there and they were crying and moaning with pain. Some of them were very badly wounded. We could hear tapping all over the ship, SOS taps, no voices, just those eerie taps from all over. There was nothing we could do for most of them."

The U.S. also lost 188 planes on Oahu, 96 army and 92 navy, which was more than half the aircraft of the Pacific Fleet. Most of the losses occurred on the ground, where the planes had been conveniently parked in tight clusters, wing tip to wing tip, as a measure to guard against enemy saboteurs. Many of the destroyed planes were obsolescent types such as the Curtis P-36 fighter.

Just as the second wave swept over Oahu, an unarmed flight of American B-17s from the mainland arrived after a fourteen-hour trip. Low on fuel, they had to scramble for their lives. Several were shot down and others crash-landed amid the wreckage scattered on the runways of Wheeler and Hickam Fields.

The Japanese had 29 of their aircraft shot down in the raid, 20 of them during the second wave when American gunners had finally been supplied with ammunition and began to find the range.

Pearl Harbor was awash in flotsam and human bodies. Metallic debris and severed limbs were thrown into the air by the explosions and rained down upon nearby ships and buildings. The waters were a mass of bobbing, oil-covered heads. Hundreds of men were splashing about in the thick, greasy water trying to avoid the burning oil and reach safety. Others were motionless or trapped below in the holds of sinking ships. Sixty percent of the casualties were due to burns. The deep, husky sounds of explosions echoed off the nearby hills while the mustard-colored warplanes with red suns on their wing tips kept on coming and coming through the smoke and fires created by the aircraft that preceded them.

The surprised Americans offered little resistance to the first wave. Hardly a shot was fired in retaliation and not a single American plane got off the ground. There were few antiaircraft guns available because those in charge had assumed they wouldn't be needed. To make matters worse, most of the antiaircraft shells were locked up in a warehouse, so virtually all of the defensive firing came from pistols, rifles, or machine guns.

As bad as the damage was, however, it could have been much worse. All three carriers of the Pacific Fleet were away from Pearl on December 7. The *Enterprise* and *Lexington* were at sea to the west and the *Saratoga* was undergoing repairs in San Diego. Had the three carriers been moored at Pearl that fateful morning, a major disaster would have become a national calamity. The Japanese, by declining to launch a third wave, left virtually untouched a 4.5-million-gallon gasoline tank farm, the destruction of which might have caused the evacuation of Hawaii and added as much as two years to the ensuing war, according to military historians.

The Japanese had also failed to destroy Pearl Harbor's shore installations, submarine pens, repair facilities, docks, ammunition depots, machine shops, power plant, and the Honolulu telephone exchange. Logistically speaking, Pearl was not as severely damaged as first thought. Thanks to Pearl's shallow waters most of the damaged ships proved salvageable. The battleships *Pennsylvania, Maryland,* and *Tennessee* were quickly repaired and ready to return to action by December 20.

Admiral Husband Kimmel, commander of the Pacific Fleet, rushed out of his quarters and was mesmerized by the destruction going on all around him.

"I knew right away that something terrible was going on, that this was not a casual raid by just a few stray planes," Kimmel said later.

A half hour later while looking over the scene at Pearl Harbor from his office, a spent bullet crashed through a window and struck the left breast of Kimmel's white uniform. It hit his glasses case and fell to the floor. He picked up the bullet, put it in his pocket, and is said to have uttered, "It would have been merciful had it killed me." Moments later, a stunned Kimmel went into an adjoining room and replaced his four-star shoulder boards with boards that displayed two stars. By his own action, he had demoted himself from his temporary rank of full admiral to rear admiral. He knew then that his career was over. It was the old naval principle that defeated admirals were expected to go down with the ship.

When VAdm. William F. "Bull" Halsey's *Enterprise* task force arrived back at Pearl later that day after delivering a dozen Marine fighter pilots in Grumman Wildcats to Wake Island, the pugnacious Halsey surveyed the wreckage and told his chief of staff, "Before we're through with 'em, the Japanese language will be spoken only in hell."

Halsey's *Enterprise* task force was supposed to have arrived back at Pearl on December 6 but was held up by bad weather that prolonged refueling. Some of the men grumbled at the delay. They had plans for Saturday night in Honolulu and Pearl City. The *Enterprise* was 200 miles from Pearl at the time of the attack and had five of its planes shot down trying to land at airfields on the island, one by friendly fire and four by the Japanese. The *Lexington* task force, which included three cruisers and five destroyers, was also headed back to Pearl that morning from a resupply mission to Midway, but was more than 500 miles away. A third carrier, the *Saratoga,* which had just arrived in San Diego for refitting when the attack occurred, was immediately loaded with munitions, stores, and planes and left for Oahu on Monday morning, finally arriving on December 13 under heightened security.

Halsey found Kimmel's headquarters in a state of chaos when he reported in. There were reports of Japanese gliders and paratroopers landing on Oahu's east coast. Halsey ridiculed the report, saying the Japanese wouldn't use their carriers for such nonsense. He thought Kimmel, a longtime friend and naval academy classmate, was in a state of nervous collapse.

Confusion reigned. Initial intelligence reports placed the attacking force to the south of Oahu. That's where Halsey's task force was sent to scout out the enemy. It was a misguided yet fortunate decision. Had he headed north, Halsey's small force of one carrier, three cruisers, and nine destroyers would have stumbled into the huge Japanese armada and probably been destroyed.

President Franklin D. Roosevelt, seething over the treachery of the Japanese and the huge loss of life, tried to calm the American people by divulging as little as possible about the sneak attack. His motives were also to deny the enemy a report of what they had destroyed and, even more importantly, what they had missed. The full report was kept secret for a full year lest the information give comfort and aid to the Japanese. Roosevelt's utter outrage and promise of vengeance against the Japanese would come the next day during his declaration-of-war speech to a joint session of Congress. Ever the shrewd politician, Roosevelt would reject advice to include Germany in his declaration-of-war speech lest it allow the isolationists an opportunity to claim he had engineered the war with Japan as a means of getting involved in Europe.

There was a very real fear both in Hawaii and on the West Coast of the mainland of an imminent invasion by the Japanese. Those living on the coastline from Vancouver to San Diego were understandably apprehensive. The media didn't help matters any by erroneously reporting on December 8 that "two squadrons of enemy planes—numbering about 15 planes to a squadron—crossed the coastline west of San Jose Monday night and reconnoitered the San Francisco Bay area and other sections of California." An Associated Press story, which was reported throughout the country, quoted the army as saying the planes "indicated in all probability that an enemy aircraft carrier was lurking off the coast, possibly as far out as 500 or 600 miles."

Roosevelt was stunned and irate at the Japanese treachery, but he tried hard not to let it show. He called Secretary of State Cordell Hull shortly after the attack and urged the latter to keep his scheduled appointment with the Japanese envoys, who were waiting in his anteroom with a message from the emperor. Roosevelt advised Hull not to tell the envoys about the attack but "to receive their reply formally and coolly bow them out."

Hull did his best to stay calm but he couldn't control his anger.

"In all my fifty years of public service I have never seen such a document that was more crowded with infamous falsehoods and distortions," Hull blurted. The envoys, who had not been told of the attack, left in an embarrassed fluster. A State Department official overheard Hull muttering under his breath at the Japanese envoys, calling them "scoundrels and pissants," as the two men left his office.

Roosevelt seemed to have an iron grip on his emotions all day.

"Though he looked strained and tired he was completely calm," Eleanor Roosevelt later wrote of her husband's demeanor that day. "His reaction to any event was always to be calm. If it was something that was bad, he just became almost like an iceberg, and there was never the slightest emotion that was allowed to show."

Roosevelt's oldest son, James, who was convalescing from recent stomach surgery, was called to the White House by his father that Sunday afternoon shortly after the Japanese attack. He recalled that his father was white as a sheet and visibly shaken by the news from Pearl Harbor. "He was sitting in a corner with no expression on his face, very calm and quiet," James Roosevelt later wrote. "He didn't even look up. I knew right away we were in deep trouble. He had out his stamp collection he loved so much and was thumbing over some of the stamps when I came in. 'It's bad, pretty bad,' he said without looking up. He showed no signs of excitement, he simply and calmly discussed who had to be notified and what the media campaign should be for the next forty-eight hours."

The president called a cabinet meeting for 9:00 P.M. When the members started arriving at the White House, Roosevelt, always a friendly and outgoing man, was off by himself trying to grasp a full understanding of all the terrible news coming in from Pearl Harbor. "He was very serious. His face and lips were pulled down, looking quite gray," Labor Secretary Frances Perkins said. "His complexion didn't have that pink-and-white look that it had when he was himself. It had a queer gray, drawn look.

"I remember the President could hardly bring himself to describe the devastation. His pride in the navy was so terrific that he was having actual physical difficulty in getting out the words that put him on record as knowing that the navy was caught unawares. . . . I remember that he twice said to Knox, 'Find out, for God's sake, why the ships were tied up in rows.' Knox said, 'That's the way they berth them.' It was obvious to me that Roosevelt was having a dreadful time just accepting the idea that the navy could be caught off guard."

The navy had always occupied a special place in Roosevelt's heart. Before polio crippled his legs, there were few things FDR enjoyed more than sailing his yacht, the *Half Moon*, during summers spent at his family retreat at Campobello Island off the coast of northern Maine.

Later that night at a meeting with congressional leaders, Roosevelt, in the same calm, factual manner, repeated what he had earlier told the cabinet members about the Pearl Harbor disaster.

"How did it happen that our warships were caught like tame ducks in Pearl Harbor?" a purple-faced Texas senator Tom Connally asked, banging his fist on the table for emphasis. "How did they catch us with our pants down? Where were our patrols? They knew these negotiations were going on. They were all asleep."

A weary Roosevelt shook his head and answered, "I don't know Tom. I just don't know."

Following the cabinet meeting, Roosevelt held an intriguing meeting with army colonel William "Wild Bill" Donovan, a lifelong friend and Medal of Honor winner in World War I, and CBS newsman Edward R. Murrow, who had eloquently reported on his experiences living through the German air attacks in London. FDR had recently named Donovan as coordinator of information (COI), a clearinghouse for intelligence gathered by all military and governmental agencies. That position eventually evolved into the Office of Strategic Services (OSS) and then into the Central Intelligence Agency (CIA). There is no written record of that meeting, but it is reasonable to assume that an infuriated Roosevelt vented his anger against Japan on the two men and made it very clear he intended some sort of retaliatory action at the earliest possible opportunity.

At every subsequent meeting with his military chiefs throughout the dark days of December and January, Roosevelt kept demanding some reprisal attacks against the Japanese, if only to lift the spirit and morale of the American people. FDR was obsessed with the idea of striking back at Japan as quickly as possible, to deliver a telling blow to her sense of national pride. The president had, as news correspondent Quentin Reynolds wrote, "a fierce, consuming hatred for the Japanese."

Two such missions were the product of FDR's constant calls for offensive action. The first was the daring raid on Japan by sixteen B-25 bombers on April 18, 1942. Led by Lt. Col. Jimmy Doolittle, the twin-engine bombers flew off the deck of the aircraft carrier *Hornet,* which had sailed within 700 miles of the Japanese coast. The surprise mission caused little actual battle damage but it did provide a badly needed psychological lift to a dispirited American public.

The second bold initiative, one that FDR personally fought for over the objections of his military chiefs, was the establishment of Marine raider battalions for use as commandos in the Pacific. The first such raid, one that was highly publicized at the time, occurred on August 17–18, 1942, when 219 Marine raiders under the command of Lt. Col. Evans F. Carlson went ashore on Makin Atoll in the Gilbert Islands, some 2,040 miles to the southwest of Hawaii. Two stripped-down companies from the 2d Raider Battalion, which included President Roosevelt's oldest son, James, as executive officer, were transported by two giant submarines on the almost 4,100-mile round trip to Makin, a small Japanese-held outpost along the sea-lanes to Australia. While the strategic significance of the raid was minimal, and the raid itself probably foolhardy, the psychological and propaganda value turned out to be enormous for a nation that was literally starving for good news from the Pacific.

This book is dedicated to those "gung-ho" Marines of the 2d Raider Battalion who left thirty of their comrades behind in an ill-advised adventure that very nearly cost all of them their lives.

One

Getting Off the Canvas

The Marine Corps recruiting offices were jammed early on Monday morning, December 8, 1941. In some towns, lines formed around the block well before the offices opened at 0800. There were so many volunteers—"Pearl Harbor Avengers" they were called—that the recruiters had to delay acceptance. There weren't enough training facilities, equipment, or qualified instructors to handle the deluge of new recruits. Soldiers who had been discharged in recent months were quickly called back into the service. Many were elevated in rank to sergeant or second lieutenant to help train the new recruits.

"We had shortages of everything but men," Marine general Holland "Howlin' Mad" Smith said. "Training was ahead of production and we ran our equipment red hot. Our greatest shortage was ammunition for rifle and artillery practice. The country had allowed its reserve to sink so low that if the Japanese had continued from Pearl Harbor with an amphibious force and landed on the West Coast they would have found that we did not have enough ammunition to fight a day's battle. This is how close the country was to disaster in 1941."

Between September of 1939 and June of 1941 authorized Marine strength doubled from 26,568 to 53,886. By December 7 it had grown to a little over 66,000, and by the war's end nearly half a million men wore the Marine uniform. The Marines prided themselves on having high recruiting standards, rejecting unemployable misfits or other human driftwood. In the three years preceding the war, the Marines received 205,000 applications for enlistment but accepted only 38,000 first-time enlistees. Of the latter, 11,300 possessed high school diplomas.

The desire to escape poverty operated as a powerful inducement to join any of the armed forces, but what most attracted men to the Marine Corps was its reputation for hard fighting, hard living, and service in exotic locales. For the son of a working-class family who had just dropped out of or graduated from high school, a four-year "cruise" in the Marines offered an opportunity to see the world, prove his manhood, and decide what he wanted to do with the rest of his life—all at government expense.

During the first month after Pearl Harbor 18,000 men joined the Marines. In Los Angeles, a city famous for its publicity stunts, some 385 recruits, symbolizing the approximate number of Marines lost in the surrender of Wake Island two days before Christmas, formed a giant W while being sworn into the navy by former heavyweight champion Gene Tunney, who was a lieutenant commander in the Navy Reserve.

More than half the initial volunteers were rejected for medical reasons, however. The long and harsh Depression had taken its toll on the health of America's youth. Many of the volunteers were suffering from anemia or malnutrition as a result of poor eating habits and the lack of vitamin-enhanced diets. Medical and dental needs had also been neglected because they simply could not afford to pay for such services.

As the war wore on, however, the armed services, particularly the army, became a lot less picky on who they accepted for military duty. Draftees were not accepted as Marines until mid-1943, and were then listed as "Selective Service Volunteers."

A story that illustrates how desperate the services became for recruits in the later days of the war, though probably embellished somewhat, was told by a member of an Arkansas draft board. It concerned a hillbilly who walked into the army recruiting office one day holding a letter written by his wife. The character, who looked as if he had just left his farm, was illiterate and couldn't read a word of the note in his hand.

The barely legible letter he was carrying was addressed, "Dear U.S. Army." It went on to say:

> Just take him.
> He ain't no good to me.
> He ain't done nothing but raise hell and drink lemon essence.
> Since I married him eight years and I got to feed seven of his kids.
> Maybe you can get him to carry a gun. He's good on squirrels and eating.

Tell him and welcome.
I need the grub and his bed's for the kids.
Don't tell him this.
Just take him.

The army did.

In Washington, D.C., John J. Pershing, the man who had commanded American forces in World War I, put on an old uniform and left his suite at Walter Reed Medical Center to offer his services to his nation. The eighty-one-year-old Pershing, steadying himself with a cane, went to the White House to meet with President Roosevelt and "reenlist."

"General, you are magnificent," Roosevelt told the old warrior, gratefully accepting Pershing's magnanimous offer. A couple of weeks later, another American icon, Charles Lindbergh, made it known that he wanted to return to duty as a colonel in the Army Air Corps. Lindbergh had been a thorn in Roosevelt's side throughout the 1930s with his isolationist views and pro-Nazi sympathies.

Roosevelt, who had been careful not to antagonize a genuine American hero in public, passed the request on to the secretary of war, Henry L. Stimson, who agreed with Interior Secretary Harold L. Ickes's opinion that Lindbergh was "a ruthless and conscious fascist" and one who "should be buried in merciful oblivion."

America was in a state of shock those first few weeks after the Pearl Harbor disaster. Even those who witnessed the carnage couldn't believe that Japan had either the audacity or sufficient skill to inflict such damage.

"We were so proud, so vain, and so ignorant of Japanese capability," said Gene LaRocque, who was aboard the USS *MacDonough* at Pearl Harbor. "It never entered our consciousness that they'd have the temerity to attack us. We knew the Japanese didn't see well, especially at night—we knew this as a matter of fact. We knew they couldn't build good weapons, they made junky equipment, they just imitated us. All we had to do was get out there and sink 'em. It turns out they could see better than we could and their torpedoes, unlike ours, worked. We'd thought they were little brown men and we were the great big white men. They were of a lesser species. The Germans were well known as tremendous fighters and builders, whereas the Japanese would be pushovers."

The Japanese, unlike the Chinese, were seen by most Americans as an inferior race. *Life* magazine described the typical Japanese as one who "betrays aboriginal antecedents in a squat, long-torsoed build, a broader, more massively boned head and face, flat, often pug nose, yellow-ocher skin, and heavier beard."

The symbolism was clear. The United States would prevail over the Japanese because it was the more civilized race.

America was frightened and vulnerable those first few weeks after Pearl Harbor. Military guards sprang up at strategic factories, ports, and shipyards. Crowds gathered outside the White House and peered through the gates, watching and waiting for something to happen. On that first night, they huddled together and sang "God Bless America." They were looking to Roosevelt for guidance and support. Roosevelt, for his part, accepted an increase in his security force but would not accede to positioning tanks around the White House, which could be interpreted by some as a sign of panic.

Many citizens were irate at the Japanese treachery. A heavy police guard was required to protect the Japanese Embassy on Massachusetts Avenue. On the first night, someone had vented his animosity toward the Japanese by chopping down four cherry trees along the Tidal Basin near the Jefferson Memorial that had been a gift from the citizens of Tokyo in 1912. A sign on the pen housing the Japanese deer in New York City's Central Park was changed to "Asiatic Deer."

On the West Coast, where the threat from invasion was thought to be more than just a possibility, antiaircraft batteries were hurried into position on the Hollywood Hills and at Long Beach and Seattle where large aircraft manufacturing plants were located. Farmers armed with pitchforks and shotguns patrolled the empty beaches of Puget Sound to help ward off expected enemy landings. Miles of barbed wire were rolled into positions along the entire coast. Lights were turned off and families huddled in basements and cellars waiting for the enemy to come ashore.

In Los Angeles, which had a Japanese-American population of nearly 50,000, FBI agents and soldiers from Fort MacArthur took "key" Japanese citizens into custody and interned them in a wire enclosure at the Sixth Street pier. The police and FBI were inundated with spy and sabotage reports against native Japanese-Americans who then and later proved to be no threat to America's war effort. Still, many Americans expressed their outrage against Japanese-Americans by smashing store windows or boycotting their businesses. It was but the first step toward a national program that would intern the entire Japanese-American population into camps for the duration of the war. By the late spring of 1942 some 120,000 Japanese-Americans in the western United States were driven from their jobs, homes, and businesses on the suspicion they were spying or plotting some form of sabotage. Not a bit of evidence was found then or ever that they were anything but completely loyal citizens, yet they were herded into camps under the point of a gun.

Eleanor Roosevelt did her best to stem a flood of prejudice and fear against Japanese-Americans, but it was to no avail. The hysteria was so strong that her calls for tolerance were thrown back at her by a media that was hell bent on crucifying anyone who could be labeled as a Jap lover.

"When she starts bemoaning the plight of the treacherous snakes we call Japanese, with apologies to all snakes, she has reached the point where she should be forced to retire from public life," proclaimed an editorial in the *Los Angeles Times*.

In the meantime, America began gearing up for an all-out war. Blackout conditions were immediately put into effect throughout the nation, though it was slow to take hold. Department and hardware stores quickly sold out stocks of black paint, blackout cloth, portable radios, flashlights, lanterns, candles, shovels, hatchets, first-aid kits, oil stoves, gas masks, Thermos bottles, earplugs, whistles, waterproof matches, and goggles.

There was also a cry for accountability within the U.S. military. Something had to be done quickly to restore the public's faith in the military and to assuage the severe morale problems in the armed services. Roosevelt came to a quick decision that the blame for the disaster at Pearl Harbor must fall on Admiral Kimmel and Lt. Gen. Walter Short, the two senior officers in charge in Hawaii, though there was plenty of evidence to point the finger of responsibility at those in Washington, namely Secretary of War Henry Stimson, Navy Secretary Frank Knox, Army Chief of Staff General George Marshall, Navy Chief Admiral Harold Stark, and President Roosevelt himself.

Some historians believe Roosevelt deliberately provoked Japan to bring the United States into the war, assuming that the attack would come in the Far East, perhaps in the Philippines. It is inconceivable that Roosevelt, had he felt the attack would come at Hawaii, would have intentionally sacrificed the heart of his Pacific Fleet and some 3,500 sailors and soldiers.

Kimmel and Short had been complaining for months about shortages of personnel, planes, and radar, but Washington's attention was focused on the Atlantic, where America's meager war materials were being convoyed to England in the desperate fight to stave off German expansion. In addition, Kimmel and Short claimed that Washington failed to consistently share intelligence information with them on Japan's intentions in the Pacific—including the precise day of the Pearl Harbor attack—often keeping them completely out of the loop. It was an argument that had a lot of truth to it.

Feelings at the time ran hot. Writer Ernest Hemingway, for example, suggested that "Knox should have been relieved as Secretary of the Navy within 24 hours of the Pearl Harbor debacle and those responsible at Oahu (Kimmel and Short) for that disaster shot."

Roosevelt, who appeared to have his mind set on relieving Kimmel and Short, sent Knox on a fact-finding trip to Hawaii on December 11. Knox arrived aboard a large flying boat loaded with plasma, antitoxin, and other medical supplies vitally needed for the wounded. Before landing at Kaneohe Bay Naval Air Station in eastern Oahu, Knox and the other passengers were given parachutes and life preservers in case their flying boat was shot out of the sky by jumpy ground personnel with short memories.

To preserve the "investigative nature" of his visit, Knox had given orders that "he would not be the guest of any senior officer." Instead the party was driven to the Royal Hawaiian Hotel, where they were met by Kimmel.

Even Knox, the veteran Rough Rider who had charged up San Juan Hill with Teddy Roosevelt during the Spanish-American War, was shocked to his boots by the shambles of Battleship Row.

Knox was told that six hundred servicemen had been buried that morning in a mass grave. On the ferry across to Ford Island he was able to see for himself the oil-soaked bodies being fished from the flotsam drifting in the harbor. He visited the wards at Hospital Point and later confided to his naval aide that "the sight of those men made me as angry as I have ever been in my life."

The visit by Knox coincided with preparations for the relief of Wake Island and the rescue of some 449 Marines, sixty-eight naval personnel, and 1,200 construction workers holding out against superior Japanese forces. When Knox left the next day, he had given Kimmel and his staff approval to implement the plan to relieve Wake Island.

As Knox boarded his plane back to the mainland, he knew he was faced with trying to reconcile two conflicting demands. First, he had approved Kimmel's plan for the relief of Wake. Second, if the admiral were prematurely removed from his command, it would prejudice the whole operation—which was vital to restoring the confidence of the fleet. Deep as his love for the navy was, Knox was first and foremost a politician. He was well aware of the damage that could be done to the administration if the demands for a public accounting of the disaster were not met promptly.

Wake fought off an attempted Japanese landing on December 11, raising Kimmel's hopes that the temporary respite the Marines had bought would allow him time to plan and mount his full-scale relief operation. The Pacific Fleet's ambitious Wake operation, which involved all three available carrier groups, might redeem Kimmel's damaged reputation if it succeeded. However, events in Washington would soon doom the operation.

Knox gave his twenty-nine-page report to President Roosevelt at 2200 on December 14. He told the president that "the damage was so horrendous" that he had not detailed everything in his report for fear of some leak. He said that "if the American people knew what had happened at Pearl, they would panic and the war would be over before we ever got into it."

With a skillful economy of words, Knox was carefully evenhanded in laying out the facts as he saw them. Although his report did not exonerate Kimmel and Short, it fell far short of leveling charges of dereliction, which both commanders were soon to face.

A displeased Roosevelt instructed War Secretary Stimson and Knox to conduct separate but similar press conferences to a waiting nation. Per instructions from Roosevelt, they would each admit that although neither the army nor navy personnel had been prepared for the air attack, once engaged, the defense was heroic. The burden of blame, by inference, was to fall on Kimmel and Short.

The command structure in Hawaii further complicated any decision to affix blame for the Pearl Harbor disaster. Neither Kimmel nor Short had been in overall command at the time, so there had been no overall defensive plan. Each commander did what he thought was best for the defense of the island. And, just as they had shared the command, they were destined to share the blame when their combined efforts proved woefully inadequate.

The press conferences greatly downplayed the actual numbers of men and ships lost. Nor was it mentioned that Kimmel and Short were not privy to the decoded Japanese message indicating a surprise move was imminent. If that aspect of the investigation had been made public, the Japanese would have known the United States was decrypting their top-secret diplomatic code, which had been broken in July of 1941. This crucial fact had to be omitted for obvious security reasons.

The facts, which were revealed only after the war, were that the United States had eight of the so-called "Purple" decoding machines in the summer of 1941. Four of them were in Washington (two each for the army and navy), one was in the Philippines, and two more were in London (in exchange for Ultra intelligence the United States was receiving from the British). The eighth Purple decoder had been slated for Hawaii, but politics got in the way. Washington wanted it and so did London. At the expense of Hawaii, and as a compromise with Washington, the machine had been sent to the British.

Roosevelt, feeling the pressure of public opinion for somebody's scalp after the Pearl Harbor debacle, moved swiftly. Kimmel, who had been FDR's naval aide when the latter was assistant secretary of the navy in World War I, and Short were relieved on December 14 while a board of inquiry was formed to thoroughly investigate what had happened at Pearl Harbor. Secretary of War Stimson called it a "housecleaning." Three days later, Roosevelt resurrected the post of commander-in-chief, U.S. Navy, which he had abolished a year earlier, and gave the job to Adm. Ernest King. Admiral Chester Nimitz was a quick choice to succeed Kimmel.

"The summary removal of the Hawaiian commanders before the presidential investigating team had even been formally announced had the effect of branding Kimmel and Short with a public charge of dereliction," Kimmel's chief of intelligence, RAdm. Edwin T. Layton, said many years later. "It served to draw attention away from any responsibility that Washington might bear for the Pearl Harbor disaster. It smacked of firing the office boys to conceal skullduggery in the boardroom.

Although [Kimmel's] dismissal was not unexpected, we all regarded it as premature. We wondered what would happen to the Wake operation. It may be an established American tradition that losing baseball teams have their manager fired, but not during the first game of the World Series.

A December victory at Wake . . . would have been a stunning blow to Japan. It would have opened the way to a transpacific relief of Corregidor and the Philippines. And it would have rallied the navy and provided a tremendous boost to the morale of the American people who were facing a bleak Christmas.

With Kimmel out of the picture and Adm. William S. Pye temporarily filling in until Nimitz could take over, a period of confusion and indecision crept over the Pacific Fleet. The end result was the cancellation of the relief mission to Wake, the subsequent occupation of the atoll by the Japanese, and the imprisonment of some four hundred Marines and a thousand American civilians.

Admiral Layton, looking back over many years, felt that Kimmel and Short were victims of a rush to judgment where other commanders were mysteriously let off the hook.

"In strategic terms the Jap raid on the Philippine airfields was a far greater triumph than the attack on Pearl Harbor," he said. "At a single blow the Japs wiped out three quarters of MacArthur's aircraft, thus removing the ability to strike back, and guaranteed the success of the impending Jap invasion of the islands. Why Admiral Kimmel and General Short were to be so publicly and immediately pilloried for a disaster they were powerless to prevent when General Douglas MacArthur escaped any charge of accountability is a question that has never been satisfactorily answered."

MacArthur not only was spared any criticism for the destruction of the U.S. air forces in the Philippines, but he was to receive the Congressional Medal of Honor three months later after his escape to Australia.

For the time being, Americans felt a little better about themselves after the removal of Kimmel and Short, but the encouragement would be short lived as the news from Wake Island went from hopeful to disastrous in a span of less than two weeks.

Wake Island, located about two thousand miles west of Hawaii and across the international dateline, was acquired by the United States in 1898. In the mid-1930s, it became a refueling stop for Pan American Airways clipper ships flying between San Francisco and the Far East. The airline promoted Wake as the place "where America's day begins." The island was also described as "the loneliest overnight stop on the world's longest air route [8,210 miles]."

As war with Japan seemed more and more likely, the American military moved to strengthen the island with air and submarine support facilities. Wake was the farthest point on the Pacific Fleet's picket line, one that offered an ideal vantage point to glimpse the gathering war clouds.

When the Japanese attacked on December 7, 1941, the island had a garrison of about four hundred and fifty Marines, twelve hundred construction workers, and assorted navy and army personnel. The main defensive weapons were eight five-inch guns, sixteen three-inch antiaircraft weapons, and two dozen .50-caliber machine guns. On December 4, a dozen F4F Wildcat fighters had been delivered to the island. Eight of them were destroyed on the ground on December 7.

On December 11, a Japanese landing party was repulsed. In radio contact with Hawaii, the defenders were asked if there was anything they needed. "Send us more Japs," came the reply. It was a rallying cry that echoed throughout the country, giving desperate Americans reason to cheer.

Meanwhile, Admiral Kimmel had begun planning a relief operation for Wake, one that would involve all three carrier groups at his disposal. Two were to act as decoys while a third, the *Saratoga*, made a dash to the island. The *Saratoga* group, under Adm. Frank Jack Fletcher, was delayed in getting to Hawaii from San Diego because of rough seas and a false submarine scare. The carrier, after a lengthy refueling at Pearl, finally left for Wake on December 16 with its covering force of three cruisers and eight destroyers. The convoy, once under way, was forced to proceed at a slower pace than normal to accommodate the highest speed of its fuel tanker.

Washington politics then entered the picture, effectively dooming the mission.

On December 16, after the convoy had left Pearl, Kimmel received a dispatch from President Roosevelt ordering him to surrender his position as commander-in-chief of the Pacific Fleet (CINCPAC) to his deputy, VAdm. William S. Pye, the turnover to take effect at 1500 the next day. The cautious Pye, who had expressed little enthusiasm for the Wake relief plan, would pull the plug on the mission when intelligence later revealed the presence of three enemy carriers near Wake.

Admiral Fletcher had moved to within 425 miles of Wake early on the morning of December 22 when he slowed for refueling. Early the next morning, the Japanese landed on Wake. Admiral Pye, who had almost canceled the operation two days before, moved quickly to abort the mission and get his carrier out of harm's way. He feared that the enemy was laying a trap for the relief forces and if that was true, the possibility existed that he could lose one or more of his precious carriers.

When the message to abort reached Fletcher, he was reported to have removed his admiral's hat and flung it to the deck in disgust. Particularly upset were the *Saratoga* pilots, who took the abandonment of their fellow Marines personally. Several threatened to climb into their fighters and fly to Wake. Others broke down and wept.

Many naval officers felt that the political moves to change fleet commanders to quickly provide a scapegoat for the Pearl Harbor disaster resulted in the loss of Wake Island. Admiral Pye's decision to write off Wake cost him the trust and respect of many of his subordinates.

Roosevelt reportedly told an aide that he considered the recall "a worse blow than Pearl Harbor." Roosevelt castigated his navy for bungling the Wake mission and sarcastically demanded that the Pacific Fleet find some way in the near future to hurt the Japanese.

When Pye turned his command over to Nimitz on December 31, he quietly stepped to the sidelines of history. He ended his naval career without ever receiving another major combat command. The navy never forgot or forgave him for the loss of Wake Island.

In hindsight, however, many military historians generally agree that Pye made the right decision. Had the *Saratoga* been lost as Pye feared might happen—a very distinct possibility—the great victory at Midway the following June might never have happened.

Two

The "Sundowner"

The stark reality of America's predicament was clearly in evidence to all those present on December 31, 1941, when Adm. Chester W. Nimitz formally accepted the position of commander-in-chief of the Pacific Fleet in ceremonies on the deck of a submarine, the USS *Grayling*, which was firmly moored to a bullet-scarred dock at Pearl Harbor.

The sun was shining and security was heavy as a makeshift band played "Anchors Aweigh" while the four-star pennant signifying Nimitz's new command was raised atop the sub's flagpole. Normally, such change-of-command ceremonies were conducted aboard battleships. Nimitz had no such option this day. All eight battleships stationed at Pearl had been either destroyed or damaged three and a half weeks earlier during Japan's surprise air raid on the Pacific Fleet headquarters. Even the music had to be improvised. The navy's best band, that of the USS *Arizona*, had perished to a man when that ship was blown apart during the Japanese attack.

Nimitz, attired in his best dress white uniform, let his mind wander a bit as a lone seagull soared above the ceremony. He wondered to himself what a wonderful view that seagull must have had of the carnage wreaked a few weeks earlier. And where were the Japanese now? He craned his sunburned neck to the west. Was the enemy fleet lurking nearby, planning another air attack or maybe an invasion?

His wife had written her congratulations to him a week earlier on his new assignment, saying, "You always wanted the Pacific Fleet. You always thought that would be the height of glory." Nimitz immediately wrote her back, saying, "Darling, the fleet's at the bottom of the sea. Nobody must know that here, but I've got to tell you."

How ironic that he should use the phrase "bottom of the sea" to describe the conditions of his new fleet. Back in 1905 upon his graduation from the U.S. Naval Academy, Nimitz had been characterized by his classmates in the school yearbook, the *Lucky Bag*, as a man of "cheerful yesterdays and confident tomorrows" and one who possessed a quality "that gets to the bottom of things."

In another odd twist of irony, the very ship Nimitz designated for his change-of-command ceremony, the submarine *Grayling*, was torpedoed and sent to the bottom of the sea six months later during the Battle of Midway.

Following the ceremony, Nimitz stepped ashore to deliver a short speech, partly for the benefit of a group of newsmen standing nearby.

"We have taken a tremendous wallop," he told the assembly, "but I have no doubt as to the ultimate outcome."

One of the newsmen asked, "What are you going to do now?"

Nimitz thought a moment and then replied with a Hawaiian expression that, as he explained, meant, "Bide your time, keep your powder dry, and take advantage of the opportunity when it's offered."

Later that day, Nimitz called a meeting with the entire staff. It was a gloomy assemblage. Most expected to be relieved and banished to far-off outposts as their punishment for the Pearl Harbor disaster. Instead of calling them to account for the recent debacle, Nimitz reacted in just the opposite fashion. He said he did not blame them for the disaster and that, in fact, he had complete and unlimited confidence in every one of them and wanted them all to stay on with him.

In that short, simple speech, Nimitz seemed to heal all wounds within the navy and lifted an incubus off the spirits of Pearl Harbor.

Nimitz was the son of a Texas cowboy, who died several months before his birth. As a youngster, he thought he might like a career in the army and applied to West Point. After learning there were no more slots available, he set his sights on the U.S. Naval Academy.

Forty years later and half a world away from the Texas flatlands of his youth, Nimitz was given command of a demoralized navy that had to be rebuilt from scratch. He didn't mind holding the change-of-command ceremonies aboard the *Grayling*. Hell, he was a former submariner himself. During World War I, as a lieutenant commander, he was an aide to RAdm. Samuel S. Robison, who was commander of submarines in the Atlantic Fleet. In 1920, Nimitz helped build the submarine base at Pearl Harbor.

Long considered one of the navy's elite officers, Nimitz had nearly been named commander-in-chief of the Pacific Fleet two years earlier, but his then four-year assignment as chief of the Bureau of Navigation (the navy's personnel department) had just begun at that time. The choice assignment in Hawaii then went to Husband Kimmel, the other shining star among the navy's up-and-coming officers.

Kimmel, who was born in Kentucky in 1882, graduated from the Naval Academy in 1904. Eight years later, he improved his prospects for promotion greatly by marrying an admiral's daughter.

"A tall, blond, red-faced man, he carried himself with the ramrod stiffness of a Prussian martinet," Admiral Layton said of his boss, adding that he had "little tolerance for laziness or indecision. He had an infectious, warm smile when pleased by something and a frosty demeanor if displeased."

Kimmel was named commander-in-chief of the U.S. Fleet on January 5, 1941, jumping over forty-six officers with greater seniority. As of February 1, when he officially assumed his new post, the command did not exist. Roosevelt created a separate Pacific Fleet under Kimmel and an Atlantic Fleet under Ernest J. King, both of whom served under Admiral Stark, chief of naval operations.

The Pearl Harbor disaster would forever alter the careers of both Kimmel and Nimitz, sending each in opposite directions. When it was decided to make Kimmel, along with army general Walter Short, the sacrificial scapegoat for the disaster at Pearl Harbor, Nimitz was immediately positioned at the top of the navy's short list of qualified replacements.

Kimmel, who had three sons in the navy, was devastated by his abrupt dismissal and the treatment he received from his superiors and fellow officers. In a letter to Admiral Stark written several months later, he sounded like a desperate man.

"I stand ready at any time to accept the consequences of my acts," he wrote, obviously in great pain. "I do not wish to embarrass the government in the conduct of the war. I do feel, however, that my crucifixion before the public has about reached the limit. I am in daily receipt of letters from irresponsible people over the country taking me to task and even threatening to kill me. . . ."

Kimmel was never given another military assignment and would fight for the rest of his life to get his good name back.

As the years went by and more and more of the truth was revealed about the Pearl Harbor disaster, the blame slowly shifted in the direction of Washington.

In 1953, Admiral Halsey, who was never called before any of the inquiries concerning the disaster, wrote Kimmel a telling letter that greatly eased the latter's heart.

"As you know," the letter began, "I have always thought and have not hesitated to say on any and all occasions, that I believe you and Short were the greatest military martyrs this country has ever produced, and that your treatment was outrageous. In the course of time I have not changed my opinion one iota. I have always felt that you were left holding the bag for something you did not know and could not control."

Nimitz traveled to Hawaii under utmost secrecy. On December 19, two days after being given his new assignment, he traveled by train to the West Coast wearing civilian clothes and under the alias of "Mr. Freeman." Freeman was his wife's maiden name. En route, he took some time to write his wife a short note that read: "As I get more sleep and rest things are looking up and I am sure that by the time I reach Pearl Harbor I will be able to meet the requirements of the situation."

After a brief delay in San Diego because of bad weather, he arrived at Pearl Harbor by flying boat at 0700 on Christmas morning. A light rain was falling when he arrived. When the plane's door was thrown open, Nimitz, still clad in civilian clothes, was struck by the stench of the oil-covered water and burned and rotting bodies. The party had to remain standing on the way to shore because the whaleboat was slick with oil. The launch zigzagged around other small boats searching the blackened waters for bodies, which were still popping to the surface. He could see the still-smoldering USS *Arizona* and the capsized USS *Oklahoma*. Thirty-two sailors from the *Oklahoma* had been rescued from the ship the first few days after the attack by cutting holes into the capsized hull. It took just over two years to refloat the *Oklahoma*, and when the final death count was added up, 415 brave men had perished, most trapped underwater within the huge battleship.

"What news of the relief of Wake?" was Nimitz's first question. He was told that the island had surrendered two days ago and the relief expedition had been recalled. Nimitz bit his lower lip and shook his head from side to side, swallowing news he found particularly distasteful.

Waiting on the dock to greet Nimitz was Kimmel. Normally a man of stiff military presence, Kimmel looked stooped and deflated.

"You have my sympathy," Nimitz said to his old friend when they shook hands. "The same thing could have happened to anybody."

Nimitz couldn't help noticing a number of wooden coffins stacked in a pile at the far end of the dock. It had to be another sobering sight, one that made him realize the enormity of the task that lay in front of him.

Later in the day, Nimitz held a brief press conference before a group of newsmen and photographers.

Nimitz delayed his change-of-command ceremony until the thirty-first so that he could assimilate all that had happened at Pearl and assess the qualifications of all the top navy officers involved. Nimitz tried to stay in the background the first few days. He reluctantly took over Kimmel's quarters and, along with Kimmel, interim commander VAdm. William S. Pye, and Pye's wife, played a foursome of cribbage almost every night. It was an awkward situation, to say the least, and it took a man of Nimitz's class and kindness to soothe the embarrassment and shame Kimmel must have been feeling.

Though he preferred a seagoing assignment, Nimitz was an exceedingly good choice to take overall command of the entire Pacific Fleet. Despite his age of fifty-six, he was a vigorous man with an immense capacity for work. He had an equal talent for obtaining the best work from others, an almost impeccable judgment of men, and a genius for making prompt, firm decisions. He seemed to grow as his responsibilities increased.

He possessed, in a shy and controlled way, the rare qualities of gentleness and firmness. His superiors admired his dedication and quiet competence, and those below him were equally impressed by his sense of compassion, justice, and humility, qualities that were rare among those in the navy who had achieved his high rank.

He was an ideal buffer between his own subordinates and his boss, the caustic Admiral King. He was not a man to walk into a situation and clear the decks. In fact, he retained all thirty-two of Kimmel's staff officers when he took command on December 31. Among them was Lt. Comdr. Joe Rochefort, one of the men most responsible for breaking Japan's secret war code in the summer of 1941. Rochefort's crew played a significant role in the subsequent victory at Midway in June of 1942, the turning point in the war.

Though only five foot nine and 180 pounds, Nimitz's broad shoulders and erect carriage made him seem much taller, and more slender. His telling facial feature was a mouth that never wavered from a thin, straight line. Early on, he rarely smiled or frowned. He was not a cold man or a bad-tempered man—quite the contrary. To the world he presented a figure of almost total complacency. He seldom lost his temper or raised his voice. His light blue eyes peered quizzically from beneath a beetling brow that was robbed of fierceness by the light hair of his eyebrows, and his fine white hair gave him the air of an elder statesman.

To junior officers, Nimitz appeared stern and completely dispassionate. The word "sundowner," which referred to a strict, rigidly uncompromising ship's officer, had sometimes been used to describe him. The term had originated as slang for a ship's captain who granted liberty only until sundown.

Nimitz was able to establish a rapport with his commanders quickly. He valued their opinions on how to improve operations. He always found time to interview and help debrief commanders returning from the front. He would stand as the officer entered his office and was friendly and enthusiastic and rarely ducked a question.

If one of his commanders got out of line, Nimitz didn't hesitate to remove him. He had a waiting bench of flag officers and was willing to give a man a chance to prove himself.

A calm, prudent man, Nimitz had a tremendous capacity for organization but he was also an inspiring leader. His appointment soon restored an air of confidence throughout the Pacific Fleet. It was one of the best decisions President Roosevelt would make in the war.

Nimitz knew before accepting his assignment that Roosevelt had agreed with British prime minister Winston Churchill that the first priority for military action would be in Europe, not the Pacific. Nimitz would have to hold on to what he had until the American war machine was able to produce enough bullets, bombs, ships, and planes to go on the offensive in the Pacific. Admiral King's first orders to Nimitz were to cover and hold the Hawaii-Midway line and maintain communications with the West Coast and Australia.

The brutal attack at Pearl Harbor had enraged the Americans and unified them in their quest for revenge. They would have to be patient, however, and that proved difficult as the war news from the Pacific kept getting worse and worse.

There was no darker period in American history than the winter and spring of 1942. The Japanese landed on northern Luzon in the Philippines on December 10 and made their first attempt to take Wake Island the next day. Guam fell on December 22, followed by Wake on December 23 and Hong Kong on December 25. Additionally, the Japanese had sunk the British battleship *Prince of Wales* and the battle cruiser *Repulse* off Malaya on December 10. They were the only two allied capital ships in the whole western Pacific. Singapore fell on February 15. General Douglas MacArthur arrived in Australia March 17 after having been evacuated from the Philippines six days earlier. The two biggest blows were the surrender of Bataan on April 9 and Corregidor on May 6. More than 75,000 men, a third of them Americans, were taken prisoner in the Philippines. It was the greatest capitulation in U.S. military history.

Among the defenders on the island of Corregidor, which was called "the Rock," were elements of the 4th Marines, the "China regiment" in which so many of the older Raiders had served during the 1920s and 1930s.

The surrenders at Bataan and Corregidor were particularly humiliating. Outnumbered and decimated by disease and battle wounds, without supplies and any hope of relief, the "army" of the Philippines was humbled by the well-disciplined and battle-hardened Japanese. The prisoners, who were forced to march about a hundred miles in six days to a prisoner-of-war camp, endured blistering heat, exhaustion, starvation, unspeakable cruelty, and murder. Thousands died along the way, either from disease or a Japanese bayonet.

By the late spring of 1942, Japan had conquered the Philippines, Singapore, Hong Kong, the Dutch East Indies, Malaya, Borneo, the Bismarck Islands, Siam, Sumatra, the Gilberts, the Celebes, Timor, Wake, Guam, most of the Solomon Islands, and half of New Guinea. Japanese bombers had pulverized the key Australian port of Darwin, and citizens of Brisbane, Melbourne, and Sydney feared an imminent invasion. The Japanese empire had expanded some five thousand miles from Tokyo in nearly every direction, covering one-seventh of the globe, some 12.5 million square miles of new territory in only five months of war.

In Washington, gloom contended with chaos. Generals and admirals were stunned by the power, speed, and skill of the Japanese advance and reached a grim conclusion: With full mobilization of manpower and resources, and at a frightful cost in casualties, it would require at least ten years to reconquer the Pacific. That was the initial assessment.

Still, there was no shortage of optimism or patriotism in those early, dark days of the war. Parents of those serving in the military proudly displayed in a front window a pennant with a blue star for each son or daughter in uniform. A gold star meant that their loved one wouldn't be coming back. By war's end, there were very few houses that didn't have either a blue star or a gold star hanging in a front window. Many houses had more than one.

The early fervor of enlistments, which produced such patriotic songs as "We'll Knock the Japs Right into the Laps of the Nazis" and "The Sun Will Soon Be Setting on the Land of the Rising Sun" gave way to more somber melodies as the bad news kept pouring in from the Pacific. By the late spring of 1942, a melancholy hung over the country like a suffocating blanket as the Japanese shocked the world with their military aggressiveness. The mood was reflected in such songs as "You'd Be So Nice to Come Home To," "Now Is the Hour," "I'll Never Smile Again," "Spring Will be a Little Late This Year," "I Had the Craziest Dream," and "I Dream of You." Two of the most popular ditties early in the war were the rallying cry of "Let's Remember Pearl Harbor" and the cocky paean of "Goodbye Mama, I'm Off to Yokohama." The first song promised Americans that they would atone for the Pearl Harbor disaster "as we did the Alamo" while the latter vowed to "teach all those Japs the Yanks are no saps" and predicted "we'll soon have all those Japs on their Japanese."

Singing was a way of taking one's mind off all the distressing news from the Pacific. It also helped to chase away the tears when the war news became personal.

The war wasn't going well in other areas of the world. In Europe, Germany was at the height of its power, occupying most of the continent and North Africa and a huge chunk of Russia. Great Britain continued to hang on by its fingernails, victims of heavy bombing attacks as well as a devastating blockade by German U-boats. The latter also took a heavy toll on American shipping in the winter and spring of 1942.

For America, however, the really bad news was in the Pacific, where the Japanese appeared to have a free hand to take whatever they wanted. The tide was about to turn, however, and Marine Raiders would help lead the way.

Three
Birth of the Raiders

The Marine Corps had experimented with the concept of amphibious raider-type forces during the late 1930s, incorporating such maneuvers in their annual Fleet Landing Exercises (FLEXs). The deployment of landing parties in rubber boats was done from high-speed transports and destroyers. In February of 1941 three units were designated as "provisional rubber-boat companies."

The Marine training was modeled somewhat after the British Army and Royal Marine commandos, which were formed in June of 1940 shortly after the debacle of Dunkirk. The army commandos were trained for cross-Channel forays, while the Royal Marine commandos were kept in the British Isles for defense against an anticipated German invasion. Roosevelt reveled in the stories told to him by Prime Minister Winston Churchill of the dash and bravery of the commandos. He became infected by Churchill's penchant for military novelty, so much so that he sent several U.S. officers to Great Britain to observe their training.

Not everyone in the British forces agreed with the commando concept. It was bitterly criticized by many officers who complained that the formation of a so-called elite force would drain the best men from their units. That's exactly what happened in both Britain and the United States.

The British Army commandos were conceived by Lt. Col. Dudley Clark, a staff officer at the War Office in Whitehall. Churchill, who was itching to get back at the Germans, took to the idea immediately, and with gusto. "Enterprises must be prepared with specially trained troops of the hunter class who can develop a reign of terror down the enemy coast," Churchill told his military chiefs.

Thus was born a breed of fighting men that combined the tactics, independence, and resourcefulness of the guerrilla with the training and discipline of the professional soldier. The mixture was to produce a military elite—the commandos. At first, they were used on "butcher-and-bolt" raids to kill, capture, and destroy. Later, they branched out to extensive operations deep behind enemy lines. They were all volunteers. They were a romantic bunch, independent, often fanatical, sometimes eccentric, and occasionally suicidal.

The first raid took place on June 24, 1940, just three weeks after their formation. Four air-sea rescue boats crossed the English Channel with 115 hastily chosen volunteers. They blackened their faces with makeup supplied by a London theatrical costumer, which they found very amusing. The plan was to land at four points along the French coast south of Boulogne to test German defenses and take prisoners.

One boat found nothing and promptly returned. Another found a German seaplane anchorage straddling its intended landing site and none made it ashore. The third group surprised two German sentries and killed both but left without searching the bodies or finding out what they were guarding. The fourth boat, with Colonel Clark aboard as an observer, nearly blundered into Boulogne harbor. A German patrol drove them off with Clark sustaining a wound to his ear.

Returning to England, one of the four boats was refused entry to Folkestone harbor until the identity of its occupants could be established. While the men drifted off the harbor boom, they drank the rum that such boats carried for reviving downed airmen who were plucked from the chilly waters of the channel. As a result, many of them were distinctly unsteady on their feet when they were at last allowed ashore. As a final indignity, they were arrested by the military police on suspicion of being deserters.

A second raid, consisting of thirty-two officers and 107 enlisted men, took place three weeks later, on July 14, 1940. The target was the Le Bourg airfield at Guernsey, one of the Channel Islands. Only forty men made it to shore, and after finding nothing, most had to swim out to their launch in heavy seas.

Both raids were comic failures, but Churchill was far from being discouraged. The prime minister decided that individual recruiting, longer training, and special equipment would be necessary before any more commando raids would be attempted. Several camps were established for this specialized training in the Scottish highlands in the fall of 1940.

The commandos did achieve a level of success in subsequent forays, particularly on the northern Norwegian island of Vagsoy on March 4, 1941, and on a German radar station on an isolated channel headland near Bruneval, France, on February 27, 1942, but their contributions to the war effort were minimal.

Nonetheless, U.S. officers like army brigadier general Lucian Truscott, army colonel Bill Donovan, and Marine captains Sam Griffith and Wally Greene were sent by Roosevelt to observe the commando training and returned to America with glowing reports of its effectiveness. It was their recommendations that helped launch the formation of the American army's ranger program and the Marine Corps's Raider battalions.

On January 13, 1942, Marine captain James Roosevelt, with the full backing of his father and the obvious encouragement of Maj. Evans Carlson, wrote the Marine commandant, Maj. Gen. Thomas Holcomb, and recommended the creation of "a unit for purposes similar to the British Commandos and the Chinese Guerrillas."

Normally, reserve Marine Corps captains don't correspond with the commandant. But, because of who Jimmy Roosevelt was, Holcomb knew he'd better take a long and hard look at it.

Marine Corps resistance to this "commando" concept, which had been talked about for nearly a year, had always been strong. Holcomb believed that the term "Marine" was alone sufficient to indicate that a man was ready for duty at any time, and the injection of a special name such as "commando" would be undesirable and superfluous.

"The organization, equipment, and training of infantry units of the Marine divisions should, in practically all respects, be identical to that of the commandos," Holcomb wrote in the fall of 1941. "In general, it may be stated that the training of all units in the two Marine divisions prepares them to carry out either offensive operations on a large scale, or small-scale amphibious raids of the type carried out by the commandos."

The attack on Pearl Harbor quickened President Roosevelt's desire to establish commando-type units within the Marine Corps. He also wanted his friend, army colonel Bill Donovan, promoted to brigadier general in the Marine Corps so that he could run the project. Holcomb asked two of his top Marine officers, Maj. Gen. Holland M. Smith, the commanding general of Amphibious Force, Atlantic Fleet and Maj. Gen. Charles F. B. Price, commanding general, Department of the Pacific, to comment on the proposal, and not surprisingly, both were steadfastly against it.

General Smith was particularly antagonistic against the appointment of Donovan on the grounds that the Marine Corps should not have to go outside of its own ranks to secure leaders. He also opposed the commando concept on philosophical grounds, noting that all Marines could be trained in raiding techniques by their own officers if it were deemed important. Smith felt that all Marines were considered as commandos, expressing a view that would become increasingly common among senior Marine officers, namely, that there was no task that the "elite" commando units could perform any more effectively than regular line units.

Smith wrote that the "appointment of Colonel Donovan to brigadier general could be compared to that of Lord Mountbatten in Great Britain—both are 'royal' and have easy access to the highest authority without reference to their own immediate superiors. The appointment would be considered by many senior officers of the Corps as political, unfair, and a publicity stunt. . . . The commandant would lose control of that number of Marines assigned as commandos. We have enough 'by-products' now. It is the unanimous opinion of the staff of this headquarters that commando raids by the British have been of little strategical value. We have not reached the stage where our men are so highly trained and restless for action that they must be employed in commando raids."

General Price warned of another problem, noting that the rapid expansion of the Marine Corps would result in an extreme shortage of qualified officers and senior NCOs with the requisite command experience. He concurred with the commando concept but only if the personnel were recruited directly rather than by drawing on already thin Marine Corps resources. Some of his contemporaries thought this opinion was formed to curry favor with his commander-in-chief.

Price also wrote a personal letter to Holcomb that delved more deeply into his true feelings about the Raider project.

"There is another thing in this connection which I could not put in my other letter and that is the grave danger that this sort of thing will develop into a tail which will wag the dog eventually," he wrote. "I know in what quarter the idea of foisting this scheme upon the Marines originated, and I opine that if it is developed along the lines of a hobby in the hands of personnel other than regular Marine officers it could very easily get far out of hand and out of control as well.

"It appears pretty clear to me that you are in a position of having to comply and that nothing can be done about it so please accept my sympathy."

Holcomb was clearly on the horns of a dilemma and admitted such in a letter he wrote to a friend in mid January of 1942.

"The Donovan affair is still uppermost in my mind. I am terrified that I may be forced to take this man," he wrote. "I feel that it will be the worst slap in the face that the Marine Corps was ever given because it involves bringing into the Marine Corps as a leader in our own specialty, that is, amphibious operations. . . . It will be bitterly resented by our personnel, both commissioned and enlisted, and I am afraid that it may serve to materially reduce my usefulness in this office, if any, because I am expected, and properly so, to protect the Marine Corps from intrusions of this kind."

President Roosevelt was insistent on establishing a commando force to help him exact revenge on the Japanese for their "dastardly attack" on Pearl Harbor. He saw the Marine commando force as a perfect vehicle to accomplish that goal. General Holcomb was equally insistent that appointing Donovan, an army man, to lead a Marine unit would be bad politics and bad for morale.

A compromise was reached. Donovan, who would later lead the Office of Strategic Services, the forerunner of today's Central Intelligence Agency, remained in the army while Holcomb accepted FDR's choice of Marine major Evans F. Carlson, a controversial reserve officer, as one of the commanders of the two initial Raider battalions. So, in a move at least partly precipitated by a desire to avoid a political appointee (Donovan) as leader of the raider units, it was decided early in February to give Lt. Col. Merritt A. Edson command of what would become the 1st Raider Battalion at Quantico, Virginia, and Major Carlson, who had gained fame marching with Communist Chinese guerrillas behind Japanese lines in the late 1930s, would be appointed as commander of the 2d Raider Battalion to be formed near San Diego.

Edson's executive officer was to be Maj. Sam B. Griffith, the man who had observed the British commando training program in Scotland. Carlson, who had become a confidant of President Roosevelt while stationed at Warm Springs, Georgia, earlier in his career, was given his choice assignment over the objections of many top Marine officers who actually had little say in the decision. His executive officer was to be the president's oldest son, Capt. Jimmy Roosevelt, who, like Carlson, was a reserve officer.

Two other names were proposed for the Marine force before "Raiders" was accepted. Colonel Edson had suggested that his unit be called the

"1st Destroyer Battalion," while General Smith came up with the moniker of "1st Shock Battalion." General Price wanted to stay with the commonly accepted term "commando" but offered "raiding battalions" as an alternative. General Holcomb shortened it to the "1st Raider Battalion," and issued the order on February 12, effective four days later. The 2d Raider Battalion was officially born February 19, though both battalions had been training for several weeks.

The basic mission of the two new raider units was threefold: to be the spearhead of amphibious landings by larger forces on beaches generally thought to be inaccessible; to conduct raiding expeditions requiring great elements of surprise and high speed; and to conduct guerrilla-type operations for protracted periods behind enemy lines.

Though President Roosevelt had lost the battle to appoint his old friend Colonel Donovan to head the Raiders, he had a very visible hand in shaping the command structure of the 2d Raider Battalion. He put the full weight of his prestige and power behind the outspoken and unorthodox Carlson, a man whom the Marine Corps brass regarded as left leaning and too individualistic to be trusted with a combat command.

Carlson was officially notified on February 5, 1942, that he was to be given command of what was to become the 2d Raider Battalion. Obviously elated, he wrote his father, Tom, at his home in Plymouth, Connecticut, the very same day.

"At last I have received a break," he wrote. "Today I was placed in command of a special unit with carte blanche to organize, train, and indoctrinate it as I see fit. There is nothing like it in existence in the country. Naturally, I'm delighted. I will hand pick my personnel. Jimmy Roosevelt is to be my executive officer. . . . Things seem to be moving in a direction I have so long urged and had almost despaired of seeing materialized. But now I have been afforded the opportunity to practice some of the precepts I have been preaching these past years."

Four
Growing Pains

Evans Fordyce Carlson had a hunger for adventure from a young age. A devotee of Ralph Waldo Emerson as a youth, he took the famous writer's advice and decided not to postpone life but to live it.

Carlson was born in Sidney, New York, on February 26, 1896, the son of an impoverished Congregationalist minister of Norwegian ancestry. On his mother's side, he was Scotch, Irish, Welsh, and English. His name is a composite of his mixed heritage: Evans is Welsh, Fordyce is English, and Carlson is Norwegian.

His mother, Joetta Evans, could trace her ancestry to before the Revolutionary War. One of her forebears was on Gen. George Washington's staff. Carlson's paternal grandfather panned for gold and silver in the mountains of eastern California before he died in 1901. His uncle Matt was a U.S. marshal in Fairbanks, Alaska.

His father, Thomas, was born in 1865 in a community of mining shacks in the high Sierras. His real name was Thorstein Alpine Carlson. He came East in his twenties to attend seminary schools. His first parish was in Sidney, New York, where Evans was born. When Evans was but six months old, the family moved to Middlebury, Vermont, where they lived for four years. The family, which then included sons Dana and Tom junior and daughter Karen, moved next to Shoreham, Vermont, near Lake Champlain. They would move again to Dracut, Massachusetts (near Lowell), Peacham, Vermont (near St. Johnsbury on the Connecticut River), and finally to Plymouth, Connecticut, in 1926.

"Evans was like every country boy of his era," Tom Carlson said. "He wore overalls and a straw hat and went barefoot in the summer. He was very good to his brothers and sister. Sometimes, when he was only nine or ten years old, Mrs. Carlson and I would have to leave him alone in the house with the children, and he always watched the younger ones with extreme care until we got back."

As a youngster, Evans exhibited a sturdy independence of thought and action, which often got him in trouble. His father remembered a time when he came upon Evans and another boy fighting in a school yard.

"They were at it hammer and tongs, and I considered stepping between the boys and admonishing them to stop the violence," Tom Carlson said. "Evans just looked at me sternly for a minute, indicating that the fight was something about which he privately felt himself to be in the right, and I had no business interfering. So I just walked away and let the two reach a settlement by themselves."

Although not mechanically inclined, Evans, like many others of his generation, was fascinated by the hundreds of new mechanical marvels of his age. He constructed his own carts and wagons of old cast-off wheels and odd bits of lumber he found around the farm.

"When he was about eleven years old, he traded some of his treasures for a broken-down Stanley steamer, one of the earliest models that ever came out," Tom Carlson recalled. "The machine wouldn't work, but it was standing in a farmyard up the road from our place, and the boy pushed it out on the road, got a fire going, and let it roll down to our place, where he could work on it. He kept that for a year or more after getting it into working order, and later traded it to a barber in St. Johnsbury for an old musket and several other trinkets."

Like most of the country boys of Vermont, Evans developed a strong interest in the outdoors. He collected his own camping equipment and knapsack, and during the summertime he and his school chums used to go off on camping trips for several days at a time.

Evans never did receive much of a formal education because of the lack of adequate schools in rural Vermont, but he was an avid reader at home. Among the books he devoured as a youngster were *Robinson Crusoe, Swiss Family Robinson, The Vicar of Wakefield,* and a popular children's series of the day, the *Five Little Peppers.* Later, he became a devotee of Ralph Waldo Emerson.

The years in Dracut, Massachusetts, were particularly harsh. Both parents were sick enough to require operations, and Evans's brother, Charles Dana, showed the first symptoms of tuberculosis. Evans left home for the first time a day short of his twelfth birthday but returned in a week when he ran out of money and had no place to live.

Carlson ran away from home again at fourteen, this time for good. He worked briefly on a farm near Vergennes, Vermont, and then as an assistant freight master on the Rutland Railroad, where he learned telegraphy. The following year, he went to New Jersey, where he had a friend who was a surveyor, and obtained a job as a chainman on a surveying crew. On election day in 1912, three-and-a-half months shy of his seventeenth birthday, Carlson bluffed his way past recruiters to enlist in the army. The legal enlistment age then was twenty-one. Asked his age, Carlson boldly told the recruiter he was twenty-two.

A few weeks later, a friend of the family discovered what Carlson had done and offered to get him out of the army because of his age.

"Mrs. Carlson and I were more than apprehensive when we learned what he had done," Tom Carlson said. "We even considered writing to our congressman to see if something could be done to get the boy out of the service. We were worried more about his extreme youth than anything else. He was only sixteen then, and we learned later that he'd lied about his age to get into the army. After considering it carefully I told his mother that perhaps it would be a good thing for him to learn a little about the consequences of impulsive acts." They felt it just might be the schooling he needed.

Over the next three years, the youthful Carlson saw service helping to construct the fortress of Corregidor in the Philippines, and at Schofield Barracks in Hawaii. Evans corresponded regularly with his father. In one of his earliest letters to his father from the Philippines, he wrote, "I know now, father, that the army will either make or break me, and I think you need not fear for me anymore."

He was discharged from the army in 1915 as a top sergeant, though he was still a teenager. After a brief period as a surveyor for the California state highway commission, he was recalled to duty in July 1916 during the border trouble with Mexico. He was commissioned a second lieutenant of artillery in September of 1917 and sent to Texas to train reserve officer material from Harvard, Yale, Princeton, and other colleges. Promoted to captain in February of 1918 and sent overseas, he was on a troop train headed for the front when World War I ended. He remained in France after the war as a member of General Pershing's staff. His job was to investigate recommendations for the Congressional Medal of Honor. He resigned from the army in December 1919.

Earlier that year, he was profoundly affected by the death of his younger brother Dana, from a bout with influenza. He also divorced his wife, Dorothy, upon his return to the States. The marriage, which took place in May of 1916, two months before he was recalled to duty, produced a son, Evans junior. Showing his abilities as a writer, Carlson wrote his parents that the divorce was obtained "without the heat of anger nor the sting of any alleged injustice. But with discretion, prudence, and deep affection."

After the war, Carlson worked as a salesman with the California Packing Corporation based in the Oakland area. He went on the road selling fruit over a territory that included Montana and Texas. Again he became restless. He couldn't resist the call of the military. The army said he could rejoin as a second lieutenant, which would mean he would be outranked by his colleagues who had remained in the service after the war. He dismissed that option and also ruled out the navy. That left the Marine Corps and the promise of new opportunities and strange places. He enlisted as a private in the spring of 1922.

The Marine recruiter was delighted to have a man of Carlson's vast experience because, as everyone in the Corps knew, a Marine private was the equal of an army captain. Carlson was equally ecstatic.

"Well, I'm back—in the service. And believe me, I'm so happy I'm almost moved to tears," he wrote his father. "Lord, I've fought off the desire to get back into harness but I'd rather be a buck private in the Marines than a captain of industry. . . . My heart is in the service—and here I must stay. . . . I shall go up, of course. Sit steady in the boat and don't worry. I'm coming out on top. . . . Hope to get out to China soon."

Interestingly, the officer who administered Carlson's oath of enlistment in the Marine Corps was Capt. James Schwerin, whose son, William, later served under Carlson as a Raider company commander.

Later that year—just two days before Christmas—Carlson was commissioned a second lieutenant.

Carlson quickly established himself as a bit of a maverick in an essay he wrote about one of his favorite topics—military ethics. He believed from an early age in "the conscious striving of men for the welfare of society as a whole." One of his early efficiency reports took note of his rather unorthodox beliefs but also commended him for his "earnestness," which was defined as his "most outstanding characteristic."

He married again in August of 1924 just before leaving for flight training at Pensacola, Florida. Carlson could see the future and he wanted to be part of it. He wrote his father:

"My main reason for desiring aviation training is the fact that the day is not far hence when this branch of the service will be the dominating factor of all wars."

Unfortunately for him, he busted out.

In 1927, he went to China as a regimental intelligence officer in Shanghai. It was to have a profound impact on his life.

In May of 1930, Carlson, now a first lieutenant, was posted to Nicaragua, where the Marines were assisting in the organization of the Nicaraguan National Guard. It didn't take him long to find some action. Responding to a report that a hundred bandits were looting a nearby town, Carlson led a twelve-man detail to quell the disturbance. Without suffering any casualties of his own, Carlson succeeded in recovering the stolen property and dispersing the bandits, who suffered two killed and seven wounded. Shortly thereafter, he was sent home with fatigue and malaria and a Navy Cross for "extraordinary heroism."

Sam Griffith, one of Carlson's contemporaries in the Marine Corps who would later become commanding officer of the 1st Raider Battalion, enjoyed repeating a story he had heard about his friend's service in Nicaragua.

"It seems that Carlson was at a hill station called Jalapa," Griffith said. "He had to travel about twenty miles through hill country that was pretty much controlled by bandits. The area was near the Honduran border where the Sandinistas used to get most of their weapons.

"So he got himself a mule and started off. He was dressed like a native with a serape covering his body. You know, one of those long waterproof cloths with a slit in the middle for your head; it hangs over your shoulder. And underneath the serape he had a Thompson submachine gun. And that's the way, all alone, he rode those twenty miles. How's that for guts?"

In the spring of 1933, Carlson returned to China to his old job as an intelligence officer of the 4th Regiment, this time in Peking. The scene had changed. Japan had moved into Manchuria and the Chinese Red Army, organized in the southern provinces under Mao Tse-tung, had fought off four extermination campaigns directed against them by Chiang Kai-shek.

If Shanghai had been Carlson's school of Chinese politics, Peking was his university of Chinese culture. He studied art and architecture and the Chinese language. He entertained and enjoyed the good life, making friends with intellectuals and well-known writers such as Edgar

Snow and Agnes Smedley, who wrote many books on their adopted homeland.

Snow, a lifelong friend who exerted a profound influence on Carlson, was a passionate advocate of Communism. Carlson was not so much interested in China's politics as he was the tactics and esprit de corps of its military establishment.

"Evans Carlson was no Communist," Snow wrote. "He was one of those people whom Dostoyevsky's policeman called 'far more dreadful'—a Christian who believed in God and also believed in socialism."

Promoted to captain on his return to the States in 1935, Carlson became an aide to Maj. Gen. Charles Lyman at President Roosevelt's detachment at Warm Springs, Georgia. Carlson, the president, and FDR's oldest son, Jimmy, would talk for hours about the unstable situation in Asia and Japan's growing designs on China.

"President Roosevelt had an eye for interesting people," Evans Carlson Jr. said in an interview conducted in February of 2000.

Shortly before Carlson was to depart for his third tour of China in the summer of 1937, Roosevelt called him aside and asked if he would do him a favor.

"I understand you are going out to China again, Evans. I want you to do something for me while you're there," Roosevelt asked. "I want you to drop me a line now and then—direct to the White House. Let me know how you're doing. Tell me what's going on. I suspect there's going to be a great deal going on this summer in China. I'd like to hear what you have to say about it. Shall we keep these letters a secret? Just between the two of us? Shall we?"

"For as long as both of us live, Mr. President," Carlson answered.

"I've got a lot to do before I die," Roosevelt said.

Roosevelt suggested Carlson write to him through his secretary, Marguerite "Missy" LeHand, as a means of disguising where they were intended to go. It was a clear breach of military protocol.

Carlson arrived back in China just as the Japanese were expanding their sphere of influence in that country. He arrived in August shortly after the Sino-Japanese War had begun. For the following year and a half, he was attached to the Chinese armies as an official observer for the U.S. Navy Department.

During this time, Carlson became the first foreign military officer to accompany China's Eighth Route Army, or for that matter any Chinese military force, in an actual campaign. In 1938, as a Marine Corps intelligence officer, he marched the length and breadth of Shansi Province from Inner Mongolia, a five-month trip of almost twenty-five hundred miles, to study the "pattern of resistance" and make tests of the Chinese defenses against the Japanese invasion. Carlson once tramped forty-three miles with the Chinese Communists Eighth Route Army in a period of twenty hours during which they crossed eight mountains.

Over a two-year period, Carlson sent Roosevelt seventeen reports—through Missy LeHand—of his experiences as an observer with this ill-trained and ill-equipped army over some of the toughest terrain in China, an experience that shaped his own philosophy of guerrilla warfare.

Carlson's effusive praise of the discipline and determination of the ragtag Communist forces in combating the Japanese angered both his superiors in the Marine Corps and supporters of Chiang Kai-shek's Nationalist regime. He admired the Communist Eighth Army's leaders because they were unselfish and did not practice the traditional warlord custom of self-aggrandizement. He was most taken by the officers' interest in the welfare of their men.

In interviews with newspaper correspondents, Carlson said that the Red Army and the Cooperatives were the hope of China and that the United States was undermining one of its best friends by supplying Japan with scrap, oil, and other material. For this he was officially censured. When it was later discovered that Carlson had gone out of channels by secretly informing Roosevelt of his personal impressions, the Marine Corps was further incensed.

According to Jimmy Roosevelt, the Marine Corps establishment initially knew nothing of Carlson's direct reporting to his father but when it finally came to light, they came down on him to a man.

"They made life in the Marines so difficult for Evans that he actually left the service for a while," James Roosevelt wrote. "I believe Carlson's reports made father distrust Chiang Kai-shek at a time when others thought father should be supporting him. At any rate, father felt the assignment was worthwhile and he didn't care whether the generals resented his bypassing the chain of command."

Another man impressed with Carlson's report on his experiences with Eighth Route Army was Marine major general J. C. Breckinridge, who took the time to write a personal letter to Carlson in July of 1938.

My Dear Captain Carlson,
    I have just finished reading your report on the military activi-

ties in the northwest of China, dated 23 March, 1938. I compliment you on what you have done. The report is clear, understandable, interesting, and very well expressed. After great exertion that covered much territory you have compressed your observations into a valuable and creditable compactness. For the first time I feel that I have an understanding of a situation that has heretofore been nothing but an incomprehensible muddle: something like a quagmire in which very many people seemed to be floundering without aim or object. It makes me happy to know that this admirable report has been produced by a Marine officer.

As the summer of 1938 wore on, Carlson became increasingly outspoken in press conferences, calling attention to the fact that scrap iron and other raw materials sold by the United States to Japan were being turned into bullets and bombs that were killing thousands of Chinese. Carlson felt personally responsible. He could no longer talk to his Chinese friends so glibly about America and her promise of aid. He made a vow to himself that he would bring the truth to his fellow countrymen no matter what the obstacles.

Constantly muzzled by his superiors, Carlson thought it best that he resign his commission so that he could carry on his campaign of information as a civilian. The straw that convinced him he must quit the service was the response he received from his superiors on a proposed address he hoped to give in Washington on conditions in China.

"The Navy Department has no objection to the proposed talk," wrote Adm. William D. Leahy, acting for Navy Secretary Claude Swanson, "provided it reveals nothing that you learned by reason of being language officer or because of other duties assigned to you by the Naval Attaché in China."

Carlson felt the Navy Department's response was absurd and dishonest. Some of his closest friends, who respected his military promise, begged him to stay in the reserves but he rejected the suggestion. He wanted no strings attached. His mind was made up. He resigned in April of 1939, just a year before he was eligible for retirement.

"I had already strained the limits of diplomatic good form by bearing public witness to the character of Chinese resistance I had found in north China, but the story had not half been told," Carlson later wrote. "I could not do more without reverting to the status of a private citizen. And so

I submitted my resignation as an officer of the Marine Corps, and of the Naval Service. A pressing sense of duty had left me no alternative."

That was his public view. In private, according to a passage in his diary, Carlson had grown weary with narrow-minded officials in the military and all the red tape that smothered independent thought.

"I am tired of attempting to adjust my action to the arbitrary whims of a superior officer," he wrote for private consumption. "Self-preservation seems to be the first thought of an officer of the U.S. Army or Navy. His whole training tends to accentuate that inclination. As a result he inevitably takes the short view of things, considering each problem in terms of his personal economic security. He will take no action which may jeopardize his career. He is continually thinking about the next selection board, and of how his superiors in Washington will consider the decision and action he has taken. Consequently, it seems to be indicated that I should separate myself from the service if I am to be able to think and act in accordance with my own convictions. With this conviction in mind I today sent in my resignation to the Secretary of the Navy, via the [naval attaché] at Peiping. It is quite a rench [sic] to break the associations of so many years. I might retire, but the naval restrictions would continue to apply should I remain on the retired list. No, resignation is the only solution."

Simply put, his sense of personal responsibility and obligation would not permit him to stand quietly by while his own country was inviting Japanese aggression on the world by ignoring their barbarous practices in China. As he told his friends, "I have a responsibility to tell because I know."

His friends and colleagues tried hard to talk him out of it. They kept asking him why he was taking this rash position.

"I replied that I wished to be free to speak and write in accordance with my convictions. I have made my decision and will stick to it," Carlson wrote in his diary. "Everyone here very sympathetic. I do not want sympathy, though. Right now all I want is a release from a situation that has become intolerable."

He tendered his resignation in mid-September despite the fact that he had been notified that he was on a short list for promotion to major. He would not let any personal issues interfere with his mission to bring the truth to the American people. Still, it took him seven more months to officially separate himself from the Marine Corps.

While a civilian in the spring of 1939, Carlson traveled and lectured extensively in the United States and the Far East, warning the world of the strength and ambition of Japan. He wrote two books, *Twin Stars of China* and *The Chinese Army,* and numerous magazine pieces, stressing that America must stop helping Japan and that America's national interests were bound up with China's victory.

In addition, he championed an Act of Congress to embargo Japan from importing American scrap metal, oil, and other materials that might be used for waging war. Many historians believe this action proved to be the final straw in Japan's decision to strike out against the United States and its Far Eastern allies.

Popular radio news commentator Raymond Gram Swing referred often to Carlson as "probably the best informed living American in regard to Chinese affairs."

On his way home from a trip to China early in 1941, and certain that war between the United States and Japan was inevitable, he stopped off in Manila to warn General MacArthur that the Japanese would attack the Philippines. He suggested that MacArthur train his American and Filipino troops for jungle warfare and to place secret, emergency caches of food, weapons, and ammunition in the mountains to support a guerrilla campaign against the Japanese. The imperious MacArthur listened politely but did little, if anything, to comply with Carlson's suggestions.

It was probably that "cold" meeting with MacArthur that convinced Carlson he would have a better opportunity to apply his experience and knowledge as a member of the armed services rather than as a civilian.

According to Carlson's son, Evans junior, he was offered an appointment as a lieutenant colonel in the army by his old friend Jimmy Ulio, who was then the adjutant general.

"Dad felt that it was a very attractive situation, but he also felt that if he accepted it he would be taking advantage of the situation," Evans junior said. "He had an extreme set of ethical values. He felt that if he accepted the rank of lieutenant colonel in the army, he would be taking advantage of an opportunity. He would not do that."

Instead, he applied for recommissioning in the Marine Corps as a reserve major in April of 1941. Having made some enemies during his previous tour of duty, he needed the support of some powerful friends to secure the appointment, however. Some high-ranking Marine officials viewed Carlson with suspicion, as someone who had gone off "the deep end" by embracing Communism. His resignation from the Marines was also viewed as an almost treasonous act against their beloved Corps. They were not sure whether he could be trusted with a combat command.

In April of 1941, Carlson confided in a Marine Corps friend that he was thinking about returning to active duty in the army. Asked why the army, Carlson said, "Frankly, because I know what will happen if I put in my application for the Marines. My paper will come up to the Reserve board and someone will say, 'Carlson wants to come in again. What'll we do with the s.o.b.?'"

His friend had to laugh because he knew that was exactly what the Marine Corps would say.

"But we've called you [an] s.o.b. ever since you resigned; it oughtn't to be news to you," the friend said.

Carlson smiled and admitted that being called an s.o.b. took some getting used to. "Maybe," he said, "that's what will make me feel more at home in the Marines."

Carlson once again used his White House connections and the Marine Corps went along with his reappointment. The following month, Major Carlson reported for active duty at Camp Elliott in San Diego as operations and intelligence officer of the 2d Regiment. His two-year absence from the Marine Corps had cost him 250 numbers in seniority. One of the first things he did was send a memo to the commandant of the Marine Corps, volunteering for service if and when commando-type groups were to be activated.

President Roosevelt was delighted that Carlson was back in uniform and let him know that if he could be of any help to him, just ask. Roosevelt suggested that he might want to go to Scotland with a couple of other American officers to observe British commando training. Carlson, in a bit of haughtiness, declined the invitation with a reply that said he had "already studied similar tactics in Nicaragua and China."

Shortly after Pearl Harbor, Carlson, itching for action, wrote another round of letters to high officials volunteering his services for commando-type operations. This time, he included a letter to army general Joe Stilwell, who was on temporary duty in Washington. Both men were old China hands and friends for many years.

Stilwell, who was about to be sent back to the China-Burma theater as America's top military figure, answered Carlson's missive with a handwritten note dated January 17, 1942.

My Dear Carlson,
    It was a pleasure to hear from you and I appreciate the kind words. If anything should develop along the lines you indicated,

be sure that your name would at once pop into my mind, and that I would do what I could about it. Since coming [to Washington], I have been at work on several tentative plans and do not yet know what will be decided, but should know within ten days now. It is a comfort to know that you are ready to be leaned on. Best wishes, and hoping we'll get our chance, sincerely yours, J. W. Stilwell.

Carlson was still viewed as something of an oddball as far as the Corps was concerned, but his friendship with Roosevelt helped temper any overt criticism of him within the military hierarchy. His belief in the cadre system and his idyllic accounting of the performance of the Chinese Communist guerrillas against the Japanese labeled him as a "pinko" in many circles.

Carlson knew that many of his brother officers regarded him as a maverick. They were suspicious of him. Hadn't he gone out of the chain of command to get what he wanted before? He wasn't exactly a team player.

Later, as Carlson's fame grew as the leader of "Carlson's Raiders," it only created a stubborn resentment of him in the higher echelons of the Marine Corps. As the publicity grew around the 2d Raider Battalion, the word got around that he had better be "handled." It wasn't good for the Corps to have specialized or "trick" outfits, as the Marine brass called them. Warnings from within went up that if headquarters didn't watch out, the whole Marine Corps would be a confused collection of prima donna battalions. Carlson's independence and growing fame would be constantly challenged.

Early in the war, however, Carlson had a couple of important allies who, more or less, gave him a free hand to exploit his unorthodox philosophies of warfare. President Roosevelt was one and Admiral Nimitz was another. And that was all he needed.

Five

Gung Ho

According to Carlson's biographer, Michael Blankfort, Carlson gathered most of his new battalion around him in mid-February of 1942 and introduced them to "Gung Ho," the Chinese phrase that would become their motto. As the five hundred or so Raider recruits milled around on a parade field at Camp Elliott, a jeep drove up with a portable loudspeaker that was placed atop a platform made from three ration crates. An enlisted communications man stepped to the mike and asked if he could be heard. Then a second jeep, with Carlson in the passenger seat, drove up. Sergeant Major Charles Lamb called the group to attention.

Carlson strode to the microphone looking very much like a clean-shaven Abraham Lincoln. His long nose, pointed chin, and snaggle-tooth grin gave his face a craggy look. The lines on his face, especially around the eyes and across his forehead, were evidence of the hard life he had led.

"As you were, boys," Carlson said in his deep, soft voice as he peered out over the group. Then he raised his right arm and motioned for the men to gather around him. "Come on up here. Let's get together."

The men broke ranks, with Carlson smiling and waving at familiar faces, Blankfort wrote. He had personally interviewed many of the men now standing before him. Then Carlson reached into his back pocket and took out a small harmonica, tapped it several times against his palm, put it to his lips, and blew a C.

"'The first thing we're going to do is to sing our National Anthem,'" Blankfort wrote. "Looking up at the American flag flapping above, Carlson began to sing. The men, caught by surprise, joined in, slowly at first.

Many didn't know the words. A hundred yards to the right, a small truck pulled over to the side of the road. Two Marines, who saw a group at attention singing the National Anthem, got out and, according to regulations, came to attention and saluted. It was three o'clock in the afternoon."

Once the song was over, Carlson put away his harmonica and pulled out his pipe. The "smoking lamp is lit," he said, inviting the men to sit down and smoke if they wished. He filled his pipe, lit it, and blew a cloud of smoke into the air. He had a story to tell them, he said, one he hoped would be of interest. Some of the men had heard stories about Carlson and his long march through the backcountry of China. They knew the training to come would be tough because Carlson was a tough man.

What they heard over the next twenty minutes was a speech unlike anything they had ever heard before.

Carlson told the men that they all lived in a democratic country and it was a contradiction for such a country to have an armed force that was dictatorial and undemocratic. The Prussian system of discipline that still influenced much American military thinking would not be tolerated—but there would be some form of discipline based on "knowledge and reason, not blind obedience. In a democracy, men must be thinking human beings, not puppets."

The men huddled in the audience, many of them old boots, looked at each other with a bit of bewilderment.

Furthermore, Carlson continued, there would be no caste differences in the Raiders. Officers, including himself, would not order a man to do what they themselves were not prepared to do. Officers would have no special mess or barracks or clubs. And there would be no unnecessary saluting.

The men looked at each other and smiled. A small cheer rang out and a few of the younger men pumped an arm and said, "All right." To the old hands, it sounded too good to be true.

Next, Carlson told them what to expect during training—long marches, little food or rest, and many hardships. "A time will come when our only food will be what we take off dead Japs. I promise you nothing but hardships and danger. When we get into battle, we ask no mercy, we give none."

The smiles in the audience turned into cheers. Many of them had joined the Raiders to see some action and get a little payback for Pearl Harbor. It appeared they would get it.

Then Carlson told them a true story of his experiences marching with the Chinese Communist Eighth Route Army in 1937, particularly one grueling fifty-mile march over tough terrain. The audience sat mesmerized. Carlson had their full attention.

Not one of the six-hundred-man Chinese force he was with dropped out, Carlson told the men. He knew they were dead tired and yet they kept going. He wondered how they had done it.

"If a man has only legs he gets tired," one of the weary marchers said to him.

Carlson, who now had everybody's complete attention, paused and looked out over the assembled Raiders with that withered, craggy face of his and slowly explained what the Chinese soldier meant.

"The reason those six hundred men were able to endure such hardship was because they knew why it was necessary for them to complete that march," Carlson said, using his pipe to punctuate his story. "They understood why the efforts of every single one of them was necessary for the victory of the whole Chinese people. That's what you've got to have besides legs."

It never occurred to Carlson, who was like so many idealists of his time, that the reason no one dropped out might have been a mortal fear of being punished rather than a steadfast devotion to a cause.

Carlson, taking time to relight his pipe, stressed the value of teamwork, again and again. A chain, he said, is only as strong as its weakest link. They must help each other. He was trying to build up the same sort of working spirit he had seen in China, where all the soldiers dedicated themselves to one idea and worked together to put that idea over.

"The Chinese have two words for 'working together,'" he said. "'Gung,' meaning work; 'Ho,' meaning harmony. Gung Ho! Work together. I propose that Gung Ho be the spirit and the slogan of our Raider Battalion."

He paused and moved closer to the microphone, thrusting his distinctive nose and chin at the audience. "It's a good slogan, boys. Let's hear you say it." Carlson went first, shouting out, "Gung Ho." Then the men responded, hesitantly at first but then with gusto when prompted to say it again.

Predictably, when word of this first meeting reached higher headquarters, many of the Marine brass thought the term "Gung Ho" was giving the Chinese Communists undesired publicity. The term caught on, however, and is still used today to mean someone who has a dedicated and positive attitude.

• • •

That may not be exactly how these young recruits first heard of "Gung Ho," but no one seems to have a better recollection of that initial unit meeting.

"It sure is a good story," Raider Ben Carson said fifty-seven years later. "I'm not going to say that's exactly what happened the first time we assembled. I don't remember the harmonica bit. But it could have happened. Maybe I wasn't there then."

Brian Quirk, another one of Carlson's Raiders, didn't endorse that version of the initial "Gung Ho" meeting either. "I don't remember it," he said when asked more than a half century later.

Dean Voight said he recalled an early get-together to explain the Gung Ho philosophy, but not much else. "My memory isn't that sharp, I'm afraid. I certainly don't remember any mouth organ," he said in a 1999 interview.

All three men, who would wind up in B Company of the 2d Raider Battalion and survive the blunders of the Makin Raid, vividly remember hearing of the formation of Carlson's new command and thinking, *This is for me*. Many thought it was a call to action in China or even Japan.

Carson, a Minnesota farm boy, was called a "feather merchant" by his drill instructors back in 1942 because he was only five foot six and 135 pounds. Ten weeks shy of his nineteenth birthday, he had joined the Marine Corps five days after Pearl Harbor, against the wishes of his parents, who already had a son in the navy. His older brother, George, was a gunner's mate second class aboard the USS *Maryland* at the time of the Japanese attack on Pearl Harbor. Fortunately the *Maryland* was inboard of the *Oklahoma* on that fateful Sunday and sustained only minor damage.

"Back on the farm in Minnesota we could not find out anything about the fate of my brother, but my folks finally relented and let me join the Marines," Carson said. Several weeks later after reporting to San Diego, he grew tired of polishing gear for the next guard mount, especially those damn boondocker shoes with the split leather tops. He saw an announcement on the company bulletin board that a "special" battalion was being formed in San Diego for those who wanted to see some action.

Some of the boots called it a "suicide" battalion. Carson and many others itching for action liked the ring of it.

Quirk, who enlisted the day after Pearl Harbor at a post office in Chicago, was an admitted "wise guy" because he had a couple of years of college behind him. He had dreams of becoming a Marine fighter pilot.

"I didn't exactly like all the chicken-shit discipline in boot camp," Quirk said. "Everything had to be done right and done on time. I was still enraged at the Japanese attack and I wanted at them. I heard that a new battalion was being formed and went to hear a pitch being given by a Major Carlson. A bunch of us went to hear what he had to say. He got up on a stage and told us that all he could offer was rice, raisins, bullets, a blanket, maybe death, but lots of glory. I said to myself, 'I'll show him.'"

Voight, a big, roughneck city boy from Chicago, had four years' experience as a welder before the war and could hold his own against anyone who tested his toughness. His father, who was only five foot six, gave his six-foot-two son the nickname of "High Pockets" at a young age. The son called his dad "Low Pockets." Voight enlisted in the Marines on December 8 and when he reported for boot camp in San Diego, he asked for a job as an aircraft welder.

"You know the Marines. If you're a truck driver they make a cook out of you," Voight said. "They said I didn't have enough education to be a welder. I said the hell with that, give me an infantry outfit. They sent me over to where Carlson was interviewing candidates for his new outfit."

The basic mission of Marine Corps training, then and today, is to break a man down to nothing and then build him up until he is something— a Marine. Physical pressure was applied early and often. It wasn't uncommon for a drill sergeant to backhand a recruit with the admonition, "Sonny, I can't make you do something you don't want to do, but I can make you wish you had."

Most of the recruits pouring into the San Diego area were willing fodder for whatever the Marine Corps needed in the days after Pearl Harbor. They would have to grow up in a hurry—or maybe not grow up at all. Carson, a typical wide-eyed recruit, remembered his first day as a Marine a half century later with remarkable clarity.

It was January 1, 1942, when Carson reported for duty at the U.S. Marine Recruit Depot in San Diego. After milling around for most of the day, Carson said a noncom, obviously hung over from a New Year's Eve party, finally showed up and barked, "All you guys who figure you screwed up in joining this outfit, you got sixty seconds to get through this door and the hell out of here!"

About forty recruits decided to accept the noncom's offer, according to Carson. Those who remained began to wonder why the Marines would allow so many to leave after paying for their train fare to San Diego. Moments later, they had their answer. The recruits who had left were seen marching past the barracks in the rain carrying steel bunks, rolled-up mattresses, and arms full of sheets and blankets.

That's how easy it was to "volunteer" in the Marine Corps.

Still, many of these raw recruits were ready to volunteer again for the Raiders, which made them double volunteers.

Wanting to join the Raiders and getting accepted were two different matters, however. Candidates not only had to be physically fit and able to endure extremely long marches, they had to be proficient with a variety of lethal weapons and willing to kill the enemy in close combat. Then, on top of that, they had to have a sound reason for wanting to join such an outfit.

"I won't take a man who doesn't give a damn about anything," Carlson told his officers. "But if he has a deep feeling about wanting to fight, even for the wrong reasons, take him. I know I can shape him into wanting to fight for the right reasons."

It wasn't for everybody, as Jimmy Roosevelt later wrote.

"I remember the first time a group was called together to hear us out. Carlson made a stirring plea for volunteers, but one in which he stressed the hazards involved in this sort of raiding action," Roosevelt wrote. "When, in conclusion, he asked those interested to step forward, no one budged. It was embarrassing, to say the least, the low point of our program. But finally one man moved forward. Then another."

Carlson insisted on interviewing all those who applied. He and Roosevelt did almost all the one-on-one interviews. He wanted to get behind the answers they gave on why they wanted to join his outfit. He wanted to find out what they held dear enough to die for. He had to know what they believed in. Those who were apathetic or who wanted only adventure or were too old or had personal burdens that worried them, he thanked with fatherly understanding and politely sent them on their way.

Carlson had developed an almost mystical concept of selflessness in battle and was convinced his survival depended on it. Only if he dedicated himself to helping others would he survive. That was the essence of his "Gung Ho" philosophy.

Simply being physically fit wasn't enough. Each man had to understand the things for which he fought. Did the candidate know why this war was being fought? What did he expect the world to be like after the war?

Carlson called it "ethical indoctrination." What made the Eighth Route Army function so well, and what made each soldier able to withstand great hardship without complaint, was an understanding of the "why" of the battle. Beyond that was a sense of responsibility, a matter of duty. He believed it was important that men believe in the principles they are defending and understand the enemy as a threat to those principles.

"The effectiveness of all such forces depends almost entirely on the amount of ethical indoctrination which they have assimilated," Carlson wrote. "If they are thoroughly disciplined and inspired with a high sense of duty, they are very effective. Without such training they tend to degenerate into bandits."

Carlson was particularly demanding of his officers. He let them know right from the start what he expected.

"Discipline must be based on knowledge and reason instead of blind obedience," Carlson told his officers. "Individual initiative and resourcefulness must be encouraged. You must share the hardships and privations of those you lead and prove by your character and ability your qualifications for leadership."

Officers were afforded no special privileges. They ate the same rations and shared quarters identical to those of the enlisted men. All participated in the long, grueling marches with Carlson, then forty-six, leading the way.

Among the first officers selected for the 2d Battalion was Lt. Joe Griffith. Griffith, a native of Dallas, dropped out of law school at the University of Pennsylvania in early 1941 after becoming smitten by the blue uniform of a Marine Corps recruiter. A year later, while assigned to Camp Elliott near San Diego, he heard that a Major Carlson was forming a handpicked battalion to engage in unorthodox action against the enemy.

"Everybody wants to be in an elite outfit," Griffith remembers. "I went for an interview and when Carlson found out I was a graduate of the famous Jim Crowe Scout Sniper School, he took me immediately."

Carlson and his staff processed more than three thousand applications and would eventually take one thousand. The recruits came mostly from the main Marine base in San Diego, nearby Camp Elliott, and a new recruit depot up the coast at Camp Matthews. A great many of the volunteers Carlson took were farm boys, those who had experience in tramping through the woods, camping, and hunting.

Carlson, then a major, and Roosevelt, a captain (they would each be promoted a rank in early May en route to Hawaii), conducted most of

the interviews in a big room of one of the permanent buildings alongside the parade ground at Camp Elliott. Each man sat behind a big table
at opposite ends of the room. On the tables were personnel files, a couple of notebooks, and several pencils. The candidates filed in one at a
time, saluted, gave their name, rank, and serial number, and were asked
to sit down.

Roosevelt interviewed Private Carson, who tried not to act nervous.
Carson told him he was a farm boy from Minnesota and how his brother
had survived the Pearl Harbor attack aboard the battleship *Maryland*. He
wanted to avenge the attack on his country and his brother.

"Can you swim?" Roosevelt asked.

"Yes, sir," answered Carson, adding that he'd grown up near several
lakes close to his home in Minnesota.

"Would you be able to march thirty miles on a cup of rice?" was the
next question.

"I can if anybody else can," said Carson, starting to feel more comfortable in the presence of President Roosevelt's son.

"How often do you go to Sunday school?" Roosevelt asked, a serious
look on his face.

"As often as my mother makes me," Carson answered quickly.

Both men smiled and then Carson was dismissed.

When Voight's turn came, he put on his best killer face and strode
quickly to the interview table. He saluted and took a chair, and Roosevelt
asked him what his religion was. "Mother nature," Voight said with a stern
face. Asked if he could swim, Voight said he could do anything anybody
else could do. The truth was he couldn't swim a stroke, a fact that would
nearly cost him his life six months later.

Private William McCall was interviewed by Major Carlson. McCall told
Carlson that he had been born in the Philippines to an American father,
who was currently a prisoner of war.

"I told Carlson that I wanted to join the Raiders because I thought they
might take part in the reconquest of the Philippines," McCall said. "I told
Carlson that my dad was interned by the Japs and I hoped that part of
our tour would be to invade the Philippines. I'm sure I was the only one
in that category."

McCall's father, James, had served in the U.S. Army during the Moro
Campaign in Mindanao. After his term of enlistment expired, he remained in the Philippines, where he became a schoolteacher. Impris-
oned by the Japanese at the outbreak of the war, James McCall was in-

terned at Santo Tomás Internment Camp outside Manila. When he was liberated in the spring of 1945, he weighed only ninety-seven pounds. He later came to live with his son in the United States.

William McCall came to the United States in 1939 looking for work. He enlisted in the Civilian Conservation Corps (CCC) and was sent to a camp in Pine Valley, California, approximately forty miles west of San Diego. He fought forest fires, built campsites, sawed trees for logs, and worked from sunup to sundown for a dollar a day. He made some extra money by cutting hair for twenty-five cents a man. He volunteered to go to Alaska to help construct a new camp and an airfield on Annette Island near Ketchikan. When his enlistment expired in November of 1941, he returned to California, where he later enlisted in the Marine Corps on his twenty-first birthday, January 2, 1942.

Major Carlson was impressed by McCall's CCC background and his travels to prewar China and Japan. He also thought highly of his multilingual capability, though it was restricted to Philippine dialects. Carlson determined that McCall had all the right reasons for wanting to join an independent bunch like the Raiders and took him immediately.

Many Marine recruits were alumni of the CCC, the most popular of the New Deal's work-relief programs. They lived in military-style camps administered for the most part by army officers. Most toiled in the healthful outdoors, planting trees, fighting forest fires, building wildlife shelters, digging ditches and canals, battling insect plagues, establishing parks, and restoring historic battlefields. The CCC experience enabled poverty-stricken young men to build up their bodies and sustain their pride. It also acclimated them to military discipline.

The generation that weathered the Great Depression acquired a toughness that lent itself well to the daily demands of military life. Wandering the roadways of a stricken country in search of work, dodging inhospitable policemen and railroad detectives, and living off handouts and odd jobs sharpened a man's survival skills to a fine edge.

Most of the interviews with Carlson and Roosevelt were short and to the point. Almost everybody said he wanted to avenge the Pearl Harbor attack and the sooner the better. The men were boyishly cocky, ready to say or do anything to join an outfit that appeared intent on becoming the first to take the fight to the enemy.

Could they kill a man by cutting his throat? they were asked. Hell, yes, they all answered. Bring it on.

Not everybody was accepted, of course. Carlson rejected his own son, Lieutenant Evans junior, four times because he didn't want to give anyone the opportunity to accuse him of favoritism. He relented in September after the Makin raid, finally allowing his son to join his outfit, which was preparing for a mission on Guadalcanal.

The younger Carlson, who had joined the Marine Corps in 1938 as a private and then was commissioned as a second lieutenant in May of 1941, shipped out with the 1st Marine Division and saw action early in the Guadalcanal operation. By chance, he happened to be at Espíritu Santo when the 2d Raider Battalion arrived in September of 1942. It was Major Roosevelt who intervened to convince the old man that Evans junior would be a good addition to the unit.

"Expect no favors," Carlson told his son after finally relenting. "If anything I'll be tougher on you than on anyone else. I won't mean to be, but that's what I'm sure will happen."

Evans junior did his father proud, earning a Silver Star on the famed thirty-day "long patrol" on Guadalcanal conducted by the Raiders behind enemy lines in November and December.

Unlike the 1st Raider Battalion on the East Coast, which began life as a restructured infantry battalion (1st Battalion, 5th Marines), the 2d Raider Battalion was built from scratch with men Carlson felt could adapt to his Gung Ho philosophy. The controversial Carlson encountered resistance from the Marine Corps brass all the way through training.

The brass wasn't all that happy with Jimmy Roosevelt either. Back in 1936, FDR pressured the Marines to make twenty-nine-year-old Jimmy a lieutenant colonel so that he could serve as one of his military aides on a South American goodwill tour. To his credit, Jimmy Roosevelt felt uncomfortable with this "gift" commission and wrote about it after the war.

"I quickly was infected with the esprit de corps of the leathernecks and wanted to remain a Marine, but I realized I had no right to such a high rank, which I had not earned," he wrote. He resigned in September 1939, saying, "I am impelled to take this step for the simple reason that I do not feel that my age or experience would justify my holding such a rank."

Tall, thin, and prematurely balding, Jimmy Roosevelt married soon after graduating from Harvard and went into the insurance business in California in 1930. Six years later, he joined the White House staff as his father's secretary. In 1937, he met Carlson for the first time at his father's retreat in Warm Springs, Georgia.

Initially, he was praised for his work as his father's secretary but the stress of the job, coupled with charges in the press that he was using his public office for personal gain, sent him to the hospital for treatment of a perforated ulcer. He had two-thirds of his stomach removed at the Mayo Clinic, forcing him to resign from his father's staff. In the fall of 1939 he moved to Los Angeles to become a film executive with Samuel Goldwyn Productions, an effort that proved a failure. The move coincided with the breakup of his marriage and the start of a new romance with the nurse who had cared for him when he was in the hospital.

Despite his chronic ulcer condition, bad eyesight, and foot problems (flat feet) that wouldn't allow him to wear boots, Roosevelt rejoined the Marine Corps reserve in December of 1939 as a captain. He was called to active duty in September of 1940, just prior to his father's reelection as president. One of the Republican campaign buttons of 1940 prominently featured Jimmy Roosevelt's sudden rise in the Marine Corps with a message that read, "Daddy, I want to be a captain too."

Jimmy Roosevelt's most formative experience came in April of 1941 when his father sent him and Maj. Gerald C. Thomas on a worldwide military-diplomatic mission. He visited the Philippines, China, Burma, India, Iraq, Egypt, Crete, Palestine, and areas of North Africa.

"I had numerous never-to-be-forgotten experiences on this trip," Roosevelt said. "I saw things which opened my eyes both to the ugliness of war and to the vast differences between American values and standards in other parts of the world."

Throughout the summer and fall of 1941, Jimmy Roosevelt, while acting as a liaison for his father, worked for Colonel Donovan on various intelligence projects. Donovan, though a close friend of FDR's, did not enter the presidential circle at the level of a Harry Hopkins or Steve Early, but he seemed to have unlimited access to the Oval Office. FDR looked forward to his company and gave a sympathetic ear to the colonel's reports and proposals, and, in general, enjoyed himself.

A month prior to Pearl Harbor, Jimmy Roosevelt, with the backing of Donovan, proposed to the president that the U.S. government arrange to fly a bomber load of medical supplies to Yugoslavian patriot Draza Mihajlovic. Because Yugoslavia was by then under Nazi occupation and it would be six more months before the British managed even to determine where Mihajlovic actually was hiding in the Yugoslav mountains, a more harebrained notion would be hard to imagine. But this was the kind of proposal that resulted from the Oval Office war games. It was a time when anything and everything seemed possible.

The war would take on a new degree of seriousness following the bombing of Pearl Harbor.

All four of the Roosevelt boys were called to active duty once the war broke out: Jimmy got involved with the formation of the 2d Raider Battalion, Elliott accepted a captain's commission in the Army Air Corps, while FDR junior and John were called up by the navy, the latter serving on the carrier USS *Wasp*.

Carlson, who was under the impression he was to have a free hand to form his own battalion, bristled when Marine Headquarters shipped a company (7 officers and 190 enlisted men) from Colonel Edson's 1st Raider Battalion to help stock his unit in early February. To him, it was a clear case of "interference" from on high. Carlson summarily broke up the ready-made company and insisted that each individual reapply for his battalion, subject to the same "Gung Ho" selection process that all his other volunteers underwent.

It was an equally difficult order for Edson to swallow as well. Edson was an "old China hand" who had spent several tours in Shanghai and Peking before the war, just as Carlson had. He was known throughout the Corps as "Red Mike" because of his ever-present sunburn and close-cropped reddish hair. Edson was a poster-boy Marine and an inspiration to his men. He was tough, fearless, and absolutely dedicated to the well-being of his men.

Edson had spent eight months molding the men in his outfit, only to be forced to give them up. But there was nothing he could do about it. To Edson's credit, he did not comb his battalion for the weakest links, but simply selected Capt. Wilbur Meyerhoff's Company A.

Edson felt that Carlson's treatment of his men was shabby, if not downright disrespectful. To make his men requalify to become one of Carlson's Raiders was the height of humiliation.

"This was a hell of a mess and most of us tried to qualify," said Lt. John Apergis of the 1st Raiders. "We were proud and just could not stand rejection by the West Coast mob."

Apergis had sent his former commander, Edson, a letter describing the treatment he and the rest of A Company received from the 2d Raider Battalion. According to Apergis, Carlson greeted the company at a formation by asking who among them wanted to volunteer for a commando outfit. Only half stepped forward. Those who remained were subjected to not only physical testing but psychological testing as well. According to Apergis, the latter testing took place in "a darkened room where occasionally a knife flew by and thudded into the wall, or firecrackers went off under the interviewee's chair." Few of the newcomers from the 1st Raider Battalion seemed to meet the unorthodox standards Carlson set.

Carlson's treatment of Edson's company ignited a firestorm within the Marine Corps. General Price, who was keenly aware of President Roosevelt's friendship with Carlson, bluntly wrote Edson that the company he had sent to the West Coast had made "a very bad impression" on Carlson, so bad that he had accepted only a quarter of them for his command.

"Either there is an entirely different impression in the East as to what these men are to do and the type of men required effectively to do it or someone has made a serious bust," said Price in a letter to Edson, which preceded the one the latter had received from Lieutenant Apergis.

"I am trying to stop an official complaint on the case," Price wrote, obviously trying to cool off a steamed Edson, "not because I feel that one is not warranted but because I hate to see you get hurt over the matter. This commando business is a hobby with high authorities in our nation and Capt. James R. is the Exec of the Battalion."

By this time, Edson was thoroughly disgusted with Carlson, and though several grades junior to General Price, he pulled no punches in venting his anger in his reply.

"Whatever Carlson's so-called standards may be, his refusal to accept three out of four of these men only confirmed my opinion that the Marine Corps had lost nothing by his resignation a few years ago and has gained nothing by his return to active duty as a reserve major," Edson wrote.

The statement in your letter to the effect that the men rejected by Carlson were distributed to units in the 2d Division "where no one wanted them" is not so much a reflection upon the quality of men sent as upon this prejudicial attitude and ignorance of the officers under your command. It is true that Jimmy Roosevelt has connections with high officials in this country. It is also true that he is a reserve captain with very limited military experience as an officer in the Marine Corps. I have already stated my opinion of Major Carlson.

I have given you many years of loyal, faithful, and, I believe, efficient service. . . . If, as implied in your letter, you feel that an official complaint is warranted based on Carlson's report to you, I shall not ask you to withhold it on my account. I have no apologies to make nor anything to conceal in the transfer of this draft to the West Coast.

Edson was further piqued a week or so later when he received a letter from Captain Meyerhoff, who was among those "dismissed" by Carlson and reassigned to units in the 2d Marine Division.

"We would gladly pay our fare back to get into our former outfit again if such is possible," Meyerhoff wrote Edson. It was signed by twenty-seven former members of the 1st Raider Battalion. Edson made a few inquiries on their behalf, but there was nothing he could do to get them back.

Edson would harbor a grudge against Carlson that would last even after the latter's death.

Despite Carlson's misgivings, this East Coast group was more mature and better trained than the bulk of his volunteers and would go on to play prominent roles in the battalion's successes. Two, Sergeants Robert V. Allard and Dallas H. Cook, would win Navy Crosses but lose their lives on the Makin raid.

To fill the vacancies in the 1st Raider Battalion, Edson, who would later win the Congressional Medal of Honor at Guadalcanal, went out and handpicked replacements from the 1st Marine Division, which was then organizing and training at New River, North Carolina, later called Camp Lejeune. It didn't make him a popular man within the Corps.

"Merritt Edson, armed with appropriate orders, arrived to comb our units for officers and men deemed suitable for his 1st Raider Battalion— a new organization," 1st Division commander Maj. Gen. Alexander A. Vandegrift wrote in his memoirs many years later. "I had known about the Raiders in Washington. Neither General Holcomb nor I favored forming elite units from units already elite. But Secretary of the Navy Col. Frank Knox and President Roosevelt, both of whom fancied the British commandos, directed us to come up with a similar organization. Edson's levy against our division, coming at such a critical time, annoyed the devil out of me, but there wasn't one earthly thing I could do about it."

In addition to disrupting personnel and training in regular units, the formation of Raider battalions generated a variety of requests for new and exotic equipment. The Raiders were to be given first priority on new weaponry and equipment being developed. Typical requests were for riot-type shotguns, Lewis machine guns, collapsible bicycles, chain saws, scaling ropes, rubber boats, bangalore torpedoes, and sufficient automatic pistols to issue one per Raider.

Carlson irritated the Marine Corps in another way. He wanted to change the basic makeup of the Marine squad to comply with the mission of Raider forces. Carlson saw the pillars of his new battalion as mobility, flexibility, and heavy firepower. A regulation eight-man Marine infantry squad was equipped with six World War I–era Springfield bolt-action rifles and two Browning automatic rifles (BAR). Carlson wanted his squads to consist of three three-man fire teams, each equipped with a BAR, Thompson submachine gun, and the new Garand semiautomatic M1 rifle, which would provide each fire team with more firepower than a squad of regular Marines.

Carlson felt that because his Raiders would often be operating in secret or behind enemy lines or engaged in prolonged marches far from regular units, they would not have the luxury of supporting fire such as mortars, tanks, artillery, air cover, and naval gunfire. Therefore they needed to carry their own firepower with them. The weapons had to be light, easy to maintain, and effective at close range.

All Carlson had to do was convince Marine Corps Headquarters to change their Table of Organization. Predictably, the Marine Corps said no.

Carlson didn't discourage easily, however. He wrote of his need for more firepower directly to the commandant, with a copy to President Roosevelt. He was able to get FDR's ear rather easily by asking his executive officer, the president's son, to call direct.

"Carlson once let me read the reply to a letter he had written to President Roosevelt about Raider training," Raider Oscar F. Peatross wrote in his book *Bless 'em All*, which was published in 1995, "And I suspected that he had greased the ways for the launching of his proposal by sending the President a copy well before the commandant received the recommendation through regular channels. Hence, the conjecture that strong encouragement for the adoption of Carlson's proposal came from the very top—the President—through the secretary of the navy to the commandant of the Marine Corps."

Knowing which strings to pull, Carlson didn't take very long getting his fire-team concept approved. Later, it would be adopted by other traditional outfits in both the Marines and army. Carlson's battalion got the newest weapons, helmets, and boots, the latter a high-priority item because of the emphasis on long marches. They were steel-tipped Otto Bergman boots, manufactured in Oregon for loggers. They were very durable and comfortable on long marches and a vast improvement over the standard boondockers. They were soon known as "Raider Boots." The helmets were the new "turtle" design, much more protective than the old World War I "washbowl" style. Each company was also authorized a doctor and two corpsmen.

Later on, the battalion was also provided with three Japanese-language interpreters—two Korean civilians, who were promptly named "Gung" and "Ho," and Marine lieutenant Gerald Holtom, who had lived for many years in Japan with his missionary family. All three read, wrote, and spoke fluent Japanese.

All Carlson had to do to get what he wanted was to ask Jimmy Roosevelt to make one well-placed call—out of channels, of course.

Carlson's maneuverings infuriated the Marine Corps brass, but there wasn't a damn thing they could do about it.

Jimmy Roosevelt was not only obeying the order of a superior (Carlson), he was being a good executive officer.

"I was able to use my influence to get Carlson's Raiders the special equipment we needed, such as boots which would hold up under the rigors of wet landings on coral reefs," Roosevelt later wrote. "And of course there was some resentment at our getting equipment others could not get."

The 2d Raider Battalion was initially composed of companies A, B, C, and D and were moved out of Camp Elliott in late February to a more private area at nearby Jacques Farm. Companies E and F joined the battalion on April 14 once they were formed.

Six

Life on the Farm

Jacques Farm (now part of Camp Pendleton) was situated in the middle of an olive grove and adjacent to Camp Elliott. Consisting of a small house, a barn, a chicken house, and a well, it had been abandoned for several years when the government bought it, shortly after the war started. Away from the prying and meddlesome influence of the "regular" Marine Corps, it provided just the remoteness Carlson wanted to conduct his own brand of training, and also afforded an opportunity for his men to bond as a specialized strike force.

The Raiders pitched tents in the olive grove and got to work creating a firing range and a bayonet course and cleaning out the hen house so it could be used as a galley. The farm boys were particularly helpful with the latter, moving mountains of dry, year-old chicken manure to a site downwind of the soon-to-be mess hall.

The barn was converted to an outdoor stage where shows and speeches were given. Officers mixed with the enlisted men. Nobody wore any rank. No insignia, no stripes, and no name tags. Everyone knew who the officers were. Seldom was a salute seen. Visitors from the regular Marine Corps and other services were shocked to see an officer, perhaps Carlson himself, sitting next to a tree eating with an enlisted man or bumming a cigarette.

Jimmy Roosevelt was just as easy to get along with too.

"Carlson and Roosevelt were 'enlisted men' friendly," remembered Private McCall.

The main emphasis was on conditioning, and the hikes grew longer and longer as the training progressed. They were designed to separate the men from the boys. They did. More than a hundred fell by the wayside and out of the battalion in the first week. Most of the casualties were the old-timers who had grown a little lazy in peacetime service.

On the first day of training, Carlson gathered his battalion around him and said, "Fellas, I'm twice as old as you are, but I'm going to teach you how to march and how to march without griping. I'm going to march you until blood runs out of your shoes. And, at the end, I'm going to be there."

The young recruits found out that Carlson was as good as his word.

"Carlson would get us all together early in the morning and say to us, "See that mountain peak over there? We'll be there by evening.' And, off we'd go," Voight said. "He would do anything we could do, plus some. He was a gutsy old man. I think he could walk forever."

Raider Al Flores never forgot the look in Carlson's eyes whenever he gave one of his speeches.

"His eyes were stern," Flores said. "They made me feel like my preacher was looking at me."

The men took to Carlson almost immediately. His low-key approach and ability to laugh at himself, and with the men, were endearing.

"Gentlemen," he would announce before a march into what looked to be some daunting real estate, "it's only twenty-two miles as the crow flies."

Someone in the rear sounded off: "Yeah, Major, but we ain't crows."

Everybody laughed. Then, off they would march, following Carlson every step of the way. Later on, when the unit marched and fought in the thick jungles of Guadalcanal, someone would invariably try to lift some sagging spirits by saying, "What does the colonel think we are, crows?"

Lieutenant Holtom captured the mood of the men in a letter he wrote to his older brother, Tom, on February 25, 1942.

Dear Tom,

We are now camped out in pup tents on a farm undergoing intensive training designed to familiarize us with our weapons and condition us so that we can eventually walk fifty miles a day with ease.

For once I seem to have struck an outfit that seems to know what the score is. Of course some of the officers seem a bit on the stupid side but the commanding officer, Major Evans Carlson, seems a corker and everyone works hard without exception.

The life is very healthful and while I don't get much chance to study Japanese, it is such a change from the inefficiencies I met at San Luis Obispo and practically everywhere else in the Marine Corps that I am well satisfied.

The idea is that we be attached to the Navy for raids and general demolition work. Major Carlson is the Marine officer who went off with the Eighth Route Army of Chinese guerillas. He lived with them eighteen months behind the Japanese lines, marched about five hundred miles, and generally studied their tactics so he should know his stuff on hit-and-run warfare. He is the author of *Twin Stars of China,* which is an account of his experiences with this outfit.

Much of the marching near Jacques Farm took place along the roads, sometimes with an ice cream truck following close behind. There would be no time for ice cream, however.

Great care was taken in the positioning of packs to avoid load shifting and chafing. Checks were made for dangling or noisy equipment. Carlson's Raiders emphasized speed, comfort, and stealth. They would set distance and time records on their marches that were measuring sticks within the Marine Corps for years to come.

"As we went along I told the boys everything we were doing and invited criticism and suggestions. And we got them," Carlson said. "I was trying to build up the same sort of working spirit I had seen in China, where all the soldiers dedicated themselves to one idea and worked together to put that idea over. I told the boys about it again and again. I told them of the motto of the Chinese Cooperatives, Gung Ho. It means Work Together—Work in Harmony. It was hard at first to make them understand, since we are essentially a selfish people. But gradually, the longer we were together and the more I had a chance to talk with them, they began to feel it. My motto caught on and they began to call themselves the Gung Ho Battalion.

"When I designed a field jacket to replace the bulky and orthodox pack, they even called it the Gung Ho jacket. And they named every new thing Gung Ho. It became the watchword. I also told them they would never be given an unnecessary order. They weren't, and that meant that whenever an order was given in the field it was carried out to the end without question."

Each Raider was issued two knives, a stiletto type and a heartier Jim Bowie type. Knife and bayonet experts were invited to Jacques Farm to share their expertise. An emphasis was placed on close-in combat and where best to demobilize an enemy.

The men took their knife training seriously.

"It was dangerous to walk around at night because you might be hit by someone throwing a knife at a tree," Brian Quirk remembered. "We had a lot of young, crazy guys in the outfit."

Most of the young Raiders enjoyed every minute of the training.

"It was interesting that such a variety of Marines existed to pass on to us recruits their knowledge and experience," Ben Carson remembered. "We had Marine Corps captains left over from World War I who taught us how to shoot a BAR from the hip. Some officers, commissioned after fighting in the Lincoln Brigade in Spain during the Spanish Civil War, demonstrated the effectiveness of indirect fire with automatic weapons when repulsing a human-wave attack. According to one of these officers, the Spanish Loyalists fired their automatic weapons into the pavement ahead of attacking waves of troops so the ripping and tearing effect of the cobblestones and ricocheting bullets would amplify the firepower."

The rifle range the Raiders had built at Jacques Farm got plenty of use, both from an individual aspect and in small-unit training.

"I know there was a shortage of ammunition, but I don't think we ever had a shortage," Brian Quirk recalled. He was right. The Raiders had first priority on ammunition too.

Extra training was devoted to knife and bayonet practice. They learned how to kill silently and quickly. They became, according to one writer, highly polished dealers in death who, had they not had a purpose, might well have been regarded as assassins.

The war came a little closer to the Raiders on February 23 when a Japanese submarine surfaced off the coast near Santa Barbara, California, and lobbed a couple of shells in the vicinity of a nearby oil field.

The appearance of the enemy sub, which threw the West Coast into a heightened state of alert, added a new dimension of training for the Raiders, who were temporarily pressed into duty as coast watchers or formed beach patrols and searching parties for any Japanese who may have come ashore. Even though nothing was discovered, it provided a degree of realism to their training and added some seriousness to their preparation.

Gung Ho meetings were held every Friday or as often as necessary. They were used to air gripes and discuss ways to improve training. Other topics open for discussion were military and political issues such as the kind of social order they wanted after the war. Many of the meetings included group sing-alongs around a campfire, movies, and guest speakers.

Since there were no authorized leaves or passes allowed during training, these Gung Ho meetings served as social events to bring the men closer together as a unit, minus the women, beer, and gambling, of course. The whole purpose was to demonstrate that every man was important and that each had a personal stake in the success of their mission. With this established, each man could be more aggressive in battle rather than sit back and wait for orders and possibly let opportunities slip away.

One of the most popular features of the Gung Ho meetings was the periodic talks given by Jimmy Roosevelt on world issues and global strategy. Roosevelt, who had been an aide to his father on many of the latter's trips, had met most of the world leaders and his insights were very educational. Roosevelt even brought his mother, Eleanor, to one of the meetings at Jacques Farm, as well as Navy Secretary Frank Knox.

"The pièce de résistance was a visit by Jimmy Roosevelt's mother, Eleanor herself," Private McCall said. "Her visit was a boost in morale and she also visited us overseas on the island of New Caledonia."

Another Raider, Pvt. Dean Voight, had another view of Eleanor Roosevelt's visit. Voight stormed out of the meeting in a huff and walked right past Jimmy Roosevelt. Later, Roosevelt asked Voight why he had embarrassed his mother like that by walking out on her.

"If I don't know what I'm fighting for she's not going to tell me," Voight told the president's son.

Individual thought like this was encouraged by Carlson, though Roosevelt was obviously not entirely convinced when it involved his mother. For the most part, however, the Gung Ho meetings were open to any and all subjects, without regard to rank or any possible repercussions. It was certainly a unique adaptation of military behavior.

"Back in camp we had passed evenings discussing life and taking votes on our feelings," Roosevelt wrote some twenty years later. "I remember how surprised [Carlson] was when the men once voted against his suggestion that all men be limited to $25,000 a year income as a means of spreading the wealth of the nation. Their reason was that if they survived the war, they did not want to return to a world in which they would be denied the opportunity to become one of the wealthy."

The weekly Friday-night forums, as they were called, were something the men looked forward to. The format was often left up to the men. There might be some singing and perhaps a brief skit, with Raiders happily volunteering to play the parts of women. Guest speakers continued to show up from time to time. Sometimes the men broke into groups to discuss different matters. One time, Carlson invited a young chaplain to join his outfit. Some of the men saw this as an attempt to force religion on them and took it out on the young lieutenant. Carlson took the hint and withdrew the invitation.

There were some typical bumps in the road for Carlson during the training. After the initial enthusiasm wore off, some of the men began to take advantage of the informality to see how much they could get away with. It caused Carlson to question his convictions and himself. He was always considerate and patient with his men because he knew it was a new experience for them. He treated them as equals, on and off duty, but certain rules had to be obeyed for the good of all. Those who tested the limits of his patience were given time to become part of the team, but there were limits. Carlson recognized the wants and needs of his troops and was willing to overlook minor infractions up to a limit. He would not compromise the seriousness of the training, however, and if one of his troops continually failed to measure up, he didn't hesitate to dismiss him.

The main causes of disciplinary problems were a lack of creature comforts and the absence of any liberty and all that that implied, namely no beer and no women.

There were more than a few adventurous Raiders who went "over the hill" to San Diego once taps sounded and then regaled their mates the next day with their exploits. But this practice diminished after a couple of 0300 company assemblies discovered the absence of some of the troops. A few of them were brought up on charges. Usually, however, it took at least two strikes to be ushered out of the battalion.

"We never got leave while at Jacques Farm, we took leave," Raider Dean Voight said. "We'd arrange for a cab to meet us beyond the creek running around the farm and head into town after taps. San Diego was crawling with hustlers back in those days. One time, I had my money belt cut away from me by a razor and never felt a thing. After that we stayed away from San Diego and went to other towns instead."

Asked what kind of punishment Carlson assessed to those caught leaving the base for a night on the town, Voight said, "I don't know what it was. I never got caught."

The Raiders were issued innovative equipment to evaluate. One item was a packsack that the Raiders labeled the "camel" pack because it placed a hump in the middle of the back rather than higher on the shoulders. Strips of light canvas attached to the packsack could be laced up around the chest to prevent the pack from flopping around during running. It was supposed to replace the old World War I pack that always seemed to wind up around your ears when you hit the deck.

In an effort to build more esprit de corps, Carlson designed an unofficial battalion logo to be pasted on camp buildings and seabags. It was not a cloth shoulder or pocket patch but a glue-backed paper cutout. It featured a black death's head (half skull, half face) on crossed yellow scimitars on a scarlet background. Hundreds of these stickers were issued to soldiers of the 2d Raider Battalion at Jacques Farm and later in Hawaii. Those issued in Hawaii were earmarked as a psychological marker to be pasted on enemy dead and equipment in future actions. Most of the emblems stuck together in the tropical heat and never got to be used anywhere. They are collector's items today.

By the time Carlson's battalion reached Guadalcanal in the fall of 1942, the emblem had evolved into a skull backed by a crossed Gung Ho knife and lightning bolt. An official Raider cloth shoulder patch was authorized by the Marine Corps in 1943. It featured a skull within a diamond surrounded by the five-star constellation of the Southern Cross. That patch adorned the left shoulder of Jimmy Roosevelt in a photo taken in January of 1945 at the swearing-in ceremony of his father for his fourth term as president.

By late March, training at or near Jacques Farm had increased to between twelve and fourteen hours a day. The hikes grew longer and longer and still there were no liberty passes.

Sergeant Clyde Thomason described just how tough the training was in a letter he wrote to his buddies back in Atlanta. "We're bivouacked out in the mountains away from anywhere. There's been nothing but manual labor—marching five, eight, ten miles and calisthenics to get into shape," he said. "Twice a week . . . a thirty-five-mile hike, and once a week a seventy-mile overnight hike. We never ride. Every man will be a walking arsenal, including . . . a knife which we are learning to throw. Hope

I haven't bitten off more than I can chew. We all have crew haircuts. O, my beautiful waves! For such a small outfit we have been getting quite a lot of attention. I'm really thrilled I've gotten into this outfit."

Thomason would be the first enlisted Marine to earn the Congressional Medal of Honor when he was killed by a sniper on the Makin raid on August 17.

Near the end of March, the battalion moved out of Jacques Farm for three weeks of ship-to-shore training off the southern California coast and San Clemente Island. It consisted of inflating, launching, and learning to paddle in unison the eleven-man rubber boats they would later use in the real thing. The Raiders disembarked from old World War I destroyers, climbing down and then back up cargo nets. At first, the rubber boats were towed into position by Higgins boats so as not to expend unnecessary energy paddling in from far offshore.

There would be much more of this training later when the 2d Raider Battalion was sent to Hawaii.

In mid-April, the battalion moved to Camp Elliott and was joined by two newly formed companies (E and F) for more unit training. They were just about ready for deployment.

The war news during February, March, and April continued to be depressing. The surrender at Bataan on April 9 and the certain fate of Corregidor, which capitulated May 6 with the capture of almost twenty-five thousand Americans, cast a gloom over the entire country.

Then came news of the Jimmy Doolittle Raid on April 18, giving Americans their first chance to smile in more than four months. Lieutenant Colonel Doolittle, an army pilot, led a flight of sixteen B-25s off the deck of the carrier USS *Hornet* on a daylight bombing raid of Japan. Thirteen of the planes, each carrying four five-hundred-pound bombs, made runs over Tokyo while the other three, armed with incendiary bombs, flew over Kobe, Nagoya, and Osaka. All of the planes were scheduled to immediately fly off toward friendly airfields deep in the heart of China.

Roosevelt had envisioned staging such an air raid way back in December. Within a week after Pearl Harbor, he tried to persuade the Russians to bomb Japan in retaliation but Joe Stalin, hard pressed by the Germans in the west, was not willing to antagonize Japan in the east and fight a war on two fronts. FDR then asked Stalin for permission to use the Russian seaport of Vladivostok, located on the Sea of Japan about six hundred miles north of Tokyo, as a base for an American attack on

Japan. Again he was turned down. The Americans would have to do it on their own.

The raid turned out to be more symbolic than destructive, but the psychological harm to Japan was enormous. It proved that the Japanese homeland was not invulnerable and forced the enemy to divert more planes and ships to the home islands to ensure it wouldn't happen again.

The Doolittle Raid had been a risky endeavor right from the start. It was supposed to be a night raid and all planes were scheduled to land at predetermined airfields deep in China behind Japanese lines. The carrier task force under Admiral Halsey had been spotted some seven hundred miles east of Japan and had been forced to take off early, which would put them over Japan about noon. Amazingly, none of the planes were shot down over Japan.

Flying on to China and running low on fuel, the squadron ran into a heavy rainsquall just as night fell. Eleven of the sixteen crews had to bail out, another four crash-landed, and the remaining crew got disoriented and wound up landing in Russian-held territory near Vladivostok. Two of the crews (eight men) were captured when they were forced to crash-land or bail out over China.

All but nine of the eighty aviators on the raid survived. Four drowned and another was killed in a parachute mishap. Of the eight crewmen captured in China, three were executed by a Japanese firing squad after a sham war-crimes trial and another died in captivity. The executions of the airmen, who were accused of intentionally shooting up a school yard, infuriated America, which now had another rallying cry to go along with "Remember Pearl Harbor" and "Remember Wake Island."

The Japanese, who were unable to determine the size or direction of the attack, were humiliated.

"Even though there wasn't much damage, it's a disgrace that the skies over the imperial capital should have been defiled without a single enemy plane shot down," Adm. Isoroku Yamamoto wrote. "It provides a regrettably graphic illustration of the saying that a bungling attack is better than the most skillful defense."

President Roosevelt was delighted with the bombing raid and called it just the tonic the Americans needed after months of nothing but bad news. When asked by the media where the planes had come from, he smiled, leaned back in his chair in the oval office, and said, "They came from a secret base in Shangri-la," referring to the mythical land in James Hilton's *Lost Horizon*.

A month later in a White House ceremony, Roosevelt presented the Congressional Medal of Honor to a reluctant Doolittle, who had been promoted two ranks to brigadier general. Doolittle felt he had done nothing more than anyone else in his squadron and thus did not deserve to be singled out for such an individual honor.

Doolittle's daring raid turned out to be the psychological blow that altered the course of the war in the Pacific and ultimately spelled Japan's doom. Within days, Yamamoto had convinced the military regime to delay a planned thrust southward to capture Samoa, Fiji, and New Caledonia, which would have cut off the shipping lanes between the United States and Australia, and to coordinate a strike eastward against Midway in the central Pacific. The Americans, he told the militarists, must not be allowed to hold any territory from which they could launch more air attacks on the Japanese homeland.

In addition, the invasion of Midway would bring Yamamoto what he desired most, a major sea battle with the U.S. Pacific Fleet. This time he would destroy the carriers, a job left undone at Pearl Harbor six months earlier.

Japan's military leaders, deeply embarrassed by the Doolittle Raid, quickly approved Yamamoto's eastward plan of attack and set the date for the first week of June.

The rest is history.

Time was fast approaching for the 2d Raider Battalion to get into the war. The men had grown close during ten weeks of training at Jacques Farm, San Clemente, and Camp Elliott and were aching to get at the Japanese.

Their interest heightened when they saw the advance units of the 1st Raider Battalion leave for American Samoa in the South Pacific from San Diego on April 13. The 1st Raiders joined four army divisions (Americal, 32d, 37th, and 41st) already in the Australian–New Zealand theater of operations and would later be joined by scattered elements of the 1st Marine Division (1st, 5th, and 7th Marines) and the 2d Marines of the 2d Marine Division. By July, the Americans would have a force of some 41,000 army troops and 15,000 Marines scattered all across the South Pacific awaiting orders to go on the offensive. That would come on August 7 with the invasion of Guadalcanal.

The home front was also preparing itself for a long, hard war. Rationing began in March, first with sugar and coffee and then gasoline, the latter with limits of three gallons a week. Aircraft and munitions factories were operating twenty-four hours a day. The automobile and steel industries had shifted gears from civilian to military production. The government had ordered 60,000 planes, 45,000 tanks, 20,000 antiaircraft guns, and 8 million tons of shipping—all for 1942.

Ford was building an aircraft plant at Willow Run, west of Detroit, that was a half mile long and a quarter mile wide, promising to roll out a four-engine Liberator bomber every hour once it started production. Chrysler began turning out tanks, Boeing was building B-17s, Kaiser was making ships, and General Motors, trucks. Studebaker was building B-17 and B-29 engines, and Packard arranged to construct 6,000 Rolls-Royce aircraft engines for Great Britain and U. S. consumption. The Depression was but a bitter memory. There was plenty of work for everybody.

San Diego was a bustling metropolis in the late spring of 1942, teeming with navy and civilian personnel. There wasn't a room or a billet to be had in the entire city, a fact that was humorously described in the following not-so-far-fetched anecdote.

It seems that a construction worker desperate for a room happened to come upon a man who was floundering in the water, obviously drowning. Answering the man's shouts for help, the construction worker removed his coat and shoes and jumped in to try and save him. Grabbing the drowning man's flailing arms and holding his head out of the water, the Good Samaritan asked the man what his name was.

"John Doe," the man sputtered.

"What's your address?" the rescuer asked.

The man told him and with that, the would-be rescuer let go and swam back to shore. After putting his coat and shoes back on as fast as he could, he hailed a cab and drove to the address the drowning man had given him.

Still panting heavily and dripping wet, he ran up to the door and knocked. The woman who opened the door was advised that her tenant, John Doe, had just drowned, and—was his room available?

The woman shook her head and said no.

Incredulous, the caller demanded, "Who could possibly have rented it?"

"The man who pushed him in," the woman said matter-of-factly.

On April 23, Admiral Nimitz wrote his boss, Admiral King, that the 2d Raider Battalion was "pushable," which meant it was ready for further assignment. Nimitz said that the battalion had "reached a morale peak which can be maintained only by engaging in active operations or by changing the locale and nature of its training." He proposed that the unit be moved to Hawaii for specialized training in landing from submarines and rubber boats, calling the unit "a striking force with strength out of proportion to its numbers."

The Raiders were given a few days liberty in early May before shipping out. It was their first official leave since joining the outfit. It wasn't long enough to go home, however, and it was just short enough to keep most of them from getting into any serious off-duty trouble. The Raiders had trained in total isolation for more than two months and didn't realize how much civilian life had changed since they enlisted or how secret their training had been to the general populace.

"A couple of us hitchhiked to San Clemente and the guy who picked us up asked about what we were wearing. He didn't know what a Marine Corps uniform looked like," Pvt. Dean Voight said.

Most of the Raiders headed for downtown San Diego, where the local merchants were only too happy to relieve them of their back pay. Because of the shortage of hotel rooms, many of the Raiders spent their leaves as guests of local families.

As night fell on May 8, the 2d Raider Battalion was trucked to a pier in San Diego, where they were crammed aboard the USS *J. Franklin Bell,* an old World War 1 China-run troop transport. They sailed later that night.

Among those seeing the Raiders off that night was Lt. Evans Carlson Jr. He had spent much of the day in a last-ditch effort to convince his father to take him along as a member of the unit.

"He would have none of it," Evans junior remarked fifty-eight years later.

Private Ben Carson had a name for the *J. Franklin Bell.* He called her "old strawbottom. The only thing that kept her afloat was a coat of paint on her bottom," he said with a bit of sarcasm.

It didn't take long for the Raiders to have a bad reaction to their ship. Jammed in like sardines, the Raiders were ordered to stay below and out of the way of the navy personnel. The quarters were barely fit for humans. They were dark, poorly ventilated, and very claustrophobic. Although they didn't know it, the experience proved to be a good training exercise for their long submarine voyage three months later.

Their first shipboard meal, which came after everyone else had been fed, consisted of leftover beans and cold ham. The ham turned out to be tainted.

"Within forty-five minutes, about a third of B Company was groaning, puking, and rolling about on the deck," Carson wrote.

Virtually everybody got seasick on the trip. Private McCall wasn't one of them, however. McCall had experienced hundreds of hours aboard ship coming to the United States from the Philippines and traveling to Alaska on army transports.

"Lots of guys were green around the gills and hanging on to the ship's rails, increasing the liquid content of the Pacific with vociferous regurgitations," McCall said in a 1999 interview. "I told one puking Raider to remember to swallow real hard when he tastes something brown and furry coming up his throat because it might be from his rectum."

That's how the 2d Raider Battalion went off to war.

Seven

One Step Closer to the War

The USS *J. Franklin Bell* sneaked out of San Diego in the middle of the night without an escort and zigzagged westward on a nine-day journey to Pearl Harbor. The Raiders had been assigned no specific mission, so speculation on where they might be deployed ran rampant on the long voyage to Hawaii.

Carlson, who would learn of his promotion to lieutenant colonel and that of Roosevelt to major when he reached Hawaii, thought the 2d Raiders had been chosen to spearhead the first offensive action against the Japanese. He composed a solemn and inspirational message for his men that he ordered read over the loudspeaker midway on the trip.

"This battalion is now headed for the theater of operations in the Pacific. . . . We become the first of our land forces of our nation to carry the war to the enemy," he wrote. "By our faith, our energy, our courage, and our intelligence—perhaps most of all by our willingness to sacrifice comfort and convenience—we shall march on to victory. Even more important, we will set the pace and blaze the trail for those behind, inspiring them with confidence and showing them that we Americans have what it takes to win battles. It means work and sacrifice, Raiders, but let's go."

While the ship slowly plodded across the Pacific, the Raiders had plenty of time to speculate about what awaited them in the coming months. They had little to do aboard except KP duty, head details, and fire watches. Showers were taken with seawater. Laundry was done by attaching articles to a long rope and dragging it aft of the fantail. Special care was taken with garbage so that an enemy sub couldn't track the ship.

Private McCall had a great time on the passage.

"It was fortunate for me that all the messmen in 'Officer's Country' were from the Philippines. I was a big hero to them," McCall said. "I got special food for my meals. I volunteered for KP duty in the officer's mess and even slept in the above-deck compartments for the messmen. The rest of the troops slept belowdecks and I would visit them from time to time and bring some goodies with me like cakes, cookies, and ice cream."

Some of the Raiders would sneak out of the troop compartments at night and try to sleep on the deck, where the air was cooler and clean, unfouled by the fetid stench of the unwashed bodies below. Little did they know they would have to overcome the same circumstances three months later.

Many of the men lay awake at night thinking about why they had joined the Raiders and wondering where it would all end. Many of them were farm boys who had never been more than a hundred miles from home. Here they were crossing the Pacific Ocean to far-off lands they had never heard of before. Many would not come back. They may not have known much about war, but they were certain many of them would be killed.

"I have wondered all these years about each one's motivation," Mc-Call said in January of 2000. "Was there a chauvinist inkling of the duty they were doing for America? I doubt it. For my part I was hoping that the 'leapfrog' method of the Pacific war would eventually head the Raiders towards the Philippine Islands and I would be able to rescue my dad from a Japanese internment camp in Manila. It was General MacArthur who went that route and made good his 'I shall return' promise to the Filipinos. 'Deo gratias,' I say to that."

By now recovered from their bouts of seasickness, most of the men couldn't wait to get at the Japanese. They felt they were ready to be tested and eager to see how they measured up.

One of the passengers on the trip to Hawaii was Lt. Comdr. John R. "Happy Jack" Pierce, a submarine captain who was heading for a new assignment. Pierce talked to Carlson and Roosevelt about the possibility of using the navy's large submarines, the *Narwhal, Argonaut,* and *Nautilus,* for commando-type raids. His enthusiasm was contagious.

Using submarines had never been seriously discussed before. Carlson just assumed that because his Raiders had been trained to disembark from transports, that would be the case in any real operation. The more Carlson talked with Lieutenant Commander Pierce, the more it sounded as if it could happen.

The two men, along with Jimmy Roosevelt, stayed up late at night discussing strategy and where the Raiders might be best used. Pierce called the submarine the ultimate guerrilla weapon. Carlson broke into a broad smile. He liked the sound of that.

Their paths would cross again on the controversial Makin Raid.

It was early morning on May 18 when the Raiders passed through the antisubmarine nets and entered Pearl Harbor. The sights were a sobering reminder of the power and audacity of Japan's military force.

"It occurred to me that 'battleship death row' might now be a more fitting name," Lieutenant Peatross later wrote. "On all sides we could see the almost unbelievable results of the Japanese attack: the pitiful wreckage of once proud warships, some on their sides, some bow up, others stern up, but all looking irretrievably lost."

The Raiders leaned against the railings of the ship and drank in the scene of one of the worst disasters in naval history. Inwardly and outwardly, they vowed to make Japan pay for this brutal attack on their country.

"I had read stories of the Pearl Harbor raid in the *Minneapolis Star-Journal,* but I was not prepared for the devastation I saw that May morning," Pvt. Ben Carson wrote. "On our port side as we entered the harbor lay the USS *Oklahoma,* looking every bit like a beached whale carcass."

Everywhere the Raiders looked they could see work crews busily repairing damaged ships. The harbor was a buzz of activity, both on the surface and high above where dozens of warplanes swooped past the *J. Franklin Bell* on some mission far out to sea. The Raiders had never seen that many planes before.

After nine days aboard ship without much to do, the Raiders looked forward to getting their land legs back.

Carlson turned the battalion over to the company commanders while he and Roosevelt reported in to Nimitz, who was eagerly awaiting their arrival. The president had called to congratulate Carlson and his son on their promotions, which became effective on May 12. FDR had called Nimitz often, ever anxious to promote some offensive action. With the Raiders now in Hawaii, he would continue to call for news of his "pet" unit as well as his oldest son.

FDR's interest in his son is certainly understandable, but it did cause some embarrassment for the latter.

"I have reason to believe that Father tried to keep up with my activities, though he took pains not to let me know he was inquiring about me," Jimmy Roosevelt later wrote in a book about his father. "I have seen one letter in which he commented to Carlson: 'I am . . . glad that Jimmy is working with you—but don't forget that he had part of his stomach taken out and that a diet of condensed cubes would probably lay him low in forty-eight hours. For heaven's sake don't let him know I mentioned this or he would slay me."

Carlson and Jimmy Roosevelt had enjoyed presidential favors for a long time and benefited greatly by the commander-in-chief's personal interest in the 2d Raider Battalion. Over the preceding few months, FDR had convinced Nimitz that the 2d Raider Battalion was a special bunch that should be given a special assignment, and the sooner the better. The home front needed a boost to its sagging morale.

Nimitz, who owed his present job to Roosevelt, was very receptive to utilizing the Raiders in some spectacular mission. Though disappointed that the president hadn't told the country about the navy's participation in the Doolittle Raid, Nimitz understood the need for secrecy in not revealing the role played by the USS *Hornet* on the mission. Here was a chance for the Raiders, which were, after all, part of the navy, to get a bit of glory of their own—perhaps in conjunction with the planned invasion of Guadalcanal.

The idea of getting Carlson's Raiders to a point of action by submarine came from Nimitz. He had instructed his planners months earlier to come up with operational plans to utilize submarines, his one naval force that hadn't been crippled by the attack at Pearl Harbor back on December 7.

Nimitz warmly welcomed Carlson and Roosevelt and assigned a liaison officer from his staff to coordinate training and planning so that everybody was kept up to the minute on the latest intelligence. Carlson's Raiders, which some regarded as Nimitz's personal army, were the only land force personnel attached to Nimitz, and he could order the battalion into action whenever he wanted without going through the conventional chain of command.

If the Raiders were looking for action, they didn't have to wait long. Nimitz told Carlson he expected a Japanese attack at Midway and that he was counting on his battalion to help defend the island should the situation develop as he expected. He ordered Carlson to meet with his planning staff and stand by for new assignments.

Meanwhile, the six companies of the 2d Raider Battalion had begun to settle in at Camp Catlin, a small encampment off the main road between Pearl Harbor and Honolulu. The camp was named for a World War I hero, Brig. Gen. Albertus W. Catlin, who had been the recipient of the Congressional Medal of Honor at Vera Cruz in 1914.

One of the first chores at Camp Catlin was to remove the remains of a Japanese Zero that had crashed at the site back on December 7. It had, for some inexplicable reason, been left there as a reminder of the attack. The wreck became a kind of tourist attraction.

"We took axes and hacksaws to it and got it out of the area," Private Carson said.

The camp itself was not more than half a square mile, hardly sufficient for training purposes. Major Roosevelt was instrumental in getting permission from the surrounding landowners for the Raiders to use their property for training exercises, with a promise that they would not do any damage to buildings and fences or eat the pineapples.

The latter stipulation was a tough promise to keep. The temptation to tear into a juicy pineapple, especially after a particularly long hike, often was too great to overcome. Although the Raiders argued that they were merely exercising what they had been taught—to live off the land—it became a real disciplinary problem. Severe punishment and fines limited the problem, but never did stop the Raiders from partaking of the forbidden fruit.

Over the next several weeks, the long marches continued as the Raiders toughened up for their impending baptism of fire. As the days dragged on, many an exhausted Raider headed for his bunk at night with the words uttered by an actor in the movie *Gung Ho!*

"All I want to know is when does the war start? I'm going to need it to take a rest."

When Carlson arrived at Camp Catlin after his meeting with Nimitz, he put two of his companies, C and D, on alert for a possible deployment to Midway. Two days later, on May 20, Carlson and Roosevelt and the two company commanders (Capt. Donald H. Hastie and 1st Lt. John Apergis respectively) met with navy planners and, after being sworn to secrecy, were informed that the two companies would indeed move to Midway to help defend the island from an expected invasion force of between five thousand and six thousand Japanese Marines. The alert orders sounded ominous. They were instructed to "make the Japs pay dearly for every man they landed" and both company commanders were told to defend "to the last man and the last bullet."

The two companies deployed on May 22 and, sailing at flank speed, completed the thirteen-hundred-mile trip to Midway in only three days. C Company was assigned to Sand Island, where the seaplane base, fuel tanks, cable station, radio station, and Pan Am Airways terminal were located. D Company was deployed to Eastern Island, the site of the three-runway airfield.

The Raiders were immediately put to work unloading supplies and manufacturing mines to be planted on suspected landing sites. After their three-day sea voyage to Midway, many of them looked a little rough around the edges. One writer described them as "a wild-looking bunch" with bandoliers of cartridges hanging over their shoulders and their pockets bulging with grenades. "Their belts concealed knives, which they flung at the palm trees with casual skill. They stuck to themselves, mostly, and were rarely visible to the rest of the defenders. The naval reservists regarded them with cautious awe. They knew that it could cost a man's life to go near them after dark without knowing the password."

The other four Raider companies, A, B, E, and F, remained on alert back at Camp Catlin, grumbling about being left behind in Hawaii. Their orders were "to be prepared to embark on designated ships for landings or counterlandings at places to be designated." In the meantime, many of the Raiders were put to work scattering drums of gasoline around the island just in case the Japanese decided to attack Oahu again.

As it turned out, there was no invasion of Midway or any other island in the Hawaiian chain, and the other four Raider companies were not needed for any landings or counterlandings. The Battle of Midway was primarily an air and naval battle that resulted in the near destruction of the Japanese force.

On June 8, two days after the remnants of the Japanese naval force retreated, Jimmy Roosevelt was detailed to Midway on a fact-finding mission. After a one-day inspection where he interviewed many of the top officers involved, he flew on to Washington to deliver a detailed report to his father.

While Roosevelt was in Washington, Companies A, B, E, and F boarded ships for possible deployment to the Aleutian islands of Attu and Kiska, which were occupied by the Japanese on June 6 and 7. The convoy left Hawaii on June 21, the day after C and D Companies returned to Oahu from Midway, but were diverted to Midway shortly after leaving port. On June 28, the same four companies, after being issued maps and aerial photographs of Attu and Kiska, got under way again toward the

Aleutians, only to be turned back to Hawaii rather than rush into what could have become a risky operation.

The 2d Raiders had arrived in Hawaii just in time to help the United States turn back a major effort by the Japanese at Midway, designed to force the Americans out of the Hawaiian Islands. The Japanese, embarrassed by the Doolittle Raid back on April 18, were determined to draw the remaining U.S. naval forces into a major confrontation in the hopes of completely crippling America's sea and air capability. Japan felt that had they succeeded, they could have opened peace talks with the United States from a position of power.

Admiral Isoroku Yamamoto, the commander-in-chief of the Japanese combined fleet and planner of the attack on Pearl Harbor, sent an overwhelming force of 185 ships, including 10 battleships, 4 aircraft carriers, and 70 destroyers, to seize Midway Island, the farthest outpost of the Hawaiian chain.

The Americans, who had broken the Japanese code, were waiting in ambush to the northeast of Midway. Their attack on June 4 caught the Japanese by surprise and resulted in the destruction of all four carriers, one heavy cruiser, three battleships, and 372 aircraft. An estimated thirty-five hundred Japanese sailors were killed and the cadre of experienced pilots was nearly wiped out.

The Battle of Midway tilted the balance of naval power in the Pacific to the Americans and signaled the beginning of the end for Japan.

Eight

Target Makin

Upon returning to Hawaii on July 3, Carlson met with Nimitz and his staff to plan future operations. The navy brass was refining the operational plans for the first offensive of the war, the invasion of Guadalcanal, and since the 1st Raider Battalion would be a key player in that operation, Carlson wanted a piece of it for his battalion.

Nimitz, flush from his overwhelming victory at Midway, was all for it. The talk centered on an amphibious raid from submarines. Both Nimitz and President Roosevelt believed that the most spectacular use of the 2d Raider Battalion would be a payback raid on Wake Island, which the Japanese had taken from the Americans back on December 23.

Available intelligence in July of 1942 put the Japanese occupational force on Wake at between two and four thousand troops, a figure much too high for one Raider battalion to handle, and it was quickly dismissed as a reasonable target. Ironically, the Americans never did invade Wake during the war, deciding to bypass the island. The Japanese garrison on Wake consisted of some twelve hundred troops when the island was surrendered on September 4, 1945, two days after Japan's formal surrender in Tokyo Bay.

Nimitz and his staff quickly shifted their emphasis away from Wake Island to other targets in the summer of 1942, targets that could be tied in with the planned invasion of Guadalcanal. It was agreed that Carlson's Raiders could best be used as a diversionary force, one that would divert or delay any Japanese reinforcements and supplies from being used on Guadalcanal.

According to Carlson's biographer, Nimitz asked the Raider com-

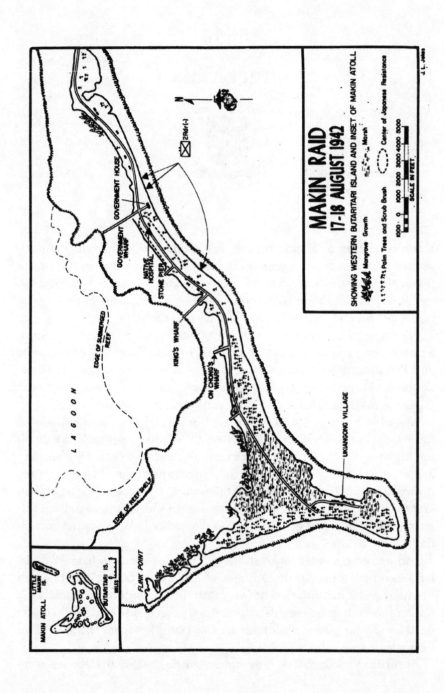

mander how many submarines he thought he would need for such a small-scale amphibious operation.

"Twenty," Carlson answered in a flash, bringing a laugh from Nimitz.

"I can let you have two to practice landings from. You're lucky you can have a real sub to practice with instead of a mock-up," Nimitz said with that calm demeanor of his. "We're short of men, short of ships, and short of planes. Your ideas are sound enough, but find out what you can do with the subs, and I'll take up the question of hit-and-run raids with the staff."

The next issue involved a target. It must be a lightly defended island that afforded the Raiders a good chance of success.

Carlson was originally told to investigate the possibilities of raids on Wake, Tinian, Hokkaido, Tulagi, and Attu. By the first week of July, four of the sites were eliminated because they were too heavily defended and too far from Guadalcanal. The fifth site, Tulagi, which was about twenty-five miles from Guadalcanal, had been eliminated because it had been assigned to the 1st Raider Battalion as part of the Guadalcanal operation. A decision was made, probably by mid-July, to go for Makin Atoll in the Gilbert Islands, a small, lightly defended outpost about a thousand miles northeast of Guadalcanal.

"After considering all factors, an objective in the Gilbert Islands seemed the most realistic," Commodore John M. Haines later told an interviewer. "This was the area of deepest Japanese penetration . . . its exposed position might have left it sufficiently sensitive to a raid as to bring out the reaction we desired, which was to deter the immediate reinforcement of Guadalcanal. That is how we selected Makin Atoll as the target and August 17, 1942 as D day."

The navy had little intelligence on Makin. An American task force had conducted a brief air raid on the atoll back on February 1 as part of a hit-and-run mission, but it yielded few aerial photographs and little information on how heavily it was defended. Subsequently, the islands had been scouted by submarines without adding very much to the skimpy knowledge the navy already had.

It appeared that the atoll's main island, Butaritari, was used as a weather station and seaplane base and defended by an enemy force estimated at between fifty and three hundred and fifty. Butaritari was about eight miles long and a half-mile wide. It was located at the southwest point of the triangular atoll just below the main lagoon entrance. The entire island was covered by a thick growth of coconut palms that extended to the waterline. The landing would be conducted from the ocean or south side of Butaritari through a heavy surf and hopefully would catch the defenders by surprise.

The two submarines promised the Raiders were the *Argonaut* and the *Nautilus,* the two largest subs in the American fleet. The *Argonaut,* which was commissioned in 1928, was 381 feet long and had been built as a minelayer. Immediately after Pearl Harbor, she had gone through a refit at Mare Island Navy Yard, converting her to a transport submarine. Tragically, the *Argonaut* was sunk off the coast of New Guinea on January 10, 1943, with the loss of all 103 men aboard.

The *Nautilus,* completed in 1930, was 371 feet long and had undergone a complete engine overhaul in July of 1941. Both ships could do sixteen knots on the surface but only half that while submerged.

Each of the two Raider companies (A and B) picked for the raid selected a submarine liaison officer to work with the navy and figure out the logistics of the operation. It was quickly determined that there wasn't nearly enough room on the two subs to take two full companies. The larger *Argonaut* could accommodate 134 passengers, while the *Nautilus* could accommodate only 85. That would mean some 55 Raiders (25 from A Company and 30 from B Company) would have to remain at Pearl.

Carlson didn't want to leave that many behind. He wanted a third submarine, the *Narwhal,* but this time his "connections" couldn't help him. Nimitz told him that he would have to make do with two and be thankful it wasn't one. Nimitz had good reason to deny this request. With his battleships virtually wiped out seven months earlier and with a severe shortage of carriers, he needed his submarine fleet to provide security for Hawaii and the shipping lanes to Australia until the United States could replace all the combat surface ships that had been lost back on December 7.

Another problem Carlson couldn't overcome was the availability of the submarines during training. Once again, Nimitz couldn't spare the *Nautilus* and *Argonaut* for training missions. They were needed for patrol duty. They would become available a day or two before the mission and not a minute before, Nimitz told Carlson. With the Guadalcanal invasion slated for August 7, there wasn't much time to get the Raiders ready to play a meaningful role in the offensive.

Companies A and B moved to Barber's Point at the southwest corner of Oahu for their highly secret rubber-boat training in mid-July. Barber's Point was picked because it had surf as rough as they would find at Makin, so rough in fact that there was no need to protect the beaches from an enemy invasion with barbed wire. It was believed that an enemy force couldn't land over such a surf.

The Raiders would use the standard eleven-man rubber boat, which could and did accommodate up to thirteen or fourteen men. Each boat came equipped with a two-cycle outboard motor that had an exposed ignition system. Attempts to build a cover over the ignition system largely failed, which made the motors difficult to start and keep running in heavy seas.

Each boat came with ten paddles, humorously referred to as the auxiliary power source, a large five-gallon gas can, and a portable tank of carbon dioxide for inflating the boat when pressurized air was not available. Some of the boats came equipped with straps to tie down special equipment such as medical supplies, demolition supplies, heavy weapons, and stretchers.

Each crewman had specific tasks he was responsible for while aboard. The senior man was the boat captain, one was the outboard motor mechanic and usually the coxswain, another was in charge of the gas can, and still another was responsible for the paddles.

Two buoys, signifying the *Argonaut* and *Nautilus*, were anchored some two thousand yards offshore. Onshore, the Raiders would practice inflating their rubber boats with hand pumps and then walking the boats out into the surf, where they would jump in and start the motors. When they had reached the buoys, the boats would line up and try to effect a coordinated landing. Once ashore, they would camouflage their boats, move inland, and carry out specific assignments against mock-up targets that were supposed to represent those on Butaritari. The targets were actually stakes in the ground.

The training started slowly, without equipment at first and then with full gear, helmets and all. Later, they graduated to night maneuvers.

"The training with rubber boats at Barber's Point was fun," Private McCall remembered. "We trained in our skivvies and some were dressed in their 'wherewithals.' The sun baked our skin brown and there wasn't a woman in sight."

The training was difficult and filled with mishaps. Many of the boats were flipped over by huge breakers, and the two-cylinder Evinrude motors often sputtered out because the salt water shorted out either the exposed coil or the spark plugs, or both.

Private Carson remembered his battle with the surf as a life-and-death experience. He was saved from death by an alert crewmate after he was knocked out cold when his capsized boat landed on top of him.

"Sometimes the rubber boat would hit the breaker so hard that it would bend right in the middle," Carson said. "As we would top the wave, the boat would unbend itself so fast that those seated in the back half of the boat would get airborne and, most often, end up outside the boat."

That's what happened to Carson. The boat flipped over and Carson's head collided with a metal pressure gauge affixed to the bow, and he was knocked unconscious. Fortunately, the coxswain, Pfc. William Gallagher, saw what had happened and grabbed Carson, keeping him afloat until the boat was righted. Once ashore, Carson came to and, except for a bump on the head and a sore throat from swallowing salt water, was able to resume training. Gallagher was later killed on the Makin Raid.

"We practiced rowing out to the buoy and back to shore," McCall said. "The boat teams trained between the buoys and the beach for every possible eventuality—so we thought at the time—by boating through the surf with and without paddles, with and without motors, with full teams and reduced teams, with full equipment and no equipment at all, and in combinations of these factors."

Captain James "Blast" Davis also conducted demolitions training at Barber's Point, assembling a six-man crew to handle these duties once on the objective. Four of the team members had had experience with dynamite as civilians. The former powder monkeys, as they were called, were Pvt. Fred Helm, Pfc. John Kerns, Pfc. Lamar Mazzei, and Pvt. Richard Olbert. The two neophytes were Pvt. Brian Quirk and Pvt. Don Roberton.

"To this day I don't know why they picked me," Quirk said six decades later. "My kids laugh at me when I tell them I was a powder monkey in the war. I have trouble turning on a light switch. I guess [the Raiders] thought I was a screw-up, so they volunteered me to be a demolition man. Captain Davis knew his stuff, though, and we had a lot of experienced people in the crew."

The Raiders used little half-pound blocks of TNT, attaching them to the object of destruction with black putty and primer cord.

"We blew up some grass huts, small buildings, and gas cans. We even set some off in the water," Quirk said.

When the Raiders hit Makin, all six men went ashore with their rifles and ammunition as well as a twenty-pound knapsack filled with dynamite. Kerns and Roberton would not come back from the raid.

The training at Barber's Point was completed by the end of July.

"We had no doubts as to our readiness to handle anything that might await us at the objective," Lt. Peatross wrote, "and it was with feelings of great self-confidence and no little self-satisfaction that we broke camp and boarded trucks for the move back to Camp Catlin."

The Raiders had one "sanctioned" leave while in Hawaii, a one-day pass. But, just as they had at Jacques Farm, more than a few Raiders sampled the nightspots on their own during "unofficial" furloughs after curfew.

There was also a dance held at Camp Catlin a few days before they left on the raid. It was arranged by Major Roosevelt as a reward for their hard work.

"Major Roosevelt lent us his station wagon to go and pick up some girls at the Alexander Young Hotel and bring them back to the dance," recalled Pvt. Dean Voight. "At the time I hung around with Pvt. Charlie Selby. He was the best-looking guy in the outfit and really had a way with the girls. He was from Ontonagon, Michigan. I called him the Duke of Ontonagon.

"Anyway, I let Duke do all the talking at the hotel and he had no trouble convincing the girls to come along back to camp with us. We never got to dance with them, though. All the big shots, the officers, took care of the girls."

Booze was never very difficult to acquire in Hawaii.

"What we couldn't buy we made," Voight said.

Prewar Honolulu was famous for its nightlife. Just the name Hotel Street put a smile on a swabbie's face. The street was a mile long and featured a wide and colorful collection of glittery strip bars, brothels, and other fancy clip joints. At various navy clubs, called slop chutes, you could get a pitcher of beer for a quarter. For fifty cents you could get pretty sloshed. A mixed drink cost a quarter. Prices went up sharply a few months after the war broke out and the demand exceeded the supply. Most of the honky-tonk establishments in town had back doors for quick exits, just in case the shore patrol showed up to break up fights or check to see who did and didn't have legitimate passes.

Hotel Street and nearby River Street, the address of many of Honolulu's ladies of the evening, were hives of entrepreneurial excess. The former was no wider than a good-sized alley. There was room for one lane of traffic, some parking, and not much else. The street meandered among two- and three-story buildings that appeared ready to collapse on any unsuspecting automobile or pedestrian. Many of the buildings were covered in battleship gray. Scuttlebutt had it that gray paint was the color of choice because it was provided by the yardbirds in exchange for beer and other necessities.

Sailor Theodore Mason, who was aboard the battleship *California* at the time of Pearl Harbor, described Hotel Street as crammed with "narrow-fronted business establishments offering every type of profit-making escapism" a young sailor could ever hope for.

"Side by side were dim bars with jukeboxes blaring the latest Stateside and hapa haole hits (Hawaiian music modified to American tastes); photo studios where one could pose with a dusky lass in a grass skirt before a painted backdrop of Waikiki and Diamond Head; trinket and souvenir counters; shooting galleries operated by White Russians from Shanghai; jewelry and clothing stores; barber shops where flirtatious Japanese girls wielded the clippers; tattoo parlors whose tiny windows were filled with sketches and designs strange and wondrous; peep-show and pinball-machine joints; saimin (pork and noodles) stands; an occasional respectable restaurant like Wo Fat's with its green-tiled pagoda tower," Mason wrote.

"And pervading all this was the unique smell of Honolulu: a malodorous infusion of decaying pork, overripe fish, and a variety of pungent spices unknown to Western nostrils.

"On the second and third floors, reached by narrow wooden stairways, were the offices of small, secretive businesses and professions, massage parlors advertising their electrical delights in gaudy neon, and hotels of two types. One kind actually rented rooms by the day or week. The other had the names such establishments always have: Rex, Ritz, Anchor, New Senator. If still in doubt about what these hotels had to offer, one had only to follow the uniforms."

Many of the Raiders made friends with the sailors they met on the submarines. The sailors, who had been in Hawaii for a longer time, knew a whole lot more about downtown Honolulu and Pearl City than the Raiders. They also were experts in distilling their own liquor.

"One of the things we used to do was get feeling good on the home-made liquor and then swap uniforms before going into town," Voight said. "I was six foot two and my sailor buddy was five foot six. You should have seen us. It was pretty funny."

The Honolulu of mid-1942, which had to conduct business under strict blackout conditions, was pretty tame compared to its prewar days. There wasn't all that much to do, which was revealed in a letter Lieutenant Holtom sent to his aunt, dated August 3, 1942, just a few days before he shipped out on the Makin Raid.

"Well, as you know, I am over the briny drink, in an unnamed spot, as the censors would have it. We have a splendid climate, plenty of mosquitoes, and lots of sitting around. We get a liberty once in a while, and then go down to see the vastly overrated town. I have been down to see the town four times since we came, and would be just as willing to spend my liberties in camp, since there is very little to do when you do get to the burg.

"The great dissipation here is the show in the evening," Holtom wrote. "You ought to see the old wrecks they trot out occasionally. We are all looking forward to *The Covered Wagon* or maybe something with Rudolph Valentino.

"We live in barracks, which are supposed to be temporary, but which are actually very comfortable, especially if you come in from a week of sleeping on the ground. We gripe about the food, but it actually isn't so bad, though beans are emphasized unduly. Aside from the beans, the potatoes, the lack of vegetables, the lousy deserts [*sic*], the spoiled meat (the lads evidently find a dead cow once in a while), the old-sock coffee, and lack of milk, the food is quite good, since, after all, we do have good bread. We had some chili con carne the other day that was really hard to take; I don't know what they had done to it, but something was terribly wrong, as about fifty percent of the camp found two hours later, when the great trek began."

There were still many problems the Raiders had to overcome before they could even begin to think of shoving off on a combat mission, however. Continuing difficulties getting the outboard motors to work worried the Raiders, as did the stuffy conditions belowdecks on the submarines and a general lack of reliable intelligence on the objective.

It was too late to get new and more effective motors. They would have to make do with what they had. The mechanics worked overtime to create some kind of shield over the exposed ignition system to try and keep out the seawater, but there was no time to test the handmade modifications.

According to Lieutenant Peatross, the raiding party held a dress rehearsal utilizing both submarines in the early-morning hours of August 6, one that was witnessed by Admiral Nimitz.

"As luck would have it, my boat landed directly in front of where Admiral Nimitz was standing," Peatross wrote in his history of the Raiders. "After supervising the securing of our boat, I introduced myself to him and we had a short conversation. Aside from Mrs. Roosevelt's three-day visit to our camp at Jacques Farm, this brief chat with Admiral Nimitz was the highlight of my life to that point."

Following the dress rehearsal, one of the major points addressed in the critique was that many Raiders appeared exhausted and dehydrated because of the intense heat aboard the submarines, which would definitely create problems on a long sea voyage. If that was the case, the men might not be able to function at peak efficiency once ashore. The problem was deemed sufficiently important to institute a last-minute, crash program to install a five-ton air-conditioner aboard each submarine. Another recommended modification was the welding of handles on the exterior of the submarines for use by the Raiders in climbing aboard the vessel in heavy seas. Of course, while these modifications, plus those necessary to accommodate the extra baggage and equipment of the Raiders, were taking place, the submarines would be unavailable to the Raiders for training missions.

One of those caught off guard by the need for so many modifications was Lieutenant Peatross.

"I personally had seen no evidence of dehydration or consequent exhaustion during the dress rehearsal, but then we hadn't spent several days, or even one day, aboard the submarines, so who was I to say?" Peatross wrote.

Peatross, who would rise to the rank of major general in the Marine Corps, is regarded as the premier historian of the Makin Raid. His well-researched book *Bless 'em All*, which was published two years after his death in 1993, is widely recognized as the most accurate and thorough account of the Raider action on Makin.

(Peatross's memory on the availability of the submarines during any of the training is disputed by Ben Carson. Carson believes that the only time the Raiders were on a submarine prior to leaving for the Makin Raid was just a few days before when they participated in a practice dive at Pearl Harbor. Most of the other Raiders, including Colonel Carlson, sided with Peatross, however, saying that at the very least, the submarine *Nautilus* was used in the dress rehearsal.)

The lack of up-to-date and reliable intelligence was the most troubling aspect of the preparation. All the navy had on Makin Atoll was some aerial photos taken back on February 1 by aircraft from the *Enterprise* and some sketchy data obtained from a native fisherman of the island who was interviewed by Lieutenant Holtom (he was promoted to captain while on the Makin Raid). Holtom had been assigned to Carlson's Raiders in late February at Jacques Farm well before the seeds for the Makin Raid were planted.

Holtom grew up in Yokohama, Japan, as the son of American missionaries. He spoke and read Japanese fluently. After earning a B.S. degree in anthropology from the University of California at Berkeley, he had returned to Japan in 1940 to work at the U.S. Consulate. He returned home and joined the Marines shortly after and was stationed at Pearl Harbor as an intelligence officer when the Japanese attacked on December 7, 1941.

Carlson was impressed with Holtom's credentials and placed great faith in his professional manner. The two grew close at Jacques Farm and closer still once the battalion reached Hawaii.

"Although he lacked military experience he made up for this lack in enthusiasm, in his knowledge of Japanese, and in his love for the rugged outdoor life," Carlson wrote to Holtom's parents shortly after their son was killed on Makin. "I made him my intelligence officer and he tore into the job with all the intelligence and energy he possessed, which was far above average. [He] was the epitome of perfection.

"One quality which Jerry possessed I particularly prize. That was the quality of thoroughness. I had only to indicate that I wished a study made of a certain area. Jerry would tear into it and work night and day until it was completed. I would find that he had exhausted every available source of information, and the bits which he included in his analysis invariably proved to be reliable."

Holtom, according to Peatross, had learned from a local fisherman that the main island, Butaritari, was manned by a garrison of about forty-five to fifty Japanese Marines under the command of a Sergeant Major Kanemitsu.

"According to the fisherman, there were no mines or booby traps and no sentries on the beaches, a most welcome bit of information," Peatross said Holtom told him.

Navy headquarters in Hawaii warned that the enemy garrison at Makin was sure to be on some kind of alert, especially after they became aware of the American landings on Guadalcanal, which were scheduled for August 7.

The conjectured size of the enemy garrison at Makin varied greatly within Nimitz's intelligence community. Some estimates as to the number of Japanese soldiers on the island ran as high as 350. If that figure was accurate, the raid should have been scratched. It would have been entirely too risky.

Raider Brian Quirk said it even better more than a half century later.

"If there really were three hundred and fifty Japs on that island it would have been good night sweetheart for us," he said.

The Raiders spent the last few days before leaving cleaning equipment and packing gear to be taken on the trip. Each Raider was told to safety-pin together a khaki shirt and pants, attach a special label with their name on it, and turn it in to the property room. The uniforms were returned the next day dyed coal-black. They were issued high-top sneakers and given a gunnysack to hold any belongings to be taken on the raid.

As the departure time neared, each of the Raiders began to exhibit his own brand of nervous energy, sometimes called butterflies. At a Gung Ho meeting shortly before leaving, Carlson said that it would be perfectly understandable for anyone to back out if he felt it would be too dangerous. If they worried about their families back home or felt that they couldn't kill someone if they had to, he would understand. He had replacements standing by for just such an occasion. A few Raiders took him up on his offer.

Among those forced to miss the Raid because of injury was Lt. Jack Miller, the second platoon leader of A Company. Miller broke his arm during training at Barber's Point. He was replaced by GySgt. Ellsbury B. Elliott. Ironically, Miller was killed four months later on Guadalcanal by an American-made Thompson submachine gun that the enemy may have captured on Makin after the raiders had left.

Corporal Cecil Bragg was scratched from the trip after he accidentally shot himself in the foot with an M1 rifle. Private First Class John Rich begged off at the last minute for religious reasons. Another cited claustrophobia as a reason. The overall attitude, however, was decidedly "Gung Ho," as most of the men were anxious to get at the Japanese and deliver a little payback for what had happened at Pearl Harbor eight months earlier.

Carlson also had a long talk with Jimmy Roosevelt and tried to convince him it wasn't necessary for him to go on the raid. Nimitz also had reservations about Roosevelt exposing himself to such danger and possibly the risk of capture. He agreed with Carlson that there was no need for Roosevelt to go on the raid and plans were made accordingly.

Jimmy Roosevelt argued that his place was with the men, and after failing to convince either Carlson or Nimitz, he put in a call to his father back in Washington. FDR is said to have called his chief of naval operations, Admiral King, and told him, "Look, my son's an officer in that battalion; if he doesn't go, no one goes."

To be sure, Jimmy Roosevelt had many concerns about his less-than-robust physical condition. His health was very much on his mind, as revealed in a letter he wrote to his mother, dated July 29 from San Francisco, where he had taken a short leave.

Dearest Mummy:
It was just swell to talk to you on the telephone and you sounded just top of the world and I hope you are. The reason for this visit [to San Francisco] is because we are about to go on our first job along the lines of our name. We leave about eight days from now and the whole business will take us about three weeks. . . . Frankly my insides are little by little getting worse. My weight is shifting a little and an increasing amount of 'gas' is for the present just uncomfortable. Originally I volunteered for this work because I felt it was my job to do a front-line job and because I feared that physically the chance would be denied unless I got at it early.

War is not a glorious or exciting thing to me. There is too much to live for at home, away from it. But right or wrong I felt that was my duty. Now comes the chance to stand by the men I've been working with and give them the confidence and leadership which being younger they will need. But Mummy, if we come through this in good shape then my brain tells me that it is foolish to go on to the point of exhaustion. Progressively my judgment and leadership get worse as I feel more lousy, and eventually I am a liability to my own group. Unfortunately I need such things as rest, milk, and food which is not greasy, to stay in shape and one just can't find and shouldn't order things to suit one individual out there or on any "front."

Mummy, I've thought so long on the angle of special interest and favoritism on this. But after all any other officer would never have been given waivers on my defects (eyes 3-20th and stomach) and when this next job is done at least inside I'll feel I have stood the test of making it no matter what the odds.

So whatever can be done or should be done about it I don't want to be retired as physically unfit and truly feel I have much to contribute in a constructive way. Father once told me he would never ask for anything for his sons and he's quite right and shouldn't be put on that kind of a spot.

Much love, Jimmy.

Early on the day they shoved off for the mission that took them to the Gilbert Islands, Lt. Col. Evans F. Carlson and Maj. James Roosevelt completed last minute plans. Roosevelt was second in command to Carlson in the 17 August 1942 raid.

Evans Carlson, left, and James Roosevelt in front of the headquarters building at Camp Catlin. Roosevelt wore sneakers because of chronic flat feet.

Raiders exercise on board USS *Nautilus* while enroute to Makin, August 11, 1942, six days before the surprise raid on Makin. Most of the trip from Pearl Harbor to Makin was made on the surface; no enemy sightings were made.

Butaritari (Makin) is seen through the periscope of the USS *Nautilus*, the evening before the landing on 17 August. (Courtesy of the Raider Patch)

Sergeant Walter Carroll, left, and Pfc. Dean Winters get ready to go topside on the *Nautilus* before the Makin Raid. (Courtesy of the Raider Patch)

Sergeant Clyde Thomason, the first enlisted Marine in World War II to receive the Medal of Honor, which was awarded posthumously. He was killed in action during the Makin Raid on 17 August 1942.

Private Dean Winters holds captured Japanese rifle on return trip from Makin.

Carlson and Roosevelt display a captured Japanese flag upon return to Pearl Harbor after the Makin Raid. (Courtesy of the Raider Patch)

Carlson, Roosevelt, and Lt. Cmdr. John "Happy Jack" Pierce talking it over aboard the USS *Argonaut* after the raid on Makin.

Lieutenant Commander John Pierce, facing camera, talks with Major Roosevelt aboard the USS *Argonaut*. Carlson is on the right. (Courtesy of the Raider Patch)

Carlson tells Brig. Gen. Harry K. Pickett, to his left, and an unidentified Marine officer the story of the Makin Raid. Carlson is holding a captured Japanese flag.

Part of the crew on stern aboard USS *Nautilus* entering Pearl Harbor. Japanese flag on gun was captured during Makin Raid.

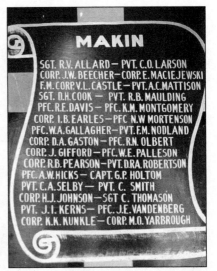

Private Brian Quirk poses at Camp Catlin with captured Japanese rifle and flag brought back from Makin Raid.

Sign shows those known who were killed in action or missing in action during the Makin Raid erected at Camp Catlin, August 1942.

MAKIN

SGT. R.V. ALLARD — PVT. C.O. LARSON
CORP. J.W. BEECHER — CORP. E. MACIEJEWSKI
F.M. CORP. V.L. CASTLE — PVT. A.C. MATTISON
SGT. D.H. COOK — PVT. R.B. MAULDING
PFC. R.E. DAVIS — PFC. K.M. MONTGOMERY
CORP. I.B. EARLES — PFC N.W MORTENSON
PFC. W.A. GALLAGHER — PVT. F.M. NODLAND
CORP. D.A. GASTON — PFC. R.N. OLBERT
CORP. J. GIFFORD — PFC. W.E. PALLESON
CORP. R.B. PEARSON — PVT. D.RA. ROBERTSON
PFC. A.W. HICKS — CAPT. G.P. HOLTOM
PVT. C.A. SELBY — PVT. C. SMITH
CORP. H.J. JOHNSON — SGT C. THOMASON
PVT. J.I. KERNS — PFC. J.E. VANDENBERG
CORP. K.K. KUNKLE — CORP. M.O. YARBROUGH

Marines shown during ceremony on Espiritu Santo where they were awarded the Navy Cross. From left, Capt. Coyte, Lt. MacCracken, Lt. Stigler, Lt. Plumley, Lt. Lamb, Sgt. Elliott, Pvt. Craven, and Pfc. Sebock.

Lieutenant Charles Lamb, left, Capt. Oscar Peatross, center, and Capt. Bud Davis pose at Camp Gung Ho on Espiritu Santo in December 1942. (courtesy of the Raider Patch)

Private William McCall, left, and Plt. Sgt. Ned E. McNussen, somewhere on Guadalcanal.

Carlson cools his feet on Guadalcanal.

Captain Oscar Peatross, right (in white undershirt) plays cards with other Raiders on Guadalcanal in November 1942.

Lieutenant Wilfred S. LeFrancois, left, Carlson, and Sgt. Victor J. Maghakian pose on the set of the movie *Gung Ho!*

Private Ben Carson, right, and Pvt. Cyrill Matelski give snappy salutes at the Royal Hawaiian Hotel after returning from the Makin Raid. Matelski was killed on Guadalcanal four months later.

Nine

The Real Deal

News of the invasion of Guadalcanal on August 7 (August 6 in Hawaii) spread like a flash throughout the Pacific and the United States. The 1st Marine Division had landed nearly unopposed on Guadalcanal and was pushing inland against very light opposition. Across Sealark Channel just off the coast of Florida Island, the 1st Raider Battalion swept across the island of Tulagi, also landing unopposed but later overcoming a determined resistance. There was a sense that at last, America was taking the fight to the Japanese.

Almost simultaneously back in Hawaii, the 2d Raider Battalion was making last-minute preparations for a mission of its own, a raid on Makin Atoll of the Gilbert Island chain. Carlson met with his officers early on August 7 to emphasize the secrecy—and danger—of the mission and then the troops got busy packing their gear. Rosters of those going on the raid were checked and double-checked and then submarine assignments were given out.

Ammunition, including grenades, was issued and individual weapons were cleaned and inspected. Unserviceable items were replaced. Several of the officers and NCOs were issued riot-type shotguns.

The Raiders would take their weapons and a gunnysack containing their personal items with them. Their seabags would remain at Camp Catlin. They would leave the following morning, August 8. Only a few of the officers knew this wasn't an ordinary training mission, but the seriousness of the preparation created an impression in everybody's mind that this, indeed, could be the real thing.

All other equipment, including the rubber boats and motors, had been taken to the pier and loaded aboard the *Nautilus* and *Argonaut* the previous night. The rubber boats were folded tightly, covered with a light coating of grease, and stored in the torpedo loading tubes on the deck. The motors and gasoline were stored below. The submarine liaison officers had figured out a way to utilize every square inch of space belowdecks.

The Raiders went about their business in a calm and quiet fashion.

"Is this it, Sarge?" one of the young Raiders asked with a burst of nervous energy.

"When you need to know, you'll be told" came the answer.

The word also went out that this might be a good time to write any letters if the men felt so inclined.

Because there wasn't room on the two submarines for two full companies, rosters had been prepared detailing who was and who wasn't to go on the raid. Some fifty-five Raiders, twenty-five from A company and thirty from B company, would have to be left behind. The stay-behinds watched their buddies pack, fully believing this was the real deal.

"What do you want for a souvenir?" one Raider asked while stuffing his green high-top sneakers and blackened uniform into his gunnysack.

"Bring me back Tojo's sword," came the reply.

Other men packed in quiet solitude lest they awaken the voice of fear within them.

Shortly after midnight on August 8, the Raiders began loading onto trucks that would take them on a short ride to the submarine base. They left camp under blackout conditions and as quietly as possible. There was no need to alert anyone else of their departure.

The trucks carrying the Raiders rolled silently through the gates of the submarine base and pulled up to a pier around 0200. Officers and senior NCOs went to the gangplank of each submarine to supervise the loading. Raiders bumped into each other trying to find the right submarine in the darkness, but slowly everything got sorted out and the loading went swiftly.

Eighty-five Raiders, eighty from B Company and five from Headquarters Company, filed aboard the *Nautilus,* disappearing one at a time down a hatch and out of sight. In order to expedite the loading, the men removed their helmets and put them in the gunnysack they were issued. The gunnysack preceded each Raider down the ladder.

Carlson and his HQ staff, which included his intelligence officer, Captain Holtom, and B Company commander Capt. Ralph Coyte, were already aboard the *Nautilus* to supervise the loading from the conning tower. The skeleton navy crew aboard the *Nautilus* included the boat's skipper, Lt. Comdr. William E. Brockman, and Commodore John M. Haines, who went along on the trip as the overall commander of the two-ship operation.

The *Argonaut* loaded at the same time, quietly and efficiently. There was no talking and no smoking as each man was checked off to see if he was on the right sub. The *Argonaut,* having more room belowdeck than the *Nautilus,* took on 134 Raiders, 105 from A Company and twenty-seven from B Company. Major Roosevelt and Capt. James "Blast" Davis, the battalion's demolition and engineer officer, and A Company commander 1st Lt. Merwyn Plumley also filed aboard. The boat's skipper was Lt. Comdr. John "Happy Jack" Pierce, the same man who had come to Hawaii with the Raiders aboard the USS *J. Franklin Bell* in May.

The submarines, each manned by a reduced navy crew, carried torpedoes only in their six firing tubes. There were no spares. Their mission was to transport troops, not to sink enemy shipping.

Most of the Raiders on board had a gut feeling this wasn't a training mission, but there were some who weren't so sure. The top officers knew the real skinny, of course, but they did a good job of keeping it to themselves.

Private Ben Carson was pretty certain they were heading into action. The evidence that convinced him was when he and his squad were issued new combat bandage kits, replacing those they had beaten flat in training.

Lines were cast off and at 0900 both ships silently made their way out of Pearl Harbor like a pair of 2,700-ton sea snakes heading off into the unknown. To those watching on shore it appeared to be two submarines embarking on a routine hunting expedition. After they cleared the harbor and reached open sea, each boat would chart a separate course to the southwest toward the Gilbert Islands and Makin Atoll so as to confuse the enemy if they were spotted. A couple of hours into the mission, the men were told it wasn't a drill. They were heading off into harm's way. The destination, however, remained a secret.

Not all that familiar with conditions aboard a submarine, many of the Raiders looked around at their cramped surroundings and silently looked for a way out. The more they thought about it, the more apprehensive they got. The key to dealing with this situation was to not think about it. That was easier said than done.

Carlson and his staff had foreseen this reaction, of course, and had made plans to deal with the problem as early as possible on the trip. Carlson had written a speech to assure the men that no matter how cramped the submarine appeared to be, the ship's generators and air conditioners would provide more than enough clean air for everybody to breathe, even when submerged. That message was delivered to all the Raiders soon after leaving Pearl.

Many of the men didn't want to hear about the availability of clean air. They wanted to know where they were going.

"That's a military secret," one NCO said.

"Hey, maybe we're going to Tokyo," a Raider blurted out.

"Nah, we're headed for Guadalcanal. That's where the action is," another answered.

Orders came from the back to "pipe down" and "save your energy."

"When the navy wants you to know where you're going they will tell you. Until then, keep those big mouths shut and try to get some rest. You're gonna need it," a Raider sergeant barked.

Almost the entire trip was made on the surface. Over the first few hundred miles, security for the submarines was provided by land-based aircraft, but as they moved farther and farther from Hawaii, they had to rely mostly on their own radar and lookouts. Remarkably, neither sub had to dive because of an enemy ship or plane sighting.

The zigzag courses each sub followed were intended not only to confuse the enemy as to their destination but to prevent a Japanese sub from locking on to them and firing off a torpedo. To that end, strict radio silence between the subs was obeyed until they reached their destination. The constant course changes added a couple of days to the trip, but the key to the operation was surprise. Without it, the mission could fail. Besides, they had no timetable to get to Makin.

Radio reports of the Guadalcanal and Tulagi invasions were piped to the Raiders as often as possible. All was going well at both locations. The men had many friends with the 1st Marine Division and the 1st Raider Battalion and were anxious to get in on the action and do their part.

"Hey, maybe the war will be all over before we get there," one eager beaver said out loud. He was greeted by laughs and playful punches to the arm.

Lieutenant Peatross had an uneasy feeling about the operation even before the submarines left Pearl Harbor. That feeling sprang from a conversation he had overheard a few days earlier while having a drink with Dr. William B. MacCracken at the Sub Fleet Officer's Club.

The two sat down near a couple of submarine officers and overheard them openly discuss the Raiders' upcoming "secret" mission.

"At best," one of the navy men said to the other, "it's going to be a risky trip. Those two old pig-iron mine-laying boats are just too big, too slow, too difficult to maneuver, and unbelievably slow in diving."

The other navy man nodded in agreement and added, "Besides all that, you just can't navigate accurately enough to pop up next to one another after making a two-thousand-mile trip, and to make it more difficult, they have to arrive after dark."

After leaving the bar, MacCracken turned to Peatross and said, "Peat, those bastards were talking about us."

Peatross kept asking himself as the submarines headed westward who else knew where the Raiders were headed. If the enemy knew exactly where the Raiders were going and when they would arrive, it could be pretty messy.

Peatross and MacCracken discussed the breach of intelligence several times on the trip westward with Colonel Carlson, and all three men came to the same conclusion. There was nothing any of them could do about it, so worrying would do no good.

Ten

Sardines at Sea

Life aboard an unusually cramped submarine became both a physical and mental challenge for the Raiders as the days began to pass. It was hard to take your mind off the physical hardships one had to endure just to turn around. Mental images of "iron coffins" were tough to blot out. Sleep came grudgingly and then only for a few minutes at a time. The restrained conditions were particularly troublesome to the biggest Raiders and those who had grown up on the spacious farms of the Midwest.

Many, many years later, Private Carson wondered how he and his mates managed to cope with these completely unfamiliar conditions.

"Navy personnel selected for submarine service were subjected to tests to determine claustrophobia, compatibility with others in a confined environment, and other attributes considered essential," Carson opined. "Apparently Raiders were assumed to have all the necessary stuff for submarine service without any training at all."

Even though new air-conditioners had been installed on both submarines, it still was extremely hot belowdecks. The temperatures registered in the upper nineties throughout the eight-day trip even though the submarines ran almost entirely on the surface. Any form of exertion produced instant sweat. As a result, the Raiders were told to refrain from any excess movement and to stay in their bunks as much as possible to allow navy personnel room to perform their duties. There was no way to block out the fetid smell of unwashed bodies. That was just something you had to get used to.

The sleeping accommodations were perhaps the worst privation they endured on the trip. Bunk space was created by stretching canvas over two-by-fours. They were like bunk beds, four tiers high and four beds deep without any room to turn over. It is a wonder that the men didn't all suffer from claustrophobia or something worse.

If someone in an inside bunk had to answer the call of nature, three other Raiders had to move to let him out. The same procedure was required to let him back in, of course. It was more than a case of inconvenience for those relegated to the bottom bunks. That's where the sweat collected from those in the top three tiers. Puddles of human sweat collected on the floor, which made walking about very slippery.

"One of the unwritten laws on the trip was that Raiders in their bunks were not allowed to break wind, no mater what," Pvt. William McCall said. "Anyone that farted was threatened to be stuffed in the number four torpedo tube and shot out into the briny."

The whole setup reminded Pvt. Ben Carson of the old root cellar on the Minnesota farm where he grew up—confined, dark, dank, and with a gamy smell all its own.

Those who grew up in large families where they had to share practically everything seemed to handle the cramped conditions much better. Many others, however, had to overcome constant attacks of claustrophobia for the entire trip. It became an exercise of mind over matter, like sitting in a dentist's chair. If you knew it wouldn't last forever, you could force your mind to bear it. Every day endured became one day closer to it being over.

Despite the shortage of clean air belowdecks, the smoking lamp was lit all the way to Makin, perhaps as a morale concession by the navy, who were respectful of the dangerous mission the Raiders were about to undertake. Usually there was barely enough oxygen to light a match or ignite a lighter, but the Raiders still enjoyed their butts. The glow from dozens of lit cigarettes looked like a swarm of fireflies in the blue light that was standard when the sub was running on the surface. The shipboard doctors, W. B. MacCracken on the *Nautilus* and Stephen L. Stigler on the *Argonaut*, assured the men that although it was difficult to light a match and keep a cigarette from going out, there was plenty of oxygen in the air for them to breathe safely.

Here, too, the men had to fight off anxiety attacks. They were taught to take small breaths and to avoid exertion that would cause them to breathe deeply and use up precious oxygen. Instead of deep drags on the cigarettes, the men made do with short puffs.

The men even got used to the smell of diesel fuel and the knocking of the engines as the subs slowly zigzagged their way westward. It became music to their ears, a kind of nautical lullaby that sent them off to dream-land every night.

A conscious effort was made to provide the men exercise periods on the deck, weather and security permitting. That first breath of clean, fresh air gave the men a welcomed jolt as each platoon took turns climb-ing the hatch to the deck. While navy lookouts and radar scanned the horizon for enemy activity, the Raiders allowed themselves a few push-ups or a series of jumping jacks.

"I only did push-ups," Private Carson remembered. "There weren't any restraining lines around the deck, and with the ship rolling and pitching you could fall right off if you were doing jumping jacks."

The number of Raiders allowed on deck at one time was limited to about two dozen because of the time it took to climb up and down the ladders. In case of an emergency, the submarine had to have the ability to dive quickly. The exercise sessions were also condensed to about ten minutes so that as many Raiders as possible could go topside during the day, once early in the morning and again after the sun went down.

"We were always glad to get on deck and not smell those body odors and other stuff that festered the olfactories. Sometimes it would smell so bad down below, it would gag a maggot," Private McCall said.

Meals were another cumbersome hassle to endure. The galleys were in almost constant operation. Each meal required three and a half hours to serve as the Raiders lined up and trooped into the mess compartment to eat in shifts. There weren't any places to sit, so most of the men ate standing up. Baking had to be done at night between feedings. The men ate two meals a day, early in the morning and again at night. Soup and crackers were available at midday and coffee was served around the clock. In fact, the only time the galley was closed was for a short period between meals to clean utensils and prepare for the next serving. The Raiders had nothing to complain about because the food was excellent.

Private McCall did have one tiny complaint, however.

"There were so many people to feed that when the cook made coffee it was so weak you could stand in a barrelful and still see your toes," he said.

With the shortage of navy personnel aboard, several Raiders were pressed into mess duty. Again, few had any complaints because it gave them easy access to the food and got them away from the cramped troop quarters.

Extra rations, mostly canned fruit and vegetables, were stashed in various nooks and crannies on the subs, providing an irresistible temptation to pilfer, which was a serious offense aboard a navy vessel during wartime. Dire warnings curtailed the thefts, but Raiders being the resourceful bunch they were never stopped completely.

Colonel Carlson kept a brief diary on the trip and his entry for August 9 read: "Wouldn't have known this is Sunday but for the title on the page. Day uneventful. Men relatively comfortable. Prefer subs to APDs. Marines up for exercise and fresh air. Cleared topside in 3 minutes."

With the reduction of navy personnel aboard, Raiders had to pitch in and learn new tasks while en route to Makin. One important job was taking care of the head, no simple task aboard a submarine. Flushing a toilet must be done properly and by the numbers or the contents would backfire and never leave the sub. "Crapper Cops," as they were euphemistically called, were assigned to each head to properly dispose of the waste, once a fellow Raider finished using the facility. Even navy personnel had difficulty executing a proper flush.

Another duty that fell to the Raiders was the disposal of the sub's garbage, again an important function while at sea. All garbage, to include cans and other solid objects, was condensed to its smallest volume by the use of a hammer before being placed in strong burlap bags. The bags were then weighted down with something heavy and tied securely before being heaved overboard. All of this was serious business. Garbage carelessly tossed overboard would leave a perfect trail for an enemy to follow. Those Raiders pressed into this chore were called "can smashers."

Raiders also stood watch or assisted naval personnel who did. More than once, Raiders reported spotting Japanese aircraft only to be told they were actually looking at sea gulls or cloud formations. Nonetheless, the navy appreciated the extra sets of eyes the Raiders provided and lauded their zeal, if not their skill at target identification.

As the trip wore on, many of the Raiders found a solution to the generally intolerable sleeping arrangements. The bigger Raiders, those over six feet and two hundred pounds, simply couldn't cope with the existing situation, which they likened to sleeping in a casket.

Private Dean Voight, who was six foot two and two hundred pounds, was among those who decided to do something about the cramped conditions, and like the resourceful Chicago city boy he was, he scouted the sub for better accommodations. He quickly made friends with one of the navy seamen and entered into an arrangement that solved his predicament.

"We became buddies and whenever he stood night watch, I'd get to sleep in his sack," Voight said. "It was a hell of a lot roomier than the one the Raiders wanted me to sleep in."

It didn't take long for other Raiders to make the same "hot-bunking" arrangements. It was common for Raiders to sack out on flat areas near the bulkhead rather than endure the hassle and aggravation of trying to sleep in that sea of condensed flesh that passed as a bunk room. A big problem with choosing one's own sleeping area was that it often interfered with movement throughout the submarine. Those who slept on the floor couldn't escape being either kicked or stepped on when others wanted to move about.

Private Carson, one of the most innovative Raiders on the journey, also had an arrangement with a sailor buddy to use his more spacious bunk, with somewhat humorous results. One night early on the trip, an exhausted Carson climbed into the vacated seaman's bunk looking for a peaceful night's rest. After removing his boondocker shoes, he tied them together and hung them by the laces over a pipe about a foot from his head.

"I had dozed off for some time when I was very abruptly awakened by the submarine Klaxon announcing a dive," Carson wrote. "Just as abruptly, that damn pipe began spinning first one way, then the other, and my boondockers were cutting a wide path right past my nose.

"I made a grab for them and almost busted my wrist. The object I thought was a pipe was the drive shaft for the bow stabilizers. Eventually the shoestrings parted and I recovered my shoes—but not before several sub sailors accused me of working for the Japs!"

Carlson's diary entry for August 10 read: "Moving steadily south at 14.8 knots per hour. All Marines on deck again today for exercise. All agree living conditions are not that bad. Today skipper opened forward torpedo room hatches and circulated air through ship. Another crash dive. No sensation going down, slight cracking in ears when coming up."

While the enlisted men were left in the hands of the NCOs, the officers met daily in the wardroom to discuss the latest intelligence and refine their operational plans once the objective was reached. When they left Pearl Harbor, only the top Raider officers, Commodore Haines, and the two submarine skippers knew precisely where they were going. Most of the Raiders had never heard of Makin Atoll. All of their training off Barber's Point in Hawaii had been conducted against an imaginary, unnamed location.

The exact mission given Carlson was to land on Makin's Butaritari Island, kill every Japanese on the island, destroy anything that might be of use to the enemy, and collect as much intelligence as they could. They were to reboard the submarines that night and land the next day on Little Makin Island just to the northeast. It turned out to be an overly ambitious undertaking, to say the least.

Makin Atoll (now part of the independent state of Kiribati) is the northernmost group of islands in the Gilbert archipelago and located between 3 and 4 degrees north of the equator. Makin is a typical Pacific atoll, a necklace of palm-shaded coral islets around a quiet, placid lagoon. The lagoon is about ten miles across at its widest point. A dirt road runs down the length of its biggest island, Butaritari, which forms the southern base of the atoll.

There are four quays jutting into the lagoon from Butaritari. From east to west they are: Government Wharf, Stone Pier, King's Wharf, and On Chong's Wharf. Most of the Japanese activity on the island centered around those four quays. On the southwestern tip of Butaritari is Ukiangong Village, the largest settlement on the atoll with a native population of several hundred. Because the island had been previously occupied by the British, some of the natives spoke and understood some English.

Among the structures along the dirt road near the quays was a two-story building at the foot of Stone Pier, which was used by the Japanese commandant as a headquarters, a steepled church located on the windward side of the road immediately south of the headquarters building, a Japanese barracks, and, opposite the Government Wharf, a building called Government House.

The operational plan called for the Raiders to attack Butaritari from the south over a coral reef, landing on a beach directly opposite Government Wharf. The Raiders hoped to take the Japanese by surprise, catching them asleep in their bunks. The plan called for an assault over the treacherous reef in twenty rubber boats, with A Company on the left and B Company on the right.

The rubber boats would be inflated and loaded on the deck of each submarine and then would float off as the latter submerged, starting their motors once free of the sub. The rubber boats would proceed to an assembly area before making a coordinated landing on the beach.

Each company, after landing and camouflaging the rubber boats, was to cross the half-mile-wide island, A Company on the left and B company on the right, veer left, and advance toward the center of the objective area, meeting in the vicinity of the church. H-hour was first set at 0600, but this was changed to 0500 when it was determined that daylight began at 0525. The time for withdrawal to the submarines was set at 1930, which meant that the Raiders would have about thirteen hours of daylight to accomplish their mission and withdraw.

The mission was to destroy enemy forces and vital installations, capture prisoners and documents, and withdraw to the submarines to prepare for an attack on Little Makin Island the next day. No one had any idea what to do with the prisoners and where to put them on an already overcrowded submarine.

The submarines would stay on the surface unless spotted by Japanese planes or enemy shipping and try to keep in constant radio contact with the Raiders ashore.

Intelligence was sketchy at best. No one seemed to have a good idea just how many Japanese were on the island or if they were waiting in ambush for them. One of the intelligence reports dated back to February 1, when an air raid was conducted on the atoll from the *Enterprise* and *Yorktown* as part of a hit-and-run operation involving several targets in the Marshall and Gilbert Islands. Those raids gave U.S. forces a badly needed boost to their morale but added relatively little to the intelligence America had on these obscure outposts.

Carlson's available intelligence varied widely. One report said Butaritari was garrisoned by about fifty Japanese and another claimed the total was close to 350. Carlson chose to believe the latter figure and conducted his planning accordingly. Even later, when on-site evidence clearly indicated that the lower figure was closer to the actual enemy strength, Carlson continued to act as if the enemy force were larger.

Carlson's diary entry for August 11 read: "Steady on our course well south of Johnston Island. Topsides again for exercise. Much warmer. Acey-deucy is the popular game on board. Marines losing good deal of their tan developed at Barber's Point and Midway."

On the following day, Carlson wrote: "We are now within 700 miles of [target]. Ready to submerge at first sight or radar indication of a plane. Happy-go-lucky life on board. No sign of nervousness or fear. Tonight we cross the 180th meridian. Tomorrow will be Friday the 14th."

His entry for August 13 simply read: "Skipped this day. Crossed 180th."

An abbreviated rehearsal was held on August 14 to familiarize the boat teams with where they had to go for the actual departure. The teams were scattered throughout the submarine. Even-numbered teams, after gathering up their weapons and gear, reported to the starboard side and odd-numbered teams to port.

"Not one Raider had a direct route to his debarkation station," wrote Lieutenant Peatross. Each had to detour to pick up something en route—a machine gun, ammunition, paddles, a radio, whatever. Then he had to help extract his team's boat from the torpedo loading scuttles, unlash it, and drag it to the appropriate air hose for inflating. In the meantime, the outboard motors, having been collected at the foot of the appropriate ladder, were tied to ropes, hauled up over the ladder and through the hatch, carried to the appropriate debarkation stations, and attached to the boats.

Similar procedures were followed with all equipment not carried by an individual, like medical supplies, stretchers, extra ammunition, crew-served weapons, and the like. The rubber boats were numbered one through eight on the *Nautilus* and one through twelve on the *Argonaut*. The number one boat on the *Nautilus* would be inflated first and then moved to the front of the sub's port side, its motor attached and fueled and cargo loaded and securely lashed down. The other odd-numbered boats followed in quick succession while simultaneously, on the starboard side, the even-numbered boats followed the same procedure. When all boats were loaded and manned, the submarines would submerge and they would motor off to the rendezvous area.

The rehearsal drill was more like a walk-through, because the submarines were in hostile waters and could not afford to have their decks full of Raiders should the enemy suddenly appear. Nonetheless, everyone got a sense of how complex and difficult the procedure was and how much was expected of everyone involved to pull it off.

The navigational feat of hitting a tiny atoll in hostile waters after a journey of some 2,100 miles (actually more than twice this if you take into account all the zigzagging the boats did to avoid enemy patrols) has to be regarded as a remarkable achievement considering the limited sophistication of the equipment involved at the time. The Raiders were fortunate to have put themselves in the hands of two of the finest submarine commanders of the time, Brockman and Pierce. The two submarines were also fortunate to have good weather and no enemy contact on the entire trip to Makin and back.

As the subs approached enemy-held territory near Makin, they spent much of the time underwater. The *Nautilus,* the speedier of the two, made landfall with Little Makin Island about 0300 on Sunday, August 16, and then slowly headed southwest to make a periscope reconnaissance of Makin's Butaritari Island during the morning and afternoon. Lieutenant Commander Brockman plotted the tidal currents and found them to be much stronger than his intelligence reports had indicated. Immediately after dark, he surfaced and made a successful rendezvous with *Argonaut* skipper Lieutenant Commander Pierce at 2116.

It began to rain and onshore winds whipped the ocean into whitecaps that crashed into and over the deck of each sub. After a quick conference to discuss the stronger-than-expected tides and menacing weather, Commodore Haines, aboard the *Nautilus,* made the decision to proceed with the raid. The two subs then moved to a designated rendezvous point about a mile south of Butaritari Island to prepare for the launch. The two subs were bobbing so much in the ten-foot swells that they had a hard time keeping from bumping into one another. They wallowed noisily in the swell like playful whales, water sloshing and wheezing through the limber holes in the superstructure. The engines would have to be kept running to negate a strong pull toward the menacing reef. The conditions were very iffy for an amphibious operation of this nature, especially since they were so far from home and so far from any help should things go wrong.

The original plan to float the rubber boats off the submarine once the latter submerged had to be scrapped. The submarines were rolling about and fighting the winds, current, and wave action to keep from being washed upon the reef. The rubber boats would have to be loaded while in the water from a pitching submarine, a much more difficult feat than loading on deck.

"We would have to do it the hard way, over the side," Peatross wrote, "but without benefit of previous practice."

The Raiders would have to adapt.

For many of the Raider enlisted men, August 16 was the first time they ever heard of Makin Atoll. Private Carson remembers getting a sneak preview of the island the night before going ashore.

"I was passing through the main control room of our sub, the USS *Argonaut,* and noticed a lot of activity around the periscope, so I eased over to learn what was sighted," he wrote many years later. "A submarine officer was viewing Makin through the periscope and other officers and sailors were taking turns looking. I was pleasantly surprised when one officer said, 'Hey, Raider, you want a look? That's where you're going in the morning!' Since it was my first periscope look ever, I was surprised to see anything: palm trees, a beach, and lots of water splashing on the lens of the periscope."

A final Gung Ho meeting was held on both subs to go over the plan one last time. They received the latest intelligence briefings, which were mostly guesses, and were encouraged to ask questions. The key to the operation, they were told, was surprise, and they appeared to have it. It wasn't known exactly how many Japanese were on the island. They would find out once they were ashore.

The men listened to a final speech over the loudspeaker system delivered by Colonel Carlson in the *Nautilus* and Major Roosevelt in the *Argonaut*. They were told they could expect tank resistance, plane attacks from nearby islands, and even an enemy landing force to strengthen their garrison. They must be off the island before any reinforcements arrived.

The men were reminded of the mission they were on, to annihilate all enemy personnel, destroy as many military installations as they could, and to gather intelligence. There would be no room for any prisoners. They were also told that there must be no cruelty to or disfigurement or mutilation of the enemy, alive or dead. The password would be "Gung" and the countersign was "Ho."

By this time the men really didn't care how many Japanese or tanks there were on the island. They just wanted to get out of their "iron coffins" and put their feet on solid ground again. They would deal with whatever was waiting for them on the island once they got there.

The troops were fed a final meal of ham and mashed potatoes, joking among themselves about this being the "last supper," in a Biblical sense. Other thoughts crept into their heads as well.

"I had thoughts that we might be on a suicide mission. Others thought the same thing too," Pfc. Brian Quirk remembered. "We knew that it wouldn't take much for things to go wrong. For most of us, we thought it was going to be a hair-raising mission. And, that was just about the case."

The Raiders got into their special uniforms, the khakis that had been dyed black back in Hawaii, and put on their high-top green sneakers, the ones that had worked so well during previous rubber-boat drills. Black makeup was available for those who wanted to paint their faces, necks, and hands. Many chose to go without. Canteens were checked for water and each man was given a D-ration chocolate bar. They would only be on the island for twelve or so hours. If they needed any more food they would have to take it from the enemy.

Weapons were checked to see that the chambers were free. That was standard operating procedure the whole trip. An accidental discharge of a weapon in a submarine could be especially lethal.

Carlson made his final diary entry written aboard the *Nautilus* on August 16: "Arrived off Makin at 0330. Scouted the eastern corner of the island down to Butaritari until 0545. Then dove to 70 feet, periscope depth. Reconnoitered by periscope throughout the day. At 1900 came to surface. Men are making ready their equipment for the raid tomorrow. Spirits excellent. At dinner, Captain announced smoking lamp lit. We reached for cigarettes but none would light. Shortage of oxygen."

Shortly after midnight of August 17, the Raiders had their final meal and began heading for the ladders leading up to the hatch, just as they had rehearsed a few days earlier on the trip. More than a few had to make a last-minute visit to the head. Sorry, they were told. You'll have to hold it until you're in the water.

You could almost hear the sound of hearts beating. The adrenaline was starting to rush through their bodies. Sweat trickled down their faces, gathering on the tip of the nose and falling, drop by drop, on the floor of the sub. The only sound was the collective sniffing of dozens of Raiders, who then wiped their noses on their sleeves. The temperature was oppressively hot. Wild thoughts of gloom and doom occupied their heads.

They were all lined up and ready to go, hanging on to anything they could grab as the submarine lurched about in the rough sea. Those charged with unpacking the rubber boats and getting them inflated were at the head of the line. The motors and gasoline for the rubber boats were stacked at the bottom of the ladder, along with crates of ammunition, ready to be passed up through the hatch on command. An air hose, just like the kind you would see at a gas station, would be brought up with one of the first guys on deck.

The two submarines, which were inching closer to the landing beach, were rocking back and forth, adding to the nervous energy everybody was feeling below. Some had to swallow hard so as not to throw up. Was it the rocking motion of the sub or was it a fear of the unknown that was responsible for the queasy feeling in the pit of so many stomachs?

Two Raiders had to be chased out of the mess area where, in full combat gear, they were scrubbing a couple of pots.

"We're all set to go," one of them said to reassure their platoon sergeant. "We just thought we had time to get things in the galley ready to fix chow after we get back."

The message was clear. Many thought, or wanted to think, that the raid would be a piece of cake. They would rush ashore, overwhelm the enemy, kill every Japanese on the island, and be back in plenty of time for a late supper.

"If anybody has a prayer he wants to say, now is the time to say it," one Raider advised. Everybody stood there in silence. Then you could hear soft voices reciting practiced verses they had learned as kids. The hushed tones spoke loudly of the dangers they knew were waiting for them.

Carlson was already topside in the conning tower with Commodore Haines and Lieutenant Commander Brockman. The three of them huddled against the driving rain and howling winds and surveyed the ten-foot swells crashing against the sub's hull. Not one of them liked the idea of shoving off in weather like this, but it couldn't be helped. After a short conversation, all three men nodded in silent unison. The mission was a go.

At about 0330, the first hatch was cracked and a loud roar swept through the submarines. There was a howling gale blowing outside and the hatch was filled with spray.

Eleven

"Organized Grabass"

A stronger-than-anticipated current was trying to drag the submarines toward the coral reef protecting Makin, forcing the submarines to run their noisy engines to keep from running aground. Hopefully the noise from the crashing surf and from the howling winds would mask the sounds of the diesel engines. The subs had gone as close to shore as they dared.

Some of the swells reached fifteen feet as the two submarines bobbed like a couple of corks on an angry sea. Butaritari Island—if the navigation had been true—was only barely visible from atop the swells. It would be easy to get disoriented in this kind of sea, Colonel Carlson told himself as he conferred with Lieutenant Commander Brockman and Commodore Haines high atop the conning tower of the *Nautilus*. All three entertained the possibility that they could be standing off the wrong island. Wouldn't that be something—to have trained so hard and come all this way only to discover that they were about to attack an island that they knew nothing about? No, they convinced themselves. This was the right island. This had better be the right island.

The troops were coming out of the hatches and scurrying over the deck. High winds sent spray over the submarines and into the faces of those trying to pull the rubber boats from their storage areas topside. Occasionally, a wave would wash across the deck, threatening to sweep everything overboard.

Lieutenant Peatross's team was the first boat crew to reach the deck of the *Nautilus*. They dragged their boat from its storage berth in the torpedo loading tube, inflated it, and dragged it again to its debarkation station at the head of the sub.

"There we fueled the outboard motor, careful shielding it to protect the fuel from contamination by the spray that blew across the deck, and loaded and lashed down our gear," Peatross wrote. "Then, with one man holding firmly to the painter, we shoved our boat over the side and jumped in one at a time, each man timing his leap to catch the bobbing boat on the uprise."

The custom-made sneakers helped the Raiders gain some traction on the slippery decks as they went about their assignments. The men dragged the rubber boats onto the deck. One by one, the boats slid out of their storage spaces and were placed side by side on the sub deck in prearranged positions. As each crew pulled its boat clear, an officer assigned a spot on the deck for inflation. A pneumatic air hose was passed up from the hatch and each boat took its turn using the hose, making certain the connection was tight before pressing the valve to inflate the boat. The connection was not tight enough on one boat and the escaping air made an earsplitting noise that everyone was certain could be heard miles away.

"I was sure we had awakened every Jap in the Pacific," Private Carson said many years later.

One by one, the boats were inflated. The motors were passed up from below and hooked to their mounting blocks on the stern of each boat. Gasoline cans came up next and then it got even trickier. The winds and spray and the rocking motion of the submarines made it very difficult to put gasoline in the motors. Gasoline spilled everywhere and a couple of men lost the caps overboard. Saving the caps was important because the five-gallon cans were being taken ashore so the motors could be refilled for the return trip to the sub.

The rubber boats were lowered over the side by ropes held fore and aft by other Raiders or navy personnel. Loading the boats, which were rising and falling fifteen or more feet in the waves, with supplies and Raiders was proving to be a Herculean task. Water running off the sub deck and out of limber holes on the side of the hull poured into the lowered boats, drenching men and equipment alike. It forced the Raiders to use their helmets as bailing instruments to keep the boats from sinking. Also, because the boats were so full of water, they were hard to distinguish from the sea.

Directions shouted by officers and noncoms were difficult to hear over the roaring winds.

It was difficult keeping the rubber boats alongside the submarines once lowered because of the strong tides. While the submarines counteracted the pulling action of the tide by keeping their engines running, the rubber boats were helpless to resist the strong current. Two rubber boats, one loaded with medical supplies and the other with ammunition, broke free and raced toward shore, unoccupied and completely at the mercy of the tide. Spare boats were quickly brought out of stowage and the debarkation routine continued.

Slowly, and with great difficulty, the Raiders jumped into the rubber boats, timing their leaps for when the boat was high against the submarine, not fifteen feet down. Many didn't wait for favorable conditions and jumped whenever they could, either crashing into their unsuspecting mates already in the boat or missing the target completely.

It was a miracle that no one was lost jumping into the boats, but there were several near misses, a handful of injuries, and a few lost weapons. More than a few Raiders, loaded down with extra ammo or equipment, bounced off the rubber boats and into the sea, only to be saved by alert comrades who grabbed on to their web gear and hung on tight. Helmets and rifle butts caused a few bumps and bruises, as well as a few curses. The Raiders could yell all they wanted in the face of the howling winds.

Corporal Ben Midulla went to jump from the *Nautilus* to his rubber boat and got his foot stuck between the ladder rung and the body of the submarine. He did all he could not to scream out in pain. By the time he reached shore, the ankle had swollen to the size of his knee and he could barely walk. Needless to say, he wasn't of much use during his stay on the island.

"Do the terms 'SNAFU' (situation normal, all fucked up), 'FUBAR' (fucked up beyond all recognition), and 'Murphy's Law' rattle your dura mater any? They were all rolled into one at departure time," Private McCall said, recalling how the Raiders stumbled over themselves trying to load the rubber boats. "You'd think you'd be happy as a clam at high tide to get off the sub, but it was 'hurry up and wait.'"

The slippery decks became crowded with Raiders looking for their boat stations. As the subs rose and fell, fully armed men staggered into each other, the wind and rain pummeling them from one end of the boat to the other. It was a miracle that these men, weighted down by so much equipment and weaponry, weren't washed overboard and lost, sinking to the bottom of the ocean like boulders dropped from a bridge.

Peatross's boat and others on the leeward side of the *Nautilus* had an easier time loading because they were sheltered somewhat from the full force of the wind and waves.

Slowly, each rubber boat became filled with its eleven-man crew and drifted off as they tried to start the motor. For the most part, the two-cylinder Evinrude motors were drenched with seawater and would not start. The salt spray had shorted out the coil and both spark plugs. They were useless hunks of dead weight. The men swore at the motors and kicked at the forty-pound hunks of iron. Even more frustrating was the fact that several motors did start, only to conk out within a few seconds. Nothing seemed to work. The boats drifted off from the submarines at a good speed, being carried by a strong current and onshore winds straight toward Makin.

This was not the plan.

By 0328, all twelve boats from the *Argonaut* were in the water and at 0334, struggling mightily with their paddles, they had reached the rendezvous point near the *Nautilus*. All boats were clear of the *Nautilus* by 0410. The boats drifted together looking for Colonel Carlson.

The rubber boats were soon out of shouting range of the submarines and the poor visibility and rolling seas made them difficult to see. Carlson, meanwhile, was still on the deck of the *Nautilus* as his troops began disappearing over the horizon. It was 0415 and all twenty rubber boats, eight from the *Nautilus* and twelve from the *Argonaut,* were clear of the submarines and drifting around without their leader. There was a little over an hour left before dawn.

Lieutenant Peatross's boat, which had thirteen men in it, motored back to the *Nautilus* to see if he could find Carlson. Finally, as he neared the submarine, he could see Colonel Carlson and his runner, Cpl. Adrian Scofield, waiting patiently by the bridge for his command boat from the *Argonaut* to arrive.

"As time crawled on and the debarkation seemed to be taking forever, tension on deck increased noticeably," Peatross wrote in his book. "Although we were still pretty much on schedule, the Commodore [Haines] began to show his concern by pacing nervously back and forth on the slippery deck. Finally, when the boat [from the *Argonaut*] was twenty minutes late, he yelled at me and motioned for me to take Carlson off in my boat."

At 0420, Peatross came alongside the *Nautilus* as first Scofield and then Carlson jumped into the bobbing boat. Carlson smacked his right cheekbone against the butt of a rifle and it began to swell immediately. Peatross, though dangerously overloaded, motored quickly to the designated assembly area, transferred the two men to another boat, and then returned to the *Nautilus* to see if there were any more stragglers. There were none, so Peatross headed off to rejoin the rest of the Raiders. After searching for five or ten minutes, he realized he must have gone in the wrong direction. Quickly realizing his mistake, Peatross returned once again to the *Nautilus* for new directions. Finally pointed in the right direction, he set course for Makin on his own.

"By this time, the storm was abating," Peatross wrote. "The rain had stopped, the wind had eased off somewhat, the cloud cover was breaking up, and a sliver of dawn was showing on the eastern horizon. We soon reached the surf line and, undoubtedly aided by the improvement in the weather and visibility and the almost flawless performance of our outboard motor, easily made it through the breakers and the surf and onto the beach.

"We landed fairly close to where we were supposed to land (I thought) and, as it turned out, only a few minutes behind the rest of the Raiders. After dragging our boat across the beach into the scrub and camouflaging it, we looked around to get our bearings."

Seeing no other Raiders, Peatross quickly thought he might have landed on another island. After further observation, however, he dismissed this possibility and surmised that he had landed too far either to the left or right of the other Raiders—but he wasn't certain. He had actually landed about a mile to the left of the main body, which had landed exactly where they wanted to.

After a few minutes of reflection, Peatross saw a rubber boat stranded at the water's edge about a hundred yards down the beach. The boat was loaded with medical supplies, but there were no signs of human activity, not even any footprints in the sand. Moments later, he discovered another abandoned boat three hundred yards away that contained two machine guns and ammunition. Again there were no signs of human life or footprints. These were obviously the two boats that had broken away from the submarines during the debarkation, Peatross told himself.

"We could not use our radio to attempt to contact the others because strict radio silence was to be maintained until firing commenced," Peatross said. "So far I had many more questions than answers, and that small, green worm of doubt began again to gnaw at the root of my self-confidence, causing me to wonder if I had misunderstood Captain Brockman's directions."

Upon further reflection, Peatross determined that it was unlikely he had landed on the wrong island. He huddled with his platoon guide, Cpl. Sam Brown, an American Indian from Oklahoma and a man Peatross respected for his survival skills, and squad leader Cpl. Mason Yarbrough. It was decided that the best course of action would be to continue on down the beach for a short distance, cut across the island, and try to locate the original rendezvous point, the steepled church.

"We had advanced only a few yards down the beach when, much to our collective relief, we caught sight of a landmark so distinctive as to leave no doubt as to what island we were on or where on it," Peatross wrote. "There before our eyes, just a short distance from the beach, was that scruffy little rifle range. Now all we had to do was to move inland about three hundred yards and we would be within a 'Hallelujah' of the church."

Carlson, meanwhile, had a devil of a time getting his landing party organized. His original plan called for A Company and B Company to come ashore on separate beaches in a coordinated landing over the reef. The rubber boats were scattered over one hundred yards at the assembly area, one company intermingling with the other. Most of the boats were being paddled because the motors wouldn't start. All of the boats were fighting strong tides and currents that were pulling them toward the island reef.

Private Dean Voight described the situation in one sentence. "It was organized grabass," he said.

Carlson had to change his original plans. All the boats would land together on one beach instead of separate beaches. They couldn't afford to wait around any longer or they would risk landing in daylight. Carlson made a quick count of all the boats he could see and it didn't add up to twenty. It wouldn't be long before it would start to get light. He couldn't wait for the rest of the boats. He stood up in his boat and, while being held steady by another Raider, waved his arm forward as the signal to head for land. While a couple of men kept busy bailing out the boats, the rest grabbed wooden paddles and headed for the sound of the breakers.

The surf was high, much higher than the one they had practiced on off Barber's Point in Hawaii.

Private Carson's boat was turned sideways at the first wave and then ended up making a full circle as everyone fought in vain to keep the bow headed toward the beach. Finally, the boat's coxswain, Pfc. William Gallagher, unhooked the nonfunctional motor and threw it away so he could better steer the boat. This seemed to help until fifty yards from shore when a huge wave flung three occupants, one of them Carson, into the surf.

"I grabbed a mouthful of air and rapidly sank to the coral reef as I was quickly dragged toward shore by the surf," Carson said. "After two or three of these rises to the surface, I was surprised to find that I could stand up and have my head above water. I finally struggled to shore and two Raiders grabbed me and walked me up the beach."

Voight's boat was flipped by the waves coming in and he was thrown out. It's a good thing he hung on to the straps of the boat, because he couldn't swim. He lost his Thompson submachine gun and his ammo and didn't get another rifle until somebody was killed. He didn't have to wait long.

Voight almost welcomed the dunking.

"My crotch was burning," Voight said. "I didn't know what the hell it was. I thought it was just something that happened to you when you went into combat. Later I learned I had been sitting in spilled gasoline on the way in."

Private First Class Harold Ryan was in the boat piloted by Major Roosevelt. Still fifty yards from shore, Roosevelt called out, "Point over the side," a cue for Ryan to jump out and take up a position to the front. The water was still way too deep. Ryan disappeared into the foam but was rescued a few seconds later by Pfc. Fred Kemp. Ryan was pulled back into the boat minus his helmet, weapon, and web belt but otherwise unharmed.

Though several boats were flipped over on the landing, there were no reports or evidence that anyone drowned.

Carlson, when informed of all the mishaps during the landing, shook his head and breathed a sigh of relief. He must have asked himself—what else could go wrong? He would find out soon enough.

Still, even with so much going wrong, the Raiders had landed on time (around 0500) and they were not detected.

The boats were scattered over several hundred yards of the beach. A Company was mingled with B Company. It looked as if they would have to wait for daylight to sort it all out.

"Because of the motors not working, the landing was all mixed up. Everything was in total disarray," Pvt. Brian Quirk said many years later.

"It took us a while to get some sense of organization. Guys were running around in the dark making things even more confused. We decided to wait until dawn to get organized, so we just stayed where we were."

The men dragged their boats up into the tree line and then stayed put until they received orders.

The first message back to the submarines from Carlson was logged in at 0513. It stated that "all Marines were on the beach."

The sky to the east was just beginning to lighten. Everyone was thankful there hadn't been a Japanese welcoming party awaiting them. Maybe it would be a cakewalk after all, a few dared to hope.

Suddenly a burst of fire from a Browning automatic rifle (BAR) split the air. Carlson ran toward the sound, trying to find out if the gunfire was coming from the Japanese. He was soon told that it had come from a Raider (Pfc. Vern Mitchell) who apparently had allowed the bolt to slam shut when he loaded a magazine.

"I thought it was two or three bursts. You could hear it in Tokyo," Pvt. Quirk said in a 1999 interview.

Carlson's second message to the *Nautilus* was recorded at 0543. It was equally terse. It simply said: "Everything lousy." He must have sent it on the heels of the accidental discharge of the BAR.

If the enemy hadn't known the Raiders were on the island before, they certainly knew it now. That's what the Raiders were thinking as they stayed put just inside the tree line waiting for orders. The only noises to be heard were from the waves bumping the shore and a few seabirds flying overhead looking for their breakfast. Officers and senior NCOs ran up and down the beach trying to sort out the two companies and get them where they were supposed to be.

Carlson, meanwhile, had radioed the sub again, this time at 0547. Oddly, the message said: "Situation expected to be well in hand shortly." The time of the message may have been logged incorrectly, because Carlson seems to be referring to his first scouting report a few minutes past 0600, which revealed he had landed right where he should have.

Despite the rubber boats having been at the mercy of the tide and currents, all but three of them landed more or less together on a two-hundred-yard stretch of the designated beach. Lieutenant Peatross's boat landed about a mile to the southwest, another boat, skippered by Cpl. Harris Johnson, got tossed about by several currents and landed about two hundred yards to the southwest, and a third boat, piloted by Sgt. William Yount, wound up a mile away to the northeast. Johnson, who was killed later in the day, and Yount managed to join up with the main body a few hours later, but Peatross's crew never did link up with the main party.

By 0600, the Raiders had pretty much regained their unit integrity and were ready to move out. The order had been given to cover the boats and carefully load their weapons. Under a bright early morning sun, the Raiders got off the beach and moved into the cover of the coconut palms. Just a few yards into the palm trees, it got very quiet. One could hardly hear the surf. With each step, some of the men began thinking this was just another training mission.

"At first, we didn't see anything," Private Quirk remembered. "After all we had been through getting ashore, it looked so easy. I remember asking myself, 'What the Marine Corps won't go through for a dummy run.' I wanted very much to believe that."

Twelve
Death from the Palms

Once the Raiders had announced their presence on the island with the accidental BAR burst, Carlson knew he had to act in a hurry or his force might be caught on the beach. He sent for Lieutenant Plumley and ordered him to send a patrol from A Company across the island to find out exactly where they had landed.

Plumley gave the assignment to Lt. Wilfred LeFrancois's platoon. LeFrancois, called "Frenchie" by his men, was a fifteen-year veteran of the Marine Corps who had served a couple of tours in China as an enlisted man. He put Cpl. Howard Young on the point just ahead of Sgt. Clyde Thomason, and the column quickly proceeded across the island. A haze had settled over the island just before sunrise. Bringing up the rear was Plt. Sgt. Mel Spotts, who was ordered to drop a man off every fifty yards so that Colonel Carlson and the main body could later follow.

In a matter of minutes, Young returned to tell LeFrancois that he had located a long pier jutting out into the water and had seen the island's flagpole. The Raiders were right where they were supposed to be, opposite Government Wharf. This must have been the news Carlson relayed to the sub saying that the "situation expected to be well in hand shortly."

Carlson got ready to give the order for A Company to move across the island, with B Company standing by to provide security on either flank should it be necessary.

About two hundred yards inland, the threesome of Lieutenant LeFrancois, Private First Class Clyde H. Norman, and Sergeant Thomason were carefully approaching a building called Government House when they were fired on by a double-barreled shotgun.

"Thomason shouted the password 'Gung' to keep our men from shooting us in a crossfire," LeFrancois said. "Then, to our amazement, the countersign 'Ho' was shouted to us from our hostile left and out came Charley Lamb with two men. [Lamb] had taken our shadowy forms for those of Japs."

They were the first intentional shots fired that day, and thankfully, they missed.

The patrol thoroughly checked out the Government House, which was empty, and then moved toward the lagoon side of the island. By this time, the sun had burned away the haze, giving the Raiders a clear view of a dirt road running down the length of the island. In front of them stood the Government Wharf, which ran out a hundred or so yards into the lagoon. Sections of it were demolished and there were no boats tied up to it.

The shotgun blasts had awakened some natives, who came running out of their huts to seek a safer location. They seemed quite friendly and began speaking in broken English once they realized the soldiers were American and not Japanese.

The natives gave Carlson his first solid intelligence information, saying that most of the Japanese were located near On Chong's Wharf to the southwest. Estimates of just how many Japanese were on the island varied, however. Some of the natives insisted that there were no more than eighty while others gave the figure of 150 or a little more.

The natives also confirmed that the Japanese had been in a state of alert the past couple of weeks as if they were expecting some kind of attack. The natives were rewarded for their cooperation with American cigarettes and D-ration chocolate bars and then told to move out of the area.

The morning sun seemed to brighten everyone's outlook. Carlson began to feel much better. Maybe, he thought to himself, the Raiders could pull this thing off after all.

LeFrancois had an uneasy feeling in the pit of his stomach, however. He was concerned that the Japanese were waiting in ambush and that his men weren't taking this operation with the seriousness that it deserved. Two of his men, Corporal Young and Cpl. Ladislaus Piskor, had found an enemy stormy-weather flag and had a tussle over it, tearing it in half. Several of the men made wisecracks about how easy everything seemed to be.

"It was one more example of the fact that none of these fellows seemed to worry about anything and took it for granted that the story was bound to have a happy ending," he later wrote.

Carlson ordered the rest of A Company to cross the island, join up with the lead platoon, and sweep southwest as far as it could.

The first platoon of A Company, under LeFrancois, led the way through a low marshy area with fairly dense vegetation, which provided good concealment for the Raiders. Of course, it did the same for the Japanese.

Corporal Young again took the point, carefully inspecting every small bog and grass hut he encountered. Ahead of them appeared a long native house with no walls and a very high pointed roof. It sat in the open just off the dirt road running down the island.

Suddenly, Young dropped to his knees and waved back to the men behind him to hit the ground. LeFrancois, who was just behind the point element, saw a truck screech to a halt about three hundred yards down the road and quickly unload fifteen to twenty enemy troops. They were joined by a dozen more who planted a large Japanese flag in the ground, probably to mark the center of their position and to serve as a rallying point. The entire enemy force then quickly deployed into the bushes on both sides of the road and began to move toward the Raiders.

"Their tree observers must have been watching us all the way and had been waiting for their troops to appear to tell them of our presence," LeFrancois wrote.

LeFrancois had no time to call up reinforcements or to set up an ambush as he had hoped. He waved his point element back, ordered up the rest of his platoon, and then deployed the entire platoon on some nearby higher ground, one that gave them frontal and flanking fire on the advancing enemy.

LeFrancois signaled to Sergeant Thomason to double-time his men up the road to a new position. Thomason, without regard for his own safety, ran up and down the line personally picking out good firing positions for his men while LeFrancois informed the command post of his position.

The Japanese came forward at a slow trot, their bayonets glistening in the morning sun. They came closer and closer.

"I could see the Japs creeping toward us in bunches along the narrow hundred-yard strip of trees and light brush between the road and the lagoon," LeFrancois later wrote in a two-part piece for the *Saturday Evening Post*. "They were perfect targets and were walking into a trap. Surely, I told myself, things like this didn't happen. No leader could be so lucky as I. I decided to swing our left flank closer to the point, so that this part of the line would form a sort of pocket with frontal and a flanking fire to welcome the Nips. It was a perfect setup. Thomason chuckled with glee and patted his shotgun. . . . Thomason shouted, 'Let 'em have it,' and poured a barrage of double-O buckshot into the enemy. There was about four minutes of inferno in which everybody in the area was blasting away at somebody or something. Anything out in the open was riddled. Then we realized we were the only ones making any noise, and let up. Later, I found our fire had been so deadly that this Jap combat group in its entirety had seen its last battle."

LeFrancois's colorful description was undoubtedly embellished by his esprit de corps and passion of the moment, but it later proved to be good movie fare. His accounting of the Makin Raid was the basis of a screenplay for the movie *Gung Ho!*, a film made in late 1943. The film, which exercised a large amount of literary license, glorified Carlson's Raiders and sold millions of dollars of war bonds.

For the next four or five minutes, the Raiders blazed away at the enemy, until much of their ammunition was gone. Corporal Young, who was part of the first squad on the left flank, described the brief but deadly firefight to Lieutenant Peatross several years later.

"A shot rang out . . . and all hell broke loose," Young said. "We had Japs in front of us, above us, alongside of us to our left, and behind us also to our left. There were man-made shallow pits about twenty inches or so deep just to the left of the road . . . and our 1st Squad . . . hit the deck in this taro patch. Two machine guns were sweeping the area above our heads; slugs were chunking into the bases of the palm trees. Snipers were coming very close, but no hits. The nearest machine gun was just about twenty yards from us.

"As [Cpl. Ladislaus] Piskor and I . . . were picking off the Japs who were trying to reinforce the group who had stopped us (i.e., those who had begun their advance from the truck), the others were trying to locate the snipers and lobbed grenades into the machine-gun nest. They knocked out the nest, but we were still pinned down by the hard-to-find snipers. Piskor and I, in the prone position, calmly squeezed them off as if we were on the two-hundred-yard range at Camp Elliott [Young was a graduate of the famous Jim Crowe Scout Sniper School]. We killed most of the Japs who came toward us in the vicinity of the road."

Sergeant Mel Spotts, who would be awarded the Navy Cross for his bravery, remembered the first encounter with the Japanese as "more or less a free-for-all. Every man was trying to move up to the front to get his score of Japs," he said.

Others were anxious to get their share as well.

"I could hear shooting up ahead, and I was getting a little 'antsy,' since at this time I was afraid the other guys were going to get them all before I could get mine," said Sgt. "Buck" Stidham, who was toting a .55-caliber Boyes antitank rifle. (Actually a British weapon, it weighed almost forty pounds when loaded on its monopad. The .55-caliber weapon, fed with a top-mounted clip, fired a tungsten-cored bullet slightly larger than the U.S. .50-caliber machine-gun round.) "I can honestly say I was excited but not experiencing any fear. It was more like a big fox hunt, and I had yet to realize how serious and dangerous this business was."

Also racing to the sound of battle was A Company's 2d Platoon, which went into action on the windward side of the road. Over the next thirty minutes, the two platoons repelled a banzai charge, overran four light machine gun positions, and dispatched a flamethrower. The 2d Platoon struggled mightily to advance under deadly sniper fire and two active machine-gun nests, suffering nine killed in action. Among the dead this day were four radio operators, whose shiny antennas attracted deadly sniper fire from enemy gunners high atop the palm trees. Also among the early dead was the baby of the Raider force, Pvt. Franklin Nodland of Marshalltown, Iowa. Nodland, nicknamed "Chicken" by many of his buddies because of his boyish looks, was only seventeen.

After a fierce explosion of fire from the Raiders, things quieted down quickly. The Japanese machine guns appeared to stop firing, but snipers kept the Raiders from moving forward.

"I stayed on the left flank for two hours, getting in a shot every now and then," Sergeant Spotts recalled. "I only got one shot at a visible target; the rest of my firing was at things that could have been Japs but probably weren't. I can say that the Japanese were near perfect at concealment and camouflage."

It became clear rather quickly that the Japanese had been expecting an attack and may even have spotted the actual landing, giving them time to position many snipers around the island. The Japanese force probably had been in an advanced state of readiness ever since August 7 as a reaction to the Marine landings on Guadalcanal.

What wasn't clear to Colonel Carlson was that his Raiders had already destroyed most of the Japanese force on the island. Carlson, to be sure he didn't lose the upper hand, called up a platoon from B Company to reinforce the right flank along the lagoon side of the road.

The only remaining problem facing the Raiders was the snipers, who had camouflaged themselves high atop the coconut palm trees. Their deadly accuracy belied the myth that the Japanese were myopic creatures who wore thick glasses and therefore couldn't shoot straight. The jungle green of their camouflage uniforms made them virtually undetectable in the palms. One of the snipers had actually tied the tops of two palms together so that if spotted, he could cut the tie separating the trees and confuse the Raiders as to which tree he was in. Others had roped themselves securely up among the fronds. They would allow the Raiders to move past their positions and then shoot them from behind.

Part of the problem was the fact that the snipers were securely strapped into their treetop positions and even though they may have been killed by previous fire, Raiders could still see a leg or part of a torso dangling from the palm fronds. As a consequence, the same Japanese body was riddled again and again by Raiders passing through the area. It was difficult to tell if the sniper was dead or not.

The Japanese snipers concentrated on the officers, noncoms, medical people, and radiomen. Whenever a Raider tried to use a walkie-talkie, he could expect to hear the pinging of bullets around him. When an officer or noncom raised his hand or head to give a command, he was shot at. It was their hand signals that gave them away. The officers and sergeants soon learned to direct their troops by voice alone and kept their hands and heads down.

Sergeant Clyde Thomason, who would become the first Marine enlisted man of World War II to earn the Congressional Medal of Honor, was killed by a sniper very early in the battle. Thomason was hit while moving along the firing line, encouraging his fellow Raiders, pointing out targets for them, and adjusting their fire. His men pleaded with him to stay down but he wouldn't listen.

Corporal Ed Wygal of B Company, called "Killer" by his mates, may have gotten the sniper that shot Thomason and was harassing LeFrancois, according to LeFrancois.

"'Killer' Wygal had located the sharpshooters in their tree nests, had borrowed an automatic rifle to take the place of his own low-velocity weapon, and had ended my worries," LeFrancois wrote. "He crawled around our right flank, along the shoreline of the lagoon, and saw a lot of dead Japs—and the live ones he was after. Huddled back of a water-cooled machine gun, they were raking our lines. Using hand grenades, his pistol, and his knife, Wygal sent those Nips to their ancestors."

Wygal received the Navy Cross for his individual acts of courage.

Later in the day, a sniper's bullet killed Capt. Gerald P. Holtom, the battalion's intelligence officer. It was a particularly bitter loss to Carlson, who had grown quite fond of the erudite Holtom.

"On the morning we landed at Makin, Jerry was with me," Carlson wrote Holtom's parents a few weeks later. "We captured the post office and Jerry came to me and said that he intended to examine some Japanese notices which were posted on the bulletin board. I told him that I would be along the road leading to the right flank of our position. The battle was in progress. He was looking for me along this road when a sniper shot him, the bullet passing through his left chest and emerging behind the right shoulder. He lived only ten seconds. He was buried near where he fell. His face indicated that he died without pain. He was wholly at peace."

Carlson wrote many of these types of letters after the Makin Raid but the toughest was probably to Holtom's parents.

"Jerry was respected and loved by all with whom he came in contact. His loss is a terrible blow to me, both because of my personal affection for him and because of the value of his capabilities. Words are futile instruments where human life is concerned. I can only say that my heart goes out to you and his other loved ones at home. He died like a man and a true patriot."

Holtom had come up to the front with the command group and was looking for Colonel Carlson when he was hit. He had found a piece of intelligence and was translating it when a sniper ended his life.

"[Holtom] was too far up in the front," Pfc. Charles Dawson said. "This would not be bad if he were needed up where he was, but he was not needed."

Private McCall saw another man, although he doesn't remember his name, cut down by a sniper's bullet. He was shot through the neck while urinating against a palm tree.

"He said he had to piss real bad and I told him to stay on the ground and pee in a prone position," McCall remembered. "I don't know if it was instinct, or what, but he couldn't resist getting up and going over to a nearby palm tree. He died with his hands in his pants."

In addition to the snipers, at least four well-camouflaged machine guns expertly raked the Raider line searching out any concealed targets.

One of the machine guns was a British-made Lewis gun that was positioned in a taro pit less than two hundred yards from the Raiders' right flank.

The gun would be knocked out, then remanned and then knocked out again. Ten enemy bodies were found around the gun when it was finally silenced.

With casualties beginning to mount at an alarming rate, Colonel Carlson decided to commit another part of his reserve, directing Lt. Joe Griffith's 2d Platoon from B Company to beef up the left flank. Griffith moved up with his platoon in a column of squads for maximum control, but Carlson overruled him and told him to advance in a skirmish line.

Griffith, in a 1999 interview, said he balked at the order, telling Carlson that it was contrary to standard operating procedure.

"They will become intermingled with A Company and I will lose all control of my platoon. I will never see them again," Griffith told Carlson.

Carlson would have none of Griffith's logic.

"Put your boys in a skirmish line," he ordered.

Peatross came down hard on Carlson when he wrote his book.

"As a result of this order, Griffith soon lost all control over his platoon, as it became hopelessly intermingled with Company A, and Carlson squandered an opportunity to maneuver and envelop the exposed right flank of the Japanese position," Peatross wrote.

Both sides had paused to regroup after the initial contact, and then the Raiders heard some yelling and shouting from the Japanese lines. They were obviously working up some courage for a banzai attack. Then came the sound of a bugle. A wave of Japanese, yelling and screaming insults at the Raiders—and President Roosevelt—burst out of the scrub growth less than a hundred yards away and charged straight into the Americans. Most of the Japanese were felled in the first Raider volley and the rest were finished off while struggling to their feet. Three more Raiders died during the attack, Corp. I. B. Earles, Pfc. William Gallagher, and Pvt. Charles Selby, and three others, Sgt. James Faulkner, Pfc. Joseph Sebock, and Pvt. William B. Murphree, were later awarded the Navy Cross for gallantry in this particular action.

Murphree had to clear up a few personal problems before he got his Navy Cross, however. It seems Murphree was a chronic army deserter who had changed his name to Howard R. Craven so that he could join the Marines. Everyone throughout training and on the trip to Makin knew him as Private Craven until he fessed up to Colonel Carlson the first day on the island. Carlson stood by Murphree and his award was presented to him several months later.

The wounded began to pile up. Platoon Sergeant Victor "Transport" Maghakian, another Navy Cross winner, was shot in the right wrist as he gave hand-and-arm signals to his men, Sgt. Norman Lenz was knocked dizzy by a grazing round to his head, and Lieutenant LeFrancois was felled by a burst from a machine gun. He was hit five times in the right arm and shoulder, which caused him to be evacuated. He, too, would later be awarded a Navy Cross.

Maghakian was another one of those tough old "China hands" who achieved almost legendary status within the Marine Corps. In 1939 while serving in China, Maghakian, then a corporal, was having drinks with a buddy at a cabaret when a Japanese major approached him and deliberately spit in his face. Maghakian rose from the table and flattened the officer with a punch to the face. When a second Japanese major struck him several times across the back with his scabbard-encased sword, Maghakian knocked him down and wrestled his pistol away from him, slowly exiting the nightclub.

The next day, he was called before his commanding officer, expecting a court martial. But a British officer who was at the scene appeared on his behalf to explain what had happened. Maghakian's commanding officer accompanied him to Japanese army headquarters, where a Japanese colonel apologized for the drunken conduct of his officers.

When Carlson formed his Raider battalion a couple of years later, Maghakian was one of the few men he sought out to join his unit. Apparently, Carlson had heard of Maghakian and felt he was just the kind of soldier he was looking for.

On Makin, Maghakian was shot in the right arm while giving directions, but after getting patched up he continued to remain in the field. Three months later on Guadalcanal, he was shot in the left arm while giving directions in a similar manner.

The most seriously wounded was LeFrancois, who absorbed five light-machine-gun bullets in his right arm and shoulder. One of them was an explosive bullet that went off inside the shoulder.

"None of them seemed to hurt me on impact," LeFrancois said, "but my clothes and the ground were soon soaked with blood. I squeezed tight against the earth in a nearby ditch.

"One of the boys crept up to me, took his belt off, and tied my arm to my body. I tried to recognize this lad, but my mind was foggy. I knew that

I was of no use anymore, that I was bleeding to death and would soon be unconscious. I rolled over and over to the cleared swamp to my right. The struggle was a painful one and my condition infuriated me. I was getting in a frame of mind to tackle the Mikado himself or just sit down in that swamp and stay there. Pulling myself up, I stumbled to the rear."

As he staggered toward the first aid station, a Japanese rifleman took a bead on LeFrancois but never had a chance to get off a shot. Private First Class Joe Bibby was quicker on the trigger and LeFrancois kept on weaving to the rear. One of the last things he remembered before passing out was hearing the sound of a bugle and what he believed to be the roar of approaching tanks. Despite what they had been told, there never were any tanks on Makin.

When LeFrancois came to, he was lying on a straw mat in a dirt hut with Dr. MacCracken looking over him.

"Frenchie, this isn't so bad as it looked at first," Dr. MacCracken told him. "You just lie here and relax until we go back to the ships. Everything is going to be all right."

LeFrancois, Maghakian, and Lenz would all survive, as would Pfc. Fred Kemp, who was nearly set afire by a stray round that plowed into his cartridge belt. The round ignited the powder in several cartridges on his belt, covering him in a cloud of smoke. Instinctively, Kemp threw himself into a moist taro pit and rolled his body back and forth to smother the smoke and fire.

Corporal I. B. Earles was grazed in the head by a sniper's bullet and became delirious, according to LeFrancois. Bleeding from the mouth, Earles had to be held down by other Raiders. He finally broke away and charged at an enemy machine-gun position, shouting and firing his weapon.

"[Earles] began to run through the thick brush, shooting dead and live Japs indiscriminately," LeFrancois said. "Then the Jap machine guns, riflemen, and the snipers opened up on him. I was never to find out how much damage Earles did before those guns murdered him."

The same machine gun that got LeFrancois was knocked out three times before it was finally silenced. The Raiders reported finding more than a dozen bodies near the gun, indicating that the enemy kept funneling in replacement crews until they ran out of men. Before the gun was silenced, however, it ended the life of Pvt. Charles Selby, the handsome Marine from Ontonagon, Michigan, whom his buddy Dean Voight called "the Duke of Ontonagon."

Private Ben Carson remembered coming across Selby's body lying near the edge of the marshy area on the windward side of the road. "[Selby] had been in one helluva firefight," Carson said. "Every one of his ammo clips was empty and he had been hit by a volley of bullets that tore up his chest."

Using covering fire from snipers high atop the palm trees, the enemy survivors of the assault, which looked to be less than a dozen infantrymen, withdrew to their rallying point to organize one last banzai attack. After several minutes of screwing up their courage, they came on again and were destroyed in their entirety. This ended what came to be known as the "Battle of the Breadfruit Trees," named for the two large breadfruit trees that stood near the point of origin of the Japanese banzai attacks.

It was a last hurrah. By 0700, organized resistance, except for the snipers, had pretty much come to an end on Butaritari.

Peatross believes that after 0700 there were no more than a dozen Japanese left alive on the island, all located in the vicinity of Stone Pier. A few minutes later, Peatross's men killed five of them manning a machine gun.

Again, Peatross faults Carlson with not moving aggressively enough to clean out the remaining Japanese and getting on with the mission. "[Carlson] cautiously kept his Raiders deployed in a long skirmish line where they bogged down in a four-hour duel between individuals or fire teams and the handful of isolated snipers," he wrote. "As a consequence of this delay, there probably would not have been enough time to complete the assigned mission in one day, even if things had gone as planned."

Asked more than a half century later why the Raiders took so many casualties from snipers, the irrepressible Private Carson said, "Nobody ever told us to look up."

It wasn't just a flippant comment by Carson. There had been no training against snipers in palm trees. It simply hadn't been anticipated. The Raiders were taught to look to their front and rear and protect their flanks. Carson was right when he said they were not taught to look up.

The college-educated doctors also were surprised by Japanese sniper fire from above. They, too, learned fast.

"I wore a red-cross arm band the first few minutes I was on Makin but I quickly took it off," Dr. Stigler said in a 1999 interview. "I never wore one again. They were too good a target."

At first, the Raiders seemed to treat the operation just like a training mission, cracking jokes and expecting an easy walk in the park. There was the instance of the two Raiders tussling over a captured Japanese flag, finally tearing it in half. Later in the morning, an attempt to run an American flag up the same flagpole by Captain Davis provided a bit of comic relief for everyone. Midway in the flag raising, a Japanese sniper seemed to be homing in on Davis, causing him to drop the halyard and hightail it for cover.

As the day wore on, however, the Raiders began treating their adventure with the seriousness it deserved. The snipers started taking their toll and the men hunkered down behind any cover they could find. The sight of one of their own lying dead and covered with blood was enough to remind the Raiders that this was the real thing and not just another training mission.

The Raiders also learned to be wary of enemy dead littering the battlefield. Sergeant Buck Stidham nearly paid with his life when he happened to come upon several Japanese bodies near a machine-gun nest.

"They were the first enemy I had seen, and I let curiosity overrule my common sense as I knelt beside one and started examining him for souvenirs," Stidham said. "To my surprise the 'dead' Jap suddenly groaned and raised up on his knees. Fortunately, I had a knife wedged down in my pistol holster, so I whipped it out and punctured his lung."

The clash between the Japanese and the Raiders had been brief, violent, and decisive for the invaders. There were probably fewer than a dozen enemy soldiers left alive on the island, but Carlson had no way of knowing for sure if they could be reinforced from nearby islands. In an earlier meeting with the natives, he had been told there were between 80 and 150 Japanese on the island. He chose to believe the latter figure, so his Raiders proceeded cautiously the rest of the day against what proved to be a handful of isolated snipers.

Thirteen

Behind the Lines

A mile to the southwest, Peatross and his twelve-man squad also heard the accidental discharge of the BAR just before dawn. It cleared up any lingering doubts they may have had that they were on the wrong island, and it provided an approximate location of the rest of the Raider force. Peatross turned on his radio. It wouldn't work. He couldn't even hear static.

Peatross knew the BAR burst had put the Japanese on full alert, and surely they would move toward the sound of the gunfire. That would put his group to the enemy rear. Therefore, he decided to move inland toward the original objectives that he was pretty sure the Japanese would vacate to seek out the source of the firing.

As Peatross's group neared the Japanese barracks building from the south, they heard the clamor of A Company's firefight with the enemy less than a mile away up the lagoon road.

"As the clatter of rifle and machine-gun fire echoed across the island, a startled Japanese burst from the barracks," Peatross wrote. "Without command and almost as one, three of our thirteen-man group fired and the luckless Japanese fell dead. These were the first shots that any of us had fired in the war; this was our first face-to-face encounter with the enemy; the first person we had met up with on Butaritari."

The squad approached the barracks building carefully. One of the men heard some noise within the building. It was a moaning sound, like someone in pain. Three men rushed the building and found it empty. The occupants must have exited in a hurry, because the bunks were unmade and the floor was littered with scattered clothing and small-arms ammunition. The noise they had heard had come from a dog and six nursing puppies.

The Raiders quickly moved to a church next door and found it pad-locked.

By this time, the firefight up the road had become intense. Peatross decided to bypass the church and immediately deploy his men into a skirmish line near the road, fully expecting to be attacked. The firing appeared to be less than a half mile away.

Suddenly, the Raiders noticed a Japanese soldier, his rifle slung across his back, pedaling a bicycle down the road in their direction. He was probably a messenger. One of the Raiders fired at him too soon and missed. The soldier halted and got off the bicycle. He calmly unslung his rifle and slowly advanced toward the Raiders. Before he could get off a shot, however, he was cut down by a hail of bullets.

"A few minutes later, another Japanese soldier came out of the bushes, picked up a bicycle, and also pedaled down the road in our direction, apparently oblivious or indifferent to the fate of the first cyclist," Peatross said. "This time, everyone held his fire until the target was opposite the center of our firing line, then we all opened up at about the same time in a classic example of overkill."

Yet another Japanese cyclist tried his luck a minute or so later and he, too, was cut down after going less than a hundred yards.

Peatross decided to cross the road and advance on the two-story building reported to be the headquarters of the island commander, Sergeant Major Kanemitsu. Though it was unoccupied, the Raiders found a radio transceiver and a small steel safe about two feet high and four feet wide. Corporal Brown managed to crack the safe, which yielded a bundle of Japanese banknotes and a quart-size bag of coins, which all the men shared as the spoils of war.

Peatross grew increasingly frustrated over his inability to contact either the submarines or Carlson. His "walkie-talkie" radio, a new model first given to the Raiders a couple of months earlier, simply would not work. He even had his radioman, Pfc. Ken Montgomery, attempt to use the captured Japanese radio to see if it could pick up a frequency to the submarines.

"All we heard was Japanese, of which none of us could understand a single word," Peatross said.

Peatross decided to keep moving up the road, where he hoped to link up with the rest of the Raiders. As they approached the next building they saw a man dressed in a white shirt, khaki shorts, and a sun helmet on the front porch, waving toward the area from which the bicyclists had come. Corporal Brown dropped him with a single bullet. Years later, Peatross discovered that the man Brown had shot was Kanemitsu, the garrison commander.

"Through sheer good fortune we had decapitated the garrison and cut off its communications with the outside," Peatross wrote.

Before Peatross's group could advance another step, however, they were taken under fire by a Japanese machine gun a hundred yards up the road, which appeared to be firing in both directions. If Peatross hoped to link up with Carlson and the rest of the Raiders, it had to be destroyed.

With Cpl. Vernon Castle on the point, the squad deployed in an echelon left between the road and the lagoon and advanced on the machine gun. As Castle drew abreast of the gun position, he turned to his right, away from the lagoon, and hit the deck. He crawled to within thirty yards of the position before he was discovered. The machine gun opened fire and hit him several times.

"With the rest of us providing such supporting fire as we could, Castle crawled and dragged himself on toward the enemy position, firing his Thompson submachine gun as he advanced," Peatross wrote. "With complete disregard for his own personal safety, ignoring wounds that proved to be mortal, and by almost superhuman effort, he struggled close enough to the enemy position to throw a hand grenade, killing the gunner and two of the crewmen. The rest of us shot two riflemen positioned near the gun."

By the time they got to Castle he was dead. Peatross called Castle's efforts "the bravest act that I witnessed in all of World War II. Had I been a little more experienced and known more about our awards system, I should have recommended Castle for the Medal of Honor."

Besides Castle, the assault on the machine gun had cost the life of Cpl. Mason Yarbrough and the radioman, Pfc. Ken Montgomery. Two others were wounded, Cpl. Sam Brown (leg) and Pfc. Ernest July (right arm).

After a brief rest to take stock of the situation, Peatross was pretty sure that all the Japanese on the island were between his squad and the main body, but he wasn't absolutely certain. Where had the bicyclists been heading? Had they been trying to reach the radio in the headquarters building or had they been going farther down the island to summon assistance?

Peatross decided to send out a patrol farther down the road to find out.

• • •

Around 0700, with the ground action seemingly over, Carlson called in a fire mission from the submarines on two suspected enemy concentrations given to him by the natives. Because of radio difficulties, the *Argonaut* never received the request but the *Nautilus* responded by firing two dozen shells from its six-inch guns across the island in the general direction of Ukiangong Point and a Japanese radio station at the head of On Chong's Wharf.

Fifteen minutes later, the Raiders spotted a small Japanese transport and a patrol boat cruising in the lagoon toward one of the quays. To redirect fire to the ships, Carlson relayed messages through Major Roosevelt, who had to return to the ocean side of the island to contact the submarines. *Nautilus* gunners could not see these targets, nor was there a forward observer available on the lagoon side with a radio to adjust the fire. Nonetheless, the *Nautilus* "blindly" scattered twenty-three salvos (forty-six shells) in the general direction of the two ships. The results were almost miraculous; both craft apparently ran themselves into the shellfire and sank. About sixty Japanese went down with the transport.

A Company Commander 1st Lt. Merwyn Plumley, who was watching from the lagoon side, called Carlson on his walkie-talkie and said, "Direct hits. The ships are on fire. Lots of Japs drowning."

Another witness to the destruction of the two ships was Lieutenant LeFrancois, who, though badly wounded, still managed to hobble around the battlefield.

"I made my way over to Major Roosevelt, who was in a clump of bushes, his bald head shining like a polished grapefruit," LeFrancois wrote. "It offered a good target, and the Japs hadn't failed to notice it. . . . The major was relaying messages to our submarine, which was bombarding the enemy's ships, and was busy telling them where their shots were falling.

"As best I could, I hurried toward a house projecting out into the lagoon, which made a swell grandstand. The Jap gunboat had opened up now but since it had no observer to check its fire, its shots were wild. Our sub scored two direct hits on the gunboat amidships, setting off its magazine in a sheet of flame and sending it to the bottom of the lagoon. The transport was sinking too."

It wasn't known how long the ships had been in the lagoon. They might have arrived a few days earlier and unloaded all their supplies and reinforcements or perhaps they hadn't had a chance to unload. Information from the natives indicated that the patrol boat had sixty Marines aboard, but it wasn't known if they had disembarked. If they had, then the enemy garrison on Butaritari was a lot bigger than the original intelligence had indicated.

Carlson knew the Japanese high command had been informed about the raid and was certain that he could expect either reinforcements or air attacks or both later in the day. He knew his Raiders would be practically defenseless against an air attack, but there wasn't much he could do about it. The two ships spotted in the lagoon worried him. Had they unloaded reinforcements before they were sunk or had they been carrying reinforcements at all? It was imperative for him to get on with the mission of destroying as much as he could and then get off the island as quickly as possible.

Carlson had committed B Company earlier to help wipe out the snipers and machine-gun pits before any Japanese reinforcements arrived. The Japanese, according to a message sent to higher command at 0905, were prepared to resist to the last man. The message, which had been intercepted by navy intelligence, simply said that "all men are dying serenely in battle."

At 0901, the *Nautilus* had its first radar contact with an enemy aircraft and then sighted a single plane before making an emergency dive. The submarines returned to the surface about an hour later before making another contact at 1039, this time consisting of two planes. The two submarines dived for cover again.

Those two planes arrived over Butaritari at 1130, circled the area for about fifteen minutes, dropped two bombs that did no damage, and promptly left. Carlson had given the order that the Raiders were not to fire on the planes, which would only show the enemy where they were.

Everyone on the ground knew they would be back, the next time in greater numbers. Sure enough, at 1255 a dozen planes of assorted makes were spotted on radar twelve to fourteen miles out by the *Nautilus,* but because of persistent communications problems they were unable to inform the Raiders ashore before submerging again.

Carlson, in the meantime, had fortuitously moved his troops back from the road as a ploy to lure some snipers out of the trees. Consequently, when the planes returned to bomb and strafe suspected Raider positions, they actually attacked their own forces, which had moved into the target area vacated by the Americans.

Private Ben Carson barely had time to reach cover when the enemy planes swooped down on the island.

"I was dashing from coconut tree to coconut tree as we were pulling back [when] all of a sudden a Jap torpedo bomber appeared just above the trees, strafing the road which was between me and the leeward beach," Carson said. "We were told not to fire at the planes. I was really glad when that plane got past me without hitting anything with his bullets when all of a sudden the lead was flying again. There was a machine gunner in the rear of the plane and he was getting his jollies blasting the hell out of the road as the plane was pulling up."

Sergeant Howard "Buck" Stidham said the strafing runs almost seemed like they happened in slow motion.

"One of the planes was a bi-wing, open-cockpit observation type," he said. "They would go over so low I could easily see the gunner from the waist up firing (it seemed) right at me. They were so slow they appeared to get off a whole belt on one pass."

According to Lieutenant LeFrancois, the planes came over the island in four waves of three planes each.

"They strafed and bombed us, dropping sticks of antipersonnel bombs, but they missed us entirely," he said.

By 1430 the raid was over and ten of the planes left. The other two, a light troop seaplane and a giant four-engine Kawanishi flying boat, landed with reinforcements in the lagoon off Stone Pier and slowly taxied toward the wharf, apparently assuming it was in Japanese hands.

LeFrancois hobbled out to a house near the lagoon for a better view of the landings and witnessed what happened next.

"[It] was a sight for sore eyes. A four-motored transport had started to land on the water, and some of our machine guns and antitank guns, as well as a few rifles, opened up on it," he wrote. "The white tracers streamed across the water and hit squarely on the plane. It nosed up, caught fire, tipped to the left, and sank swiftly out of sight."

LeFrancois was probably describing what happened to the smaller of the two planes, which had landed and was heading for the wharf.

The Raiders, firing from positions near Stone Pier, zeroed in on the two troop transports with light machine-gun fire and two .55 caliber Boyes rifles, the latter manned by Sgts. Buck Stidham and Walter "Tiny" Carroll. The small transport burst into flame on the water while the huge Kawanishi sought to make a quick exit. Taxiing frantically in circles attempting to take off, it was riddled with bullets and crashed into the la-

goon after being airborne for only a few seconds. None of the Raiders
saw any of the reinforcements aboard swim away to shore.

It took a team effort to bring down the bulky four-motor craft, and
credit was shared equally among those who were firing M-1s, BARs, machine guns, or .55 caliber rifles. Some have speculated that the flying boat
fell under the sheer weight of all the lead it absorbed trying to take off.

Stidham directed all his fire at the four-motor Kawanishi, with help
from Sergeant Maghakian, who stood behind him with binoculars to adjust his fire.

"He told me my first round was low, as it had skipped on the water,"
Stidham recalled. "I raised my aiming point, and [Maghakian] said,
'You're in the black.' I am not sure how he could be so positive of this,
but I kept firing with this sight picture and got off thirty to forty aimed
shots before the plane approached takeoff speed. At this point I secured
my gun and returned to the taro pit. Quite a few marines reported seeing the four-motor plane crash shortly after becoming airborne, but I
did not see it. What the actual cause of the crash was no one could possibly know. I am quite sure I hit it several times and like to think I had a
small part in crashing it."

The wreckage of the Kawanishi still lies today half submerged and
pretty much eaten away in the lagoon near King's Wharf.

By 0900, Lieutenant Peatross had closed the gap between his group
and the main body to less than a half mile but decided not to go any farther until he had determined for certain whether there were any
Japanese forces to his rear. He sent a three-man patrol, Cpl. Sam Brown,
Pfc. Al Donovan, and Pvt. Ray Jansen, to investigate. While they were
gone, a small Japanese car suddenly appeared and came racing down
the road heading to the southwest. The remaining forces opened up on
the car as it sped past. The car kept right on going for another five hundred yards before it went off the road and crashed. Both men in the car
were dead.

When the three-man patrol returned and reported seeing no enemy
forces, Peatross was convinced all the remaining Japanese on the island
were between his group and the main body of Raiders. With his radio
still not working, Peatross decided to send out Donovan and Jansen with
orders to find Carlson and give him the news.

Peatross instructed Jansen to stay near the windward side of the road
and Donovan to move a few yards in advance of him near the beach. They

were instructed to return if they were taken under fire by more than one gun. The pair had progressed about three hundred yards when Jansen was fired on by two riflemen. As ordered, he turned back. Donovan, however, did not return. Lieutenant Peatross could only hope that Donovan made it.

Donovan stayed close to the lagoon, dashing between trees and buildings, shouting out the password "Gung" until he heard a "Ho" in response. He reached the main body about 1400 while an enemy air raid was in progress and reported his intelligence information to Carlson.

A couple of days later, en route home aboard the *Nautilus,* a much-relieved Carlson told Peatross that Donovan's report had been the "high point" of his day thus far.

Why Carlson failed to act on the intelligence Donovan delivered remains a mystery, according to Peatross.

"[Carlson] seemed to have discounted or completely ignored Donovan's information on the enemy situation," Peatross later wrote. "Instead, he chose to remain in a defensive posture and made no attempt to link up with my group, thereby leaving the initiative in the hands of a few snipers. . . . It is difficult to understand why Carlson, a seasoned combat commander and an experienced intelligence officer, was not more aggressive in carrying out his mission and persisted in overestimating the enemy's strength or, even worse, underrating his own."

With time running short and down to only six able-bodied men, Peatross began to think of getting his men off the island. Before withdrawing to their camouflaged boat, however, he and his men set about destroying anything that could be of use to the enemy.

One of the targets was a Chevrolet truck bearing USMC markings that indicated it had been captured on Wake Island. The small truck was loaded with small-arms ammunition, hand grenades, medical supplies, and assorted picks and shovels. The Raiders tossed a couple of grenades into the cab and bed and watched it explode into flames.

The move almost backfired on the Raiders because when the enemy planes returned at about 1630, they used the burning truck as a beacon, nearly hitting the nearby Raiders with their bombs.

After the bombing, Peatross and his band moved to the lagoon shore immediately north of the headquarters building and saw some Raiders from the main body on Government Wharf still firing at the wrecked Japanese flying boat.

"Sam Brown and I quickly made our way out onto Stone Pier and waved, shouted, whistled, and fired our weapons into the air to attract their attention, which we surely did, but not as we wanted," Peatross later wrote. "Much to our surprise and no little consternation, they did not recognize us as Raiders and began firing at us. [Buck Stidham, the Boyes gunner in Company A, categorically denies this was his rifle, so it must have been Tiny Carroll's.] We hotfooted it back toward the foot of the pier; headlong at first, then slower and slower until, pooped, we were walking before we reached cover."

Peatross admitted he was stumped why the main body never made an attempt to contact his group. Surely, he believed, they must have wondered about all the shooting going on in the enemy's rear. He also wondered if Private First Class Donovan had gotten through and if he had, why wasn't Carlson making an effort to contact him? Perhaps they were on the way.

In the meantime, Peatross's group raided the enemy headquarters building, destroying a radio set and grabbing a few souvenirs, including a Japanese pistol and a flag.

After thirty minutes, Peatross decided they had waited long enough to be contacted by the main body, so he began preparations to retire to the ocean side of the island for their return to the submarine. They retraced their steps across the island and found their boat right where they had left it. They removed some palm fronds they had used as camouflage, added a little more air with a hand pump they'd brought along, and topped off the fuel tank.

They couldn't see the submarines. They would have to assume they were out there waiting for them.

"We watched the surf for about fifteen minutes to get a feel for the timing of the waves, which seemed to be coming in much faster than those at Barber's Point," Peatross later wrote. "The surf, however, was not nearly as high. We counted the incoming rollers, looking for the fifth wave, which is usually smaller than the rest, until we got on the correct count, then let the cycle repeat itself about three times to verify it. Around 1930, while the smaller wave was still two away, we dragged the boat across the beach and into the water.

"Wading and pushing until we reached the surf, we piled in one at a time, grabbed our paddles, and dug in for all we were worth. We soon got the motor started, and we motored through the last breaker and into the open sea without mishap—almost. In all of our training, I was the only member of our boat team who had never been thrown out. This time, however, as we were going over the last breaker, my turn came, and I went flying into the foam. Assisted by several pairs of willing hands and motivated by not a few smirks on the faces behind them, I quickly clambered back into the boat. In response to the questioning look on Sam Brown's face, I pointed to where I thought the submarines should appear and added, "That way, Sam, but if you can't find a submarine, just get me as close as possible to North Carolina."

Fifteen minutes after entering the water, at about 1945, they spotted the colored lights of the submarines, green on the *Nautilus* and red on the *Argonaut*. Five minutes later, they were aboard the *Nautilus*.

En route to a briefing, Peatross inquired about the rest of the Raider force. He was told that his boat was the only one to have made it back so far. Furthermore, he was told that there had been no radio contact with Carlson and his group since 1030.

Fourteen

"A Ghastly Nightmare"

By midafternoon, Colonel Carlson had begun thinking about withdrawing across the island and getting back to the submarines. The wounded, who included four stretcher cases and both doctors (MacCracken and Stigler), were, at around 1700, the first to begin moving back to the ocean side of the island, where an evacuation point was established. Major Roosevelt took charge of the area and kept trying to reestablish radio connections with the submarines, which had been busy dodging Japanese fighter planes all day.

Carlson surveyed the day's action from the lagoon side of the island and wasn't all that happy with the results. The landing had been all fouled up, and then they had lost the element of surprise when a Raider accidentally fired his BAR. Once they got going, the men had been held up by sniper fire from the palm trees along the lagoon. They hadn't known how to react. Many of his men had been frozen by the accurate fire, and as a result, a great deal of time had been spent waiting around until someone figured out a course of action.

He hadn't figured on the sniper fire from above. Any forward movement was next to impossible if they were under constant observation from a platform fifty or more feet in the air.

The inertia of his troops meant that there hadn't been enough time to accomplish everything they had come to do. His men had performed bravely, but like the rookies they were, they had made too many mistakes. Maybe he had asked too much of them. The casualties bothered him greatly. There were fourteen dead (actually eighteen) and more than twenty wounded, to the best of his accounting. These figures included the three dead that Peatross's boat crew had suffered.

He didn't know then, nor could he have imagined, that the worst of his struggles on the island was still to come.

Carlson held a farewell meeting with the natives who had helped him this day and exacted a promise from them to take care of the dead. Joe Miller, the native police chief, and his brother, William, promised to give the Raiders who had been killed on the island, including the three from Peatross's crew, a Christian burial. Carlson gave the brothers and their men some shotguns and ammunition and a few other supplies they could spare.

Enemy planes returned to the island at 1630 and for thirty minutes bombed and strafed an area previously occupied by the Raiders, without doing any damage. After a brief huddle with Captain Coyte, Lieutenant Plumley, and Major Roosevelt, Carlson decided to call it a day and begin an orderly withdrawal to the ocean side of the island so they could depart by the scheduled time of 1930.

Because there were very few Japanese left alive on the island, the withdrawal was unopposed. There was even time to take pictures.

"I had brought a small camera and ten rolls of film with me, but, up until now, I had been unable to take any pictures," Sgt. Mel Spotts said. "I decided that now was the time. I shot a few of the [government] house, shacks, trees, the front lines, wounded men, and Jap planes. I had some good ones of Jap planes but all were lost in the surf when leaving the island."

The retreating men also picked up souvenirs, including rifles, pistols, and any Japanese clothing they could find. Carlson gathered up an enemy flag and a sword, which he intended to give to President Roosevelt and Admiral Nimitz upon his return.

By 1900, most of the Raiders were on the ocean side of the island on the exact same beach they had landed on some fourteen hours earlier. When Carlson and Roosevelt looked out over the beach, the surf didn't look all that threatening. They weren't being harassed by enemy fire, so they could take their time and make an orderly withdrawal back to the sea. There was no indication of any trouble. It certainly looked doable.

Carlson assigned a detail of about a dozen men to provide cover for the debarkation. He spread them out along the tree line for about a hundred yards.

The plan called for all eighteen boats to be lined up at the water's edge ready for the command to go. The two outside boats would shove off first, to be followed by the boats inside them and so on down the line until everybody was off. Noise discipline was a key, as the Raiders didn't want to attract unwanted attention from any lingering enemy forces.

The crews quietly dragged the boats to the waterline, loaded them with supplies and war trophies, and then added any air if needed, being careful to maintain a tight fit over the air valves. Those boats with motors attached passed around community gas cans to top off the tanks. There were only a few boats with motors, and these wouldn't be started until they were in the water and under way. The crews without motors split up into paddlers and kickers and waited for the command to shove off.

The stretcher cases and the badly wounded were assigned to boats with workable motors and especially strong swimmers. The two boats in the middle of the lineup were reserved for the covering force and Carlson's command team. The latter would be the last to leave the island.

The debarkation plan looked a lot more organized than the helter-skelter embarkation plan that had put them on this devil of an island some fourteen hours earlier. But looks would prove to be deceiving. Things began to go wrong almost immediately and then progressed from bad to worse to outright disaster.

The planners had misread how quickly the sun sets on a tropic isle. By the time they were ready to go—1930—it had suddenly become pitch black. The darkness added to the confusion, preventing the boats from seeing one another, and making it hard to time the breakers.

"The hour of 1930 had been selected for the retirement because darkness would have set in and the tide would be high, enabling boats to get over the reef," Carlson wrote in his battle report. "The surf didn't look tough, not nearly as tough as other surfs we had worked in, though rollers followed each other rapidly. No one was apprehensive of getting through. However, I had failed to take into account the speed of the waves and the rapid succession in which they followed each other. The following hour provided a struggle so intense and so futile that it will forever remain a ghastly nightmare to those who participated."

Brave men were reduced to tears or a state of panic by their inability to fight through the waves. Time and again, they would fight through one wave only to be smashed by another. It was one step forward and two steps backward until finally they were too tired to keep on trying.

"Huge waves broke about a hundred yards from the beach and kept coming in rapidly with a very short interval between them," Sergeant Spotts remembered. "We would paddle until we struck the point where the surf broke. From there it was just a matter of time before we ended up back on the beach again.

"In my boat, we tried to get off for about five hours. We paddled steadily and got nowhere, staying about fifty yards from the beach all the time. Finally around midnight we gave up and decided to wait until morning when the tide changed. Our boat and one other landed back on the beach together, and we immediately took cover in a clump of bushes."

Private Carson was part of the covering force that night and lived to tell about it only because most of the boats failed to make it off the island. There was no boat left for the covering squad once the initial attempt was made. In complete darkness, Colonel Carlson had gone with the last boat, thinking that the covering force had already left.

He, too, would not get very far before the huge waves forced his boat back to the beach. This tough, wiry old campaigner, who had marched thousands of miles through the mountainous backcountry of China, proved to be no match for the power and tenacity of the relentlessness surf.

"We walked the boat out to deep water and commenced paddling," Carlson said in his after-action report. "The motor refused to work. The first three or four rollers were easy to pass. Then came the battle. Paddling rhythmically and furiously for all we were worth we would get over one roller only to be hit and thrown back by the next before we could gain momentum. The boat filled to the gunwales. We bailed. We got out and swam while pulling the boat—to no avail. We jettisoned the motor. Subsequently the boat turned over. We righted it, less equipment, and continued the battle. All this time I thought ours was the only boat having this difficulty, for the others had left ahead of us. However, after nearly an hour of struggle men swam up to our stern and reported that their boat had gone back because the men were exhausted. . . . I directed our boat be turned around and returned to the beach for our men were equally exhausted."

Many of the crews struggled with the surf for five hours or more. Only seven boats were able to break through the waves and make it to the waiting submarines.

Private Ben Carson witnessed all this futility from his guard post on the beach as part of the covering force. Looking over his shoulder, he could see the floundering boats in the glare of moonlight shining off the ten-foot breakers. He could hear the curses and see the broken, waterlogged men tossed up on the shore, rolling around in the sand, too exhausted to try again. Some of the boats drifted unoccupied and upside down a couple of hundred yards down the beach.

Carson remembers the first things he saw washed ashore were the wooden paddles, which had been ripped from the paddlers by the powerful waves that crashed into the boats. Brave men, knocked back by the waves, stood in knee-deep water near the beach and cursed the ocean in colorful language befitting a Marine.

Boats carrying the wounded had a particularly tough time because they were short paddlers and muscle. Lieutenant LeFrancois, weak from the loss of blood from five bullet wounds and tied to a stretcher, was dumped upside down and nearly drowned. He told his boat mates to leave him on the beach and they refused. Five times they tried to break through the surf and five times they failed.

LeFrancois's boat had two other wounded personnel aboard, GySgt. Lawrence Lang and Cpl. Leon Chapman. None of them was able to offer much help in getting the boat through the waves.

"The fifth time I picked myself up from the beach I took Lang aside and we made our decision. He and Chapman and I were the dead weights holding up that boat, so we gave instructions to the crew to rest and take off about midnight at low tide, carrying with them whoever was present at that time," LeFrancois wrote. "Then we three wounded men went into the bush and tried to get a good night's rest in spite of rain, pain, and worry. At midnight, the boys looked for us along the beach, then took off. When they reached the ship, they reported us missing. Soon rumor listed us among those who had been drowned."

LeFrancois, Lang, and Chapman moved to a small wooded promontory and waited for daylight.

"As far as we knew, we were the only Marines ashore, and there were no boats," LeFrancois said.

Other wounded men had a different kind of luck. Sergeant Norman J. Lenz, who had sustained a grazing gunshot wound to the head, was tied to a pole litter and laid across the stern of the boat. The rest of the crew walked the boat out through several rollers, gave it a push, and while a couple of men jumped in to paddle, the rest hung on and kicked as hard as they could. Just when it appeared they might make it, a massive wave slammed the boat, tipping it over and throwing everyone into the churning waters.

When they reached the beach there was no sign of Lenz. A few seconds later, he was spotted in the water giving the okay sign with his thumb and forefinger. The crew tried again, and again they were dumped into the water. On the third try, they made it through.

Other boat crews tried five, six, and seven times before giving up in total exhaustion. Most of them were reduced to paddling with rifle butts or palm fronds. The wooden paddles were the first things to float away and the hardest to find. The Raiders had their shoes and clothes ripped away by the jagged coral, which also caused abrasions to the hands and knees. Others stepped into huge holes in the coral and suffered sprained ankles.

Those who were thrown back upon the beach shouted at the roaring waves, beating against them with their fists in an outburst of frustration. One Raider waded about in water up to his knees and cried out, "I'm drowning, I'm drowning." It turned out he couldn't swim.

"Getting off the island the first night was a bitch of the first order," Pvt. William McCall remembered. "I tried to stay as close as I could to [Cpl.] Orin Croft, who was my squad leader and part of my boat team. No one knew that we were all going to encounter tremendous waves about a hundred yards from the beach. That's where the reef was—but it was more like a ledge than a reef.

"The outboard motor for our boat was useless, so everyone grabbed a paddle and got out to where the surf was building up. A huge wave hit us broadside and picked up our boat and hurled it back to the shore. Other boats were flipped over. We did our best to hang on to our paddles, as that was our only means of propelling the craft.

"Most of the men were down to their skivvies. I took off my boondockers and ammo belt and helmet to lighten myself. My M1 was slung over my back and over one shoulder. Time and again we tried to get past to where the surf would build up to where the sea was somewhat calmer. We knew the two subs were patrolling out there, waiting to pick us up. But every time we'd hit the area where the surf was building up, the roller-coaster waves would wash us back to the shore. At about the fifth time we were hit by the surf, I was washed overboard and separated from the boat and crew. I swam back to shore and dug a hole in the sand to keep warm."

Private Carson, who was part of the rear guard, couldn't believe all the chaos he was seeing. He wondered if they all might be marooned on this island. If so, they were doomed.

"The next five hours have got to be the most harrowing period of my life," Carson later said. "We in the perimeter guard force were to leave the beach only when we were sure that everyone else had been evacuated. As we looked toward the surf, we could see boats being turned over backwards by the onrushing waves, dumping the wounded into the surf. Raiders would stick with the wounded and drag them out of the surf back up on the beach. Nowhere could we see a boat drilling its way through that surf, and time after time the boats would wash up on the shore only to be righted by the dumped-out crews, and the struggle through the surf would begin again. After three or more tries to penetrate the surf, the Raiders would gather in small groups on the beach and rest before trying again. During all this, [they]. . . were losing their weapons, ammunition, packs, and even their shoes. We rearguard Raiders were wondering just how long this thing could go on before [we]. . . represented the remaining firepower.

"Nowhere throughout the rest of my four-year Marine Corps career did I ever observe a greater need for physical conditioning."

Somebody reported seeing Pvt. Cletus Smith swimming by himself out past the last breaker toward one of the submarines. Nobody ever saw him again. A rumor later made the rounds that a shark had got him.

Private Brian Quirk was in one of the more fortunate boats. His motor worked and he and his crew made it out on the first try, but not without a struggle. His boat drifted sideways quite a way and almost flipped over before they got the bow turned into the waves. With the motor revved as high as it would go and everybody else paddling like crazy, the boat smashed through the last wave and broke out into the open sea.

Lieutenant Joe Griffith's boat also made it through the surf that first night, but it took four or five tries to do it.

"At first we just jumped in the boat and began paddling," Griffith remembered fifty-seven years later. "We managed to get through the first wave and the second, but the third just knocked us back. We tried three, four times. Then we jettisoned our weapons and clothing and tried again. We walked the boat out and through the third wave before we jumped in and paddled like hell."

One of the men in Griffith's boat had a flashlight and he tried to signal the submarines with an SOS message, but they received no answer. Later, after climbing aboard the *Nautilus*, Griffith asked someone on the submarine why he hadn't answered the SOS. He was told the submarine hadn't wanted to give away its position.

When Griffith spotted his good friend Lt. Oscar Peatross on the deck of the *Nautilus*, he broke into a wide grin. He hadn't seen the wayward Peatross all day, and for all he'd known, he was dead.

"Peat, where in the hell have you been?" Griffith asked his friend.

"I just got lost," Peatross answered with a sheepish smile.

Doctor Stigler's boat also made it out, breaking through the last waves around midnight on about its fifth try.

"They put some real strong swimmers in my boat," Dr. Stigler remembered many years later. "On one of the attempts, I don't remember which one, I got tangled in some ropes when the boat tipped over. I was under the boat and in real trouble before somebody pulled me loose. The good Lord was looking out for me, that's for sure. Anyway, we finally pushed through and saw the *Argonaut* right in front of us. I would have gotten on a Jap sub if it had appeared."

Peatross and his crew arrived on board the *Nautilus* shortly after 2000 and were surprised to learn they were the only boat to have made it so far. Given some welcomed "medicinal" brandy, Peatross reported in to Commodore Haines before nodding off for a few minutes. He was awakened when more boats were spotted coming out from the beach.

Peatross went topside and, catching sight of an oncoming rubber boat, was shocked at what he saw.

"They all looked like pale shadows of the men I had last seen early that morning, and I knew that they had been through a terrible ordeal," he wrote in his history of the Raiders. "If the occupants of the first boat seemed pale shadows of their former selves, the later arrivals looked like nothing less than zombies. Where the first group had at least retained their weapons and most of their equipment and seemed to have preserved some semblance of organization, the later arrivals had lost everything: weapons, equipment, shoes and clothing (some of them were mother naked), and above all their sense of unity."

Peatross likened the survivors to "humanoids," who were reduced to using palm fronds and their bare hands in paddling their way to safety. They told horror stories of a killer surf and severe exhaustion. Boat after boat said the task had been made doubly difficult because the motors just wouldn't work and had had to be jettisoned to lighten the load.

Commodore Haines ordered the two subs to move as close to the beach as possible, about a half mile, and stay on the surface all night to look for any boat crews that broke through.

According to Peatross, seven boats had made it back to the submarines by midnight. The *Nautilus* had recovered four boats consisting of fifty-three Raiders while the *Argonaut* had picked up three boats and an estimated forty Raiders, including Dr. Stigler and A Company commander Lieutenant Plumley. That meant more than half the Raider force, about 125 men, were still on the island.

There had been no communication with Carlson or Roosevelt since about 1030. It seemed unlikely that the remaining Raider force had drowned in the surf, but no one aboard the submarines knew for sure. A more likely scenario, according to Peatross, was that the Raiders had worn themselves out in the surf and were attacked and wiped out by the enemy. Those on watch aboard the *Nautilus* hadn't heard or seen any gunfire, however.

Peatross even let his imagination conjure up a scenario where the remaining Raiders might have been taken prisoner, but once again, there had been no signs of a fight.

"I couldn't imagine the Raiders I knew giving up without a fight," Peatross said. "The possibility of a voluntary surrender never once crossed my mind."

Sometime around 2300 the covering force on the island heard some rustling to its front. Private Carson and Sergeant Spotts heard it. So did Pvt. Jess Hawkins. Hawkins, from South Gate, California, saw eight forms moving slowly toward him, four to his left and four to his right. He fired at one of the forms and two fired back, hitting Hawkins in the chest. Though seriously wounded, he kept on firing and later was credited with three kills.

Carson, who was only ten feet to the left of Hawkins, also opened up with his tommy gun. The tracers gave off such a bright light that Carson was reluctant to fire again for fear of giving away his position. Luckily, the enemy patrol retreated back across the island.

"We must have scored several hits," Spotts said, "for they squealed like stuck hogs and didn't bother us in this position again."

Peatross later surmised that all of the shouting during the struggle to get off the beach had acted as a sound beacon for "any surviving Japanese still seeking to die for their emperor, and there were still some of those on the prowl."

Colonel Carlson didn't know what to think of the brief skirmish. Were there more Japanese on the island than he'd thought? Had they been reinforced from some other island on the atoll? Once again, Carlson seems to have accepted the worst-case scenario.

Carlson assumed that if any of these possibilities were true, then his Raiders, most of whom had lost their weapons in the surf and been reduced to a state of exhaustion, would be easy prey for the enemy. If the enemy garrison hadn't been reinforced as yet, the chances were good that they would be in the morning. Certainly the planes would be back in even greater numbers and maybe a troopship was on the way. Carlson called this time period the "spiritual low point" of the raid.

"The situation at this point was extremely grave," Carlson wrote in his after-action report. "Our initial retirement had been orderly, but the battle with the surf had disorganized us and stripped us of our fighting power. Planes would undoubtedly return at daylight, and it was probable that a landing force would arrive. . . . A check showed that 120 men were still on the beach, and there was no assurance that others had not landed at points farther away. Rain and the fact that most of the men had even stripped themselves of their clothes in the surf added to the general misery."

By midnight the remaining Raiders were too exhausted to make any more attempts at escape. They needed rest. Carlson put out the word to get some sleep before giving it another go in the morning. As a light rain began to fall, many of the men dug themselves a shallow bed in the warm sand and fell off into a deep sleep. Others crossed the island and spent the night in a native village, where they shared some food and drink.

In the meantime, there was no way for Carlson to contact the submarines. All the radios, which had worked only sporadically during the day, had been lost in the surf.

Carlson didn't get much rest that night. He was plainly worried. He wondered if the submarines would wait for his Raiders and for how long. He was deeply concerned about the possibility of capture, especially with the president's son, Jimmy Roosevelt, still on the island. Only a few Raiders still had their weapons. How could they defend themselves if the enemy returned in force? They would have to strip the dead Japanese of their weapons and live off the land. That's what they had been trained to do. The prospects for survival certainly looked glum.

Carlson strode down the beach trying to comfort his troops. He could use a cigarette or a couple of good drags on his pipe but, under the circumstances, would have to do without. He must not let the men see how worried and concerned he was.

"Don't say I didn't warn you boys. I told you it would be tough in the Raiders," Carlson said with a forced grin.

"Gung Ho," a couple of Raiders answered with weakened voices.

"Gung Ho and don't worry," Carlson answered. "We'll be at Pearl next week this time."

Though the men may have believed him, Carlson was having a hard time convincing himself. He must make some plans if things didn't work out as he hoped. He must be ready to deal with any circumstance.

Carlson conferred with B Company commander Captain Coyte, and the first thing decided was that a maximum effort must be made to get Roosevelt off the island at any cost. Carlson, as well as Nimitz, had been dead against the idea of allowing the president's son to go on such a dangerous mission in the first place. What propaganda the Japanese could reap with the killing or the capture of the son of the president of the United States! It would be a severe blow to the morale of the whole country and a black mark against Carlson. Carlson vowed to himself that he would not let that happen.

Fifteen

The Surrender Note

Carlson made another decision later that night, one that was intentionally hidden from the public for almost half a century. Around midnight, after much soul searching, Carlson met with Captain Coyte, Dr. MacCracken, and a few key NCOs and told them he had decided to surrender the remaining forces on Makin because of his concern for the wounded and the possible fate of Jimmy Roosevelt. Roosevelt, it is believed, was not present at the meeting, although he later wrote that he was.

Roosevelt's version of what happened at the meeting appears to be pure fiction.

"We assembled in the thickest jungle growth we could find and voted on our course of action," Roosevelt wrote more than thirty years after the war in a book about his parents. "Carlson ran a democratic show. Back in camp we had passed evenings discussing life and taking votes on our feelings. . . . This night we voted on survival—whether to surrender or try to survive the night and escape when the tide went out in the morning. We voted to stay and try to escape."

Peatross, who interviewed several Raiders who were at the "surrender" meeting, believes Carlson deliberately conducted the conference behind Roosevelt's back, perhaps after the two of them held a private pep talk to keep each other's morale up.

"As far as I have been able to determine, Major Roosevelt was not present at this meeting," Peatross wrote, "and, based on my personal impression of his character and what I have heard and read about his relationship with his father, he probably would have objected strongly to being a pretext for surrender, had he been present."

Roosevelt's recollections of that fateful night are suspect in other areas as well. For example, he later wrote that "enemy aircraft bombed and strafed us" and "we kept moving about the island, leaving signs to confuse the enemy so they would misdirect their fire." There were no air attacks that night, and the men were much too exhausted to move about the island or to have gone anywhere except to sleep.

The most logical explanation of the events that night is that Roosevelt was deliberately excluded from the meeting when Carlson made his decision to surrender his force. Carlson, the consummate egalitarian, deviated from one of his core principles and apparently decided to unilaterally surrender his force without entertaining much, if any, debate at all.

The firefight with the Japanese patrol reinforced Carlson's opinion that there must still be a significant enemy presence on the island, and with the loss of so many weapons in the surf, he was fearful of being overrun and maybe taken prisoner. He apparently came to the conclusion that his only option was to surrender.

Captain Coyte recalled later that Carlson was extremely upset by their inability to get off the island and was shaken by the recent firefight with the Japanese. He regarded the enemy patrol as proof that the Japanese had landed reinforcements on the island.

Also, Carlson didn't know if the submarines would be able to stick around another day. He was most concerned that Roosevelt was still on the island. He felt responsible for the safety and well-being of the president's son and would go to any extreme to save him.

Carlson ordered Captain Coyte to contact the Japanese commander on the island to arrange for the surrender of American troops, providing they would be treated as prisoners of war. At about 0330, Coyte, along with Pvt. William McCall, who could speak a little Japanese, set out unarmed and wearing only trousers and shoes to find the garrison commander.

After traveling only a short distance, the two spotted a native hut with a light on inside. Within were two adult natives and a child. Minutes later, a Japanese soldier armed with a rifle came into the hut. According to Coyte, the Japanese soldier appeared to be unhappy.

"[The soldier] kept threatening to shoot me and was sticking the end of the rifle in my stomach. I was so tired and exhausted that it really didn't make much difference. I would push the rifle aside and . . . demand that he take me to his commanding officer," Coyte said.

The two Raiders managed to calm the Japanese soldier down and convince him to carry a surrender note to the ranking official on the island. It was almost daylight when Coyte carried out Carlson's order and composed the brief surrender message as instructed by Carlson. That note, which was later found on the body of a Japanese soldier when enemy reinforcements arrived on Makin on August 19, read:

Dear Sir:
I am a member of the American forces now on Makin.
We have suffered severe casualties and wish to make an end of the bloodshed and bombings.
We wish to surrender according to the rules of military law and be treated as prisoners of war. We would also like to bury our dead and care for our wounded.
There are approximately 60 of us left. We have all voted to surrender.
I would like to see you personally as soon as possible to prevent future bloodshed and bombing.

The signature on the document, which was later made public by the Japanese, was unreadable. Peatross says in his book that the signature was "obliterated" but in a 1992 article in *Leatherneck* magazine, Peatross said the note was signed by "Ralph H. Coyte, Captain, USMCR."

There are a couple of versions as to what happened next. Coyte said that soon after the Japanese soldier left the hut, a shot was heard. When he went out to investigate, he saw two Raiders coming down the road who said they had just shot a Japanese soldier. Coyte assumed it was the messenger.

McCall's version of the events that night hasn't changed in fifty-seven years.

"Carlson came and told me to accompany Coyte and look for some live Jap soldiers and give them a note," McCall said in a 1999 interview. "I did not read the note. I don't know who wrote it, but Coyte had it. I don't know if it was signed. My job was to go with Coyte. As far as I know, Peatross's account of the surrender was accurate.

"Coyte returned to Carlson saying the deed was done. I told Coyte I would stay with the natives for a while. I thought I would check out Ukiangong Village, and on the way I armed myself with an enemy rifle and pistol and a cartridge belt I had liberated from some dead Japs. On passing by a taro pit I heard noises and movement among the elephant-ears plants. Two Japs were hiding in the pit and tried to escape on the opposite side. One was armed and looked like the one carrying the surrender note. The other had a large pack on his back which I thought was a demolition kit.

"I shot and killed the armed Jap with the Arisaka rifle and I had to use the Nambu pistol to dispatch the other. I went to the other side of the pit and the pack-toting Jap was a medic with a large first-aid kit."

McCall brought the first-aid kit back to the Raider line and gave it to Doc MacCracken. He never thought of retrieving the surrender note. McCall then went back out to reconnoiter farther south.

"I saw some natives, spoke in pidgin English to them, and asked if they had seen any live Nips around," McCall said. "The answer was negative. I looked around some more and then returned to Carlson at the beach and reported no sign of Japs."

When Japanese reinforcements arrived on the island a day later, they recovered the surrender note, presumably on the body of the enemy soldier McCall had killed, and it later found its way into the hands of Tokyo Rose, who was only too happy to exploit a propaganda coup.

Nary a word of the surrender attempt was mentioned in any Marine Corps literature over the next half century until Peatross began writing his book on the Raiders. Peatross, ever the loyal junior officer, had learned of the surrender attempt early on the morning of August 18, 1942, but after a brief investigation, he decided to leave the issue alone. Suffering from a terminal illness in the early 1990s, Peatross wanted to set the record straight in his book before he passed on.

One of the people Peatross called to verify what he already knew was Ben Carson, who told him of a conversation between Carlson and Coyte he had overheard aboard the *Nautilus* on the return trip to Pearl after the Makin Raid. Carson heard Carlson tell Coyte to "forget about the surrender note" and that "if you want to be a hero you can't talk surrender."

Carlson was sitting on a bunk talking to Coyte in plain sight, according to Carson. When Coyte saw Carson lurking nearby, and thinking he might have overheard the conversation, he asked him in, allegedly to meet the colonel. Upon leaving, Carson said he overheard Carlson ask Coyte, "Do you think he heard what we were talking about?"

Further research by Peatross only confirmed what he knew to be true. Carlson had, indeed, planned to surrender.

Private McCall, who helped deliver the surrender note, told Peatross, "Carlson told me not to say anything about it."

Asked in 1999 if there was any need to "straighten out" any misconceptions about the surrender episode, McCall was terse and forceful in his reply.

"There was a tacit agreement between Carlson, Coyte, and I that nothing more be said between us about the surrender note," he said. "I do not have anything that I'd like to straighten out—what's done and said is over with. Carlson and Coyte are dead. Nothing needs straightening."

The other messenger, Captain Coyte, told Peatross, "We [officers] had all prepared written reports of the operation as it pertained to our participation. After they had been submitted, they were returned to us by Colonel Carlson, who advised us that Admiral Nimitz had told him that we should rewrite our report, deleting all reference to the offer to surrender."

Carlson never mentioned the surrender note in his battle report and his biographer, Michael Blankfort, refers to it only in an oblique manner in his book, *The Big Yankee*.

"Surrender?" Blankfort said, putting words in Carlson's mouth. "[Carlson] was sure that everyone on the beach was thinking of that possibility. He himself had thought of it before this night, before they even left Pearl. It was something you had to anticipate—and his decision had long been made. Courage to die had meaning only in relation to what men offered their lives for. If nothing could be gained, tactically or strategically or morally, by an all-out, suicide last-ditch fight, he would surrender his men. But the estimate of the gain would have to wait until the facts were before him. Right now his hunch was that the enemy was still quite strong, but he did not yet know how strong his own men were."

Blankfort goes out of his way to suggest that any talk of surrender came from a sobbing Raider, one who had to be slapped by an NCO to calm his hysteria. Blankfort further suggests that Carlson did have a meeting with Roosevelt and after discussing all the options, including surrender, dismissed Roosevelt by saying that there was nothing that could be done until daylight.

Word of Carlson's surrender note spread down the beach from Raider to Raider. Most of them were shocked, thinking it must be some kind of joke. Word was passed down the line that "everybody's on their own now; they're going to surrender."

Sergeant Mel Spotts wrote in his diary: "The word started around here that we would surrender in the morning [and] this didn't set so very good with anyone . . . [but] there appeared [to be] no choice. Most of the weapons had been lost in our attempts at getting off."

There are still former members of the Makin Raiders today who don't know what to make of Carlson's intention to surrender. For some, it's almost too painful to contemplate.

"Buck" Stidham still believes that Captain Coyte was the instigator of the note, not Carlson. But others are quick to disagree.

"I didn't like the sound of it then and I don't now," Stidham said in a 1999 interview. "Nobody that I talked to liked the idea. Marines don't surrender."

Private Brian Quirk, who got off the island before the decision to surrender was made, heard rumors of Carlson's action all the way back to Pearl and for many years afterward.

"I doubt Coyte made the decision," he said. "I wasn't there so I don't know, but I know that Carlson would have been in command of the situation. The fact that Peatross wrote about it in his book gives it great credibility. Peatross was a fine young officer. And if Sgt. Frank Lawson says it happened it must have, because he was a very level-headed man and a good Marine.

"But I can see Carlson's side too," said Quirk, who rose to the rank of colonel before he retired in the 1960s. "It's easy to second-guess him. He didn't know if another 250 Japs had landed on the island after dark. Half his weapons were lost in the surf, they had no ammunition and nothing to defend themselves with. I can see why this was an option for him, a course of action. Carlson certainly was not a coward. Believe me, he was one courageous guy."

The surrender news was not well received by the covering force, which hadn't yet been given a chance to give the surf a go on their own. When a couple of the rearguard crew went to Carlson to request permission to give the surf a try, Carlson seemed stunned that he had any dry, well-armed soldiers still on the island. He appeared to have been under the impression that most, if not all, of his force had lost their weapons while trying to overcome the powerful surf. It was a reasonable assumption because Carlson's boat was supposed to have left the beach last, just after the one containing the covering force. The reality was that Carlson took the last boat thinking the rear guard had already gone when, in fact, they hadn't.

About a dozen members of the covering force turned over their weapons and ammunition to other Raiders who were still trying to recover from their earlier confrontation with the surf, and got ready to give it a go on their own just as it was getting light.

Looking out beyond the breakers in the faint light of dawn, the Raiders could see both submarines silhouetted against the horizon. The men ran forward to the water's edge, waving their arms and cheering, daring any enemy snipers still remaining to fire on them from the palm trees if they wanted. It was a huge morale boost, one that seemed to lift the spirits of the entire party, especially the group's commander, Colonel Carlson.

Spurred on by the welcome sight, four more boat crews managed to overcome the heavy surf and break through to the waiting submarines in the next couple of hours. One of the boats carried a very important passenger, Maj. Jimmy Roosevelt.

Lieutenant LeFrancois, watching from his vantage point on a piece of high ground, saw Roosevelt's boat capsize shortly after dawn, throwing the men, including Lieutenant Lamb, back to the shore.

"Lamb nearly drowned," LeFrancois wrote, "and when a second attempt to reach the sub was made, he just pushed the boat off and remained behind, preferring to take his chances on the island rather than risk death in the sea. He stood there, waved to the major, and watched that boat fight its way straight through the surf and out to the submarine."

Roosevelt's boat, which also included Sgt. Buck Stidham and Sgt. Mel Spotts, arrived at the *Argonaut* at 0800, just twenty-one minutes before the sub had to dive to avoid an enemy air attack.

"Roosevelt was the last man out of the boat," said Commodore Haines, who viewed the rescue from the conning tower of the nearby *Nautilus*, "and had just barely got his tail feathers down when the first Jap plane came over and the *Argonaut* had to go under. If the plane had appeared fifteen or twenty seconds earlier, I'm afraid Major Jimmie would have been swimming around in the Pacific."

Roosevelt's journey to the submarines that morning was filled with the same difficulties that had plagued every other boat the previous night. Only this time, they were aided by experience and a little luck.

Getting through the breakers was no guarantee of safety, however. There were other dangers that awaited them beyond the crashing surf.

"Our worries were not over, because we were now in the open sea. At any minute we expected Jap planes to appear and blast us right out of the water," Sergeant Spotts remembered. "No planes appeared, at least not right then. We picked up a lone swimmer about a hundred yards from the submarine and we, in turn, were taken in tow by a motor-powered boat. Getting back aboard the submarine seemed to me as the happiest moment of my life. I was worn out."

Spotts was given a bracer, described as half alcohol and half water, and then he slept for eight hours.

Sergeant Stidham's most lasting memory of his return trip to the submarine was spotting a huge manta ray swimming along with the boat about twenty yards off the starboard beam.

"It was the size of a barn door and must have weighed a ton or more," Stidham said. "I don't recall anyone uttering a single word, but I couldn't help but notice that the rhythm of the paddles picked up a beat or two once we spotted the thing."

Stidham's other memory was the admiration he felt for Jimmy Roosevelt, who, despite his privileged background and continuing health problems, was just a regular guy who pulled his own weight.

"He was just a good egg," Stidham said fifty-seven years later. "He was a first-class guy. He was 4F material with bad eyes, bad feet, and a bad stomach, but he never complained. He pitched right in and pulled his own weight, helping to get us back to the sub."

In fact, Roosevelt was officially cited for his cool leadership and professional demeanor in helping to save three Raiders from drowning, which earned him a Navy Cross. The citation, which included earlier actions on Butaritari Island, commended Roosevelt for displaying "exemplary courage in personally rescuing three men from drowning in the heavy surf. His gallant conduct and his inspiring devotion to duty were in keeping with the highest traditions of the United States Naval Service."

There were a couple of lone wolves among the Raiders that morning, individuals who were thrown out of their boats by the crashing waves and decided to keep on swimming. One unidentified Raider tried to catch up with Roosevelt's boat and was only a few yards from the *Argonaut* when the submarine dived in response to an enemy plane sighting. He climbed into the rubber boat hurriedly vacated by Roosevelt's crew and then had to suddenly evacuate the boat when the Japanese planes arrived. He had to dive deeply under the water to escape a strafing attack and then had the energy to swim all the way back to shore, dodging bullets all the way.

Another Raider, Pvt. Herbert Oliver of Honey Grove, Texas, swam all the way out to one of the submarines that morning only to have both of them dive out of sight as he came near them. After treading water for a while, he turned around and swam all the way back, letting the tide and rolling surf carry him up on the beach.

The first two boats to break through on the morning of August 18 contained "fresh" personnel from the rearguard detachment, which included Peatross's platoon sergeant, Frank Lawson, and Pvt. Ben Carson. The latter provided the following account of his struggle.

The boat crew we assembled in the dark consisted of seven Raiders who all agreed to swim alongside the rubber boat through the surf. No one would ride in the boat. Also, everyone removed their shirts, shoes, and socks. Since we had more than four hours observing what wouldn't work in getting through the surf, we wanted to make our only try as good as we could make it. Finally, we took one last look at the sorry sight of Raiders huddled along the beach and the wounded lying near the tree line, and we shoved off.

Only then did we realize just how tough this particular surf was. We were all hanging on to the gunwale ropes on the side of the rubber boat and swimming like hell with the other arm and legs. After what seemed like a very long time, I stole a look back at the beach between breakers and was pleasantly surprised to see that we were a respectable distance from the beach. I hollered to the crew that we were better than halfway through the surf and to give her all we had. After another long struggle, I felt the breakers transcend into swells.

As soon as enough crew got aboard and started paddling, the rest of us crawled in. We were making enough speed with our paddling to churn up a luminescent wake. Everybody was really leaning into those paddles.

We had nothing to guide us to the sub other than keeping our course perpendicular to the beach. As the breaker line at the beach began to fade and no running lights of the sub were visible ahead of us, some among our crew began to express trepidation about our situation. The sea was still running pretty high, as we paddled toward Southeast Asia, when we began to hear the diesel engines of a sub being alternately muffled by the sea and then unmuffled as the sub heaved above the swell. We paddled like Olympian competitors toward the noise. Directly we could see the outline of the sub's hull against the horizon.

• • •

Carson's boat pulled alongside the *Nautilus* and the men reached out for the ladders that had been welded to the hull. The rubber boat rose and fell with the waves, allowing one Raider at a time to grab on. Waiting navy personnel reached down and helped drag the Raiders aboard and lead them to the hatches. Other personnel held on to the rubber boat to keep it from drifting off. It would be needed in a few minutes to carry a rescue party back to the island.

Sergeant Lawson's boat, which needed three tries to break through the surf, linked up with the *Nautilus* at 0719, and Carson's boat arrived at 0737. There were now an estimated seventy able-bodied Raiders still left on the island.

Peatross spotted his long-lost platoon sergeant, Frank Lawson, right away and, as soon as he was aboard, began pumping him for information on what was happening ashore.

"Lieutenant, everybody's been having a helluva time getting off the beach, and when we left, the colonel was getting ready to surrender," Lawson blurted as soon as he was pulled aboard the sub.

Peatross couldn't believe what he was hearing and asked Lawson to repeat what he had just said. Lawson described the circumstances on the island again and told Peatross he had been present at a meeting where Carlson explained why he had to surrender.

Peatross reported his conversation with Lawson to Commodore Haines. Haines gave Peatross a disbelieving look and told him he doubted strongly that Carlson would ever surrender.

"Peat," Haines told Peatross, "that crusty old boss of yours isn't going to surrender; he's just too tough for that. But I do believe he could use some help, so here's what I want you to do."

Unable to contact Carlson directly because all the functioning radios had been lost in the surf, Commodore Haines ordered Peatross to send a five-man detail back to the island to tell Carlson not to worry about the submarines leaving the area. They would wait as long as it took to rescue every man.

The five volunteers rounded up by Peatross were Sgts. Robert Allard and Dallas Cook, Pfc. Richard Olbert and Pvts. Donald Roberton and John Kerns. All were excellent swimmers and good athletes. They listened to Peatross as he relayed the commodore's promise to stay in place "until we get every living Raider off that island and, if we have to, we'll send every able-bodied man ashore, sailors included."

The volunteers would use the same boat that Carson's group had just used to reach the *Nautilus*. Carson thought he was pretty close to being "volunteered" for the mission himself. He was saved by a small vial of fermented grapes he received after climbing down the hatch.

"A Navy pharmacist mate gave me what looked like a vanilla bottle with the admonition, 'That's medicinal.' I screwed off the top and took a shot. It was brandy. Though it burned going down, I emptied that jug right there.

"As I moved toward the rear of the sub, I met Sergeant Carroll. He was recruiting a team to get back in the boat we had arrived in and head to a point just outside the surf. From there the crew would attempt to shoot a line across the surf to shore so the rubber boats could be pulled through the heavy surf by one of the submarines.

"As I stood there almost glassy eyed from the brandy, "'Tiny' Carroll said, 'Hell, you just got here—go get some sleep.' I stumbled aft until I found a spot where I could lay down. For the next half hour I slept."

Sixteen

Finally, A Little Luck

The men on the beach could see the rescue boat heading toward shore. They rushed to the water's edge and waved their arms with excitement. The exhausted men were flushed with hope that they would soon get off this godforsaken island after all.

The boat shot a line over the reef and one of the men jumped overboard to follow it to the beach. Running up to Colonel Carlson near the tree line, the unidentified Raider relayed the message he had been given that the subs would stay until every man was rescued, even if they had to tow every single rubber boat through the surf.

It was almost 0900.

Carlson, who was probably unaware that Roosevelt had made it out, smiled weakly at the good news. He looked thoroughly exhausted, like a man who had the weight of the world on his shoulders.

The unidentified Raider ran back into the water and was pulled back to his rubber boat.

Then the enemy planes were spotted.

"They flew low, hedge-hopping from the lagoon side of the island," Lieutenant LeFrancois said.

The Raiders on the island sought cover under the palm trees and the submarines quickly submerged out of sight. Those on the island watched as a Japanese Zero headed straight for the five men in the rubber boat. As the crew jumped overboard to get away from the boat, the plane riddled the area with its machine guns. The boat was ripped to shreds and no survivors could be seen. Several other planes, dive bombers, went after the submarines, dropping bombs on the giant transports, which they could easily see resting on the shallow bottom, from point-blank range.

The explosions sent huge geysers of water a hundred feet or more into the air.

The planes made several passes at the subs, dropping dozens of bombs, each one producing a giant spray of water.

The Raiders on the beach looked over the scene with shock. They turned to each other in stunned silence. They all were wondering the same thing, but nobody was brave enough to say it aloud. Had the Japanese planes sunk the submarines? If so, they were certainly doomed.

Thankfully, the planes weren't equipped with depth charges. The bombs they carried had fuses that detonated on impact, so although the submerged subs certainly felt the concussion of the blasts, they were in no real danger of suffering any crippling damage.

"[The bombs] did no damage at all, but only made a grand splash in the water," LeFrancois said.

The men on the beach didn't know that, however. A new wave of despair swept over the stranded Raiders. A few men began to weep. Others were on the verge of panic. Fear was in everyone's eyes—fear of the unknown, of death, of capture and torture.

"We were all scared," LeFrancois said, "and some of the men had folded up into balls."

This was perhaps Carlson's finest moment. He pulled the men together and tried to ease their fears. He put them to work by sending out patrols to look for enemy soldiers, food, rifles, and any intelligence. There would be no more talk of surrender. The extra day on the island would give him a chance to complete his mission of destroying anything that might be of use to the enemy. They would think about the submarines and escape later in the day, when it got dark.

Work would occupy their minds until Carlson figured out a way to get off this cursed island.

The men quickly discovered there weren't very many Japanese left on the island, which came as a great relief. Patrols were sent out to reconnoiter, to gather weapons and food, and to destroy any remaining enemy installations. A patrol to On Chong's Wharf destroyed the radio station there and killed a Japanese marine in the process. A couple of more enemy soldiers were shot by other patrols to different parts of the island as the Raiders loaded up on souvenirs and trinkets.

Among the spoils of war was a cache of blue and pink silk underwear liberated from the trading station at Stone Pier. Some of the Raiders made quite the fashion statement by wearing these colorful garments at a party held in their honor when they returned to Pearl Harbor.

As soon as the natives discovered the Raiders were going to destroy Japanese supplies, they came racing down the road to get their share. They had to be restrained to allow the demolitions men room to work.

The Raiders, including the officers, had become souvenir happy, acting like a bunch of pirates. The prime objects of their greed were Japanese weapons, particularly flags and samurai swords. A wounded Lieutenant LeFrancois, who would later write a magazine piece about the raid, recalled the following humorous anecdote about a couple of young Raiders bragging about their good fortune.

"Hey, look at the Smirnoff sword I got from one of them monkeys," one said.

"Samurai sword," a Raider corrected his pal. "That means that the bird who wore it was one of the four hundred or something."

"Oh, well, it's mine now and I can call it what I want," the first guy answered. "To me it's a genuine Smirnoff sword."

A little while later, Private McCall strolled by wearing a blue silk undershirt and a Japanese helmet, carrying a captured Japanese rifle.

"Hey, Lieutenant," McCall said when he spotted LeFrancois resting his injured body against a coconut tree. "How would you like a nice cool quart bottle of Japanese beer?"

"Get out of here, McCall," LeFrancois said with an exhausted smile on his face. "This is not the time for kidding around."

"I ain't kidding, and here's the beer," McCall said, handing it over to the lieutenant.

LeFrancois grabbed the bottle and took a slug.

By the early afternoon, Carlson had set up his headquarters at Government House where there was water, some captured Japanese food, a roof to protect the wounded, and some cover from air attacks in a nearby ditch. A patrol that had been sent to forage found supplies of canned meats, fish, and biscuits at the trading station, and they brought as much as they could carry back to Government House.

Japanese aircraft flew over the island at four different times on August 18, and, except for the first one at 0920, which destroyed the rubber boat carrying the five-man rescue party, never did any damage to the Raiders. The planes also bombed and strafed several nearby islands, obviously believing the Raider force was much larger than it was.

Carlson used the time at Government House to plan the evacuation later that night. For some reason, he felt confident that the submarines had not been blown up in the early-morning attack by the Japanese dive bombers and were still there and in good shape to take his men home. He didn't feel so confident about being able to conquer the surf, however.

For this reason, he decided that the Raiders would exit the island by way of the lagoon. There weren't enough rubber boats to transport all the remaining men, which still included four stretcher cases. Carlson noticed a forty-foot sloop with a diesel engine anchored off Stone Pier and sent a three-man detail to see if it was seaworthy. Three volunteers, led by Lt. Charlie Lamb, rowed out to the sloop to check its condition, and as they approached the craft, a pistol suddenly appeared from a porthole and a shot rang out. Lamb managed to stuff a grenade through the porthole, killing a Japanese marine who was obviously hiding out. The sloop was half full of seawater, however, and in no condition to be of use to them.

The Raiders would have to use native outriggers instead. Carlson assigned a detail to prepare the outriggers and another detail to bring the remaining three serviceable rubber boats across the island to the lagoon, where they would work on the motors. Lamb, because of his expertise with outboard engines, was in overall charge of the project.

Lamb and his crew rose to the challenge of getting the men off the island. Corporals Julius Cotton and Howard Gurman salvaged two outboard motors and had them running by early afternoon. Another crew saw to it that the makeshift raft, quickly dubbed *Lamb's Ark* by the Raiders, was lashed tight and right, or the craft would surely break up and founder once it reached the rough waters near the lagoon entrance.

"The raft was made up of three rubber boats tied together, with a seaworthy native fishing boat on either end, the whole thing being lashed securely together," LeFrancois said. "The two good motors we had were on the end [of] rubber boats. The oars of each native boat were manned by our strongest men. Our wounded occupied the center cross seats of the rubber boats."

Lamb seemed confident the motors would work fine in the lagoon. They would have to wait and see how they performed in the choppy, open water at the mouth of the lagoon.

While the raft was being readied, Carlson sent a patrol led by Captain Davis to King's Wharf to destroy a nearby fuel dump that contained between seven hundred and a thousand drums of aviation gasoline. Some of the petrol had been refined in the United States. The Raiders shot the drums full of holes and then tossed a burning fuse lighter into the gasoline pouring out onto the ground, making sure to get out of the way. The fire and smoke from the gasoline dump rose hundreds of feet in the air and could be seen for miles.

The same patrol searched the garrison administrative office and collected a chart and all the papers it could find.

"This office was in one end of the barracks that my boat team had checked early in the morning of the seventeenth," Peatross said. "At the time, we were interested only in human occupancy and couldn't have cared less about documents, which we couldn't read anyhow."

Private Cyrill Matelski was part of a patrol sent out to search the enemy dead for any intelligence information. He removed a pistol and wristwatch from a body identified as that of Sergeant Major Kanemitsu, the garrison commander. It was the only watch recovered by any of the Raiders that day. Like its owner, however, it had stopped working.

Carlson also met again with the natives and reminded Police Chief Joe Miller of his promise made the day before to give the Raider dead a proper Christian burial. According to Carlson's biographer, Michael Blankfort, Miller was given an additional fifty dollars in cash, all that Carlson could scrounge up, as an added incentive to keep his word.

The Raiders would have buried their comrades themselves, but the coral was too hard and there were no shovels available. Blankfort said Carlson stood over the bodies of eighteen Raiders (though he would report a figure of fourteen to Admiral Nimitz a couple of days later) that were covered by blankets. The dead apparently included the three casualties Peatross had the day before while fighting apart from the main body. The natives must have found them and moved them to a central spot with the rest.

"Carlson," according to Blankfort, "turned each man on his back and said a prayer." For some reason, he left their dog tags on them.

The moment of truth was now at hand. Could Carlson somehow signal the submarines to move to the mouth of the lagoon entrance for the pickup? The bigger question, of course, was whether the submarines had survived the early-morning bombing and were still in the area. There had been no contact with the submarines all day.

The Raiders had been fortunate that no enemy reinforcements had thus far shown up. Carlson knew in his heart that they would not be so lucky the next day. He knew he had to get his men off the island that night or risk either annihilation or capture the next day when enemy reinforcements were sure to arrive.

Without any workable radios, Carlson's plan was to signal the submarines by flashlight. He had had a rare stroke of good luck earlier in the day when he discovered a workable flashlight and a qualified signalman left on the island. Four signalmen had been killed the previous day and curiously, each of them had a last name that began with the letter *M* (Cpl. Edward Maciejewski, Pvt. Robert Maulding, and Pfcs. Ken Montgomery and Norman Mortensen). In an incredible coincidence, the lone remaining signalman at Carlson's disposal was another Raider with a last name that began with an *M*, Sgt. Ken McCullough.

McCullough, a wiry farm boy from southeast Oklahoma, had gone to radio school in San Diego before the war, where he learned Morse code. After having discovered McCullough's abilities earlier in the day, Carlson had made sure he would be available to him later. He insisted that McCullough stick close by him. The way his luck had gone so far, Carlson didn't want to tempt fate and lose McCullough through some accident or to an enemy sniper. He wanted to make sure McCullough would be available to send a message when the sun went down.

The two submarines, which had spent just about the entire day submerged, came to the surface shortly after 1800 and moved to the same spot they had occupied the night before, about a half mile off the reef. At 1930, according to Lieutenant Peatross, who was on the bridge of the *Nautilus* at the time, "a lookout spotted a light blinking Morse code from an area where our troops were last known to have been located."

It was McCullough, asking if the ship was the *Nautilus* or the *Argonaut*. Rather than answer the question, the *Nautilus* interrupted with the word "Who?" This happened four or five times, causing Carlson and McCullough no small measure of anxiety.

"I was scared stiff," McCullough said afterward, "because I swear I could feel about a dozen Jap rifles aimed right at me. Although we thought we had the place secure, I had been through a lot the past two days and was not quite a believer. I also thought the batteries in the light would go dead before I could get the message off."

Commodore Haines wanted to be sure he was in contact with the Raiders and not some Japanese force trying to trick the *Nautilus*. Neither submarine had been in contact with Carlson's group all day. A lot could have happened in the meantime, including their capture or destruction. He wanted some kind of authentication that only Carlson would know. On the trip to Makin, Haines and Carlson had had a friendly argument over who had relieved Haines's father as adjutant and inspector of the Marine Corps. Carlson insisted it had been "Squeegie" Long. Haines directed the signalman to flash the query, "Who followed my father as A & I?"

It took Carlson a while to figure out what answer the question was seeking. Suddenly, it came to him. He chuckled to himself, rubbed his chin, and turned to McCullough, telling him to reply, "Squeegie Long," spelling each letter of the first name slowly.

As soon as he had transmitted "Squeegie," the *Nautilus* broke in with "send your message." McCullough told the sub to meet them off Flink Point at the western entrance to the lagoon at about 2130. The message was immediately acknowledged, and Carlson was advised the submarines would be at the lagoon entrance at the time requested.

Crossing the island to Government Wharf, where *Lamb's Ark* was moored and ready for loading, Carlson gave the order to prepare to get under way. The wounded were loaded aboard the rubber boats along with some souvenir Japanese rifles and other spoils of war. An exhausted Carlson took a long look around while the last of his men boarded the ark, lost in his own thoughts. Earlier, Carlson had toyed with the idea of remaining behind so that he could organize the natives to fight the Japanese upon their return. His men wouldn't hear of it and he eventually changed his mind.

Carlson had to be disappointed with the operation, particularly the ragtag efforts at evacuating the island. The casualties bothered him greatly. He worried whether the natives would properly bury his boys. He worried if the effort had been worthwhile.

Had he done everything he could to prepare his men for this ordeal? Was he himself prepared well enough to deal with such changing conditions? No commander ever expects to fail in an operation, he told himself, but he should have a plan ready, just in case he does.

With a deep sigh, Carlson finally stepped lightly into the rear of one of the rubber boats, squeezing in among the wounded. He gave the order to go. The ungainly craft finally shoved off at 2030 and headed west for the four-mile trip to the open sea outside the lagoon entrance.

The motors remained uncooperative, each working intermittently. The paddlers dug in with all their strength to keep the craft on course so that they would meet the time deadline. The craft could barely make two knots across the calm waters of the lagoon despite a maximum effort by the paddlers.

Carlson, in a calm and detached voice, told his crew to head toward a bright star shining in the western sky.

"One of the motors coughed and stopped. It was out of gas," Lieutenant LeFrancois later wrote. "We decided to refuel slowly and carefully, to let the motor cool and also to keep both motors from running out of fuel at the same time while bouncing around on the high seas. The sudden stoppage of one motor threw the raft to port, and it took clever coordination on the part of the oarsmen to straighten us out."

They could hear some firing on Butaritari on the port side, but as long as it wasn't aimed at them, nobody cared. A flare was set off on the starboard side and that was a bit more unnerving, because no one knew what was on the other islands. It could have been a signal from Japanese destroyers convoying transports with a landing party. It could have been the U.S. Navy coming to their rescue, for all they knew.

All the while, Carlson kept assuring his crew that everything was all right and that it was only a matter of time before they spotted the submarines. He reminded everyone of their motto, "Gung Ho", and of how important it was to work together. He had faith in them and they must have faith in him. Together they would get through this.

It was 2200, a half hour behind schedule, by the time the craft reached the lagoon's entrance. They could feel the pull of the tide and currents. The wind picked up and the raft seemed to stand still as it battled both a head wind and a strong current.

"I could see that Carlson was concerned about our slow progress," Sergeant McCullough remembered. "He was also worried that the Japs had time to get a sub or surface vessel to where we were. Because we were strafed a lot the second day, they knew we were still on the island."

The fact that Carlson was clearly worried about the fate of his men was hard to discern by looking at his face.

"His expression never really changed the whole time we were on the island," McCullough said. "He would smile a lot, so you had to guess what he was really thinking."

Some of the men were beginning to grumble about the slow pace and whether there were any submarines out there at all. The boats pitched and tossed in the rough seas, snapping a few lines that held them together. Repairs were made quickly. The men hung on to the boats and each other as the waves picked the boats up and tried to break the binds that held them together. It didn't seem possible that a submarine could be waiting in water like this. The men were close to despair once again.

According to Sergeant McCullough, one of the rubber boats had been asking Carlson for permission to break off and paddle ahead of the main raft to try and locate the subs. Carlson, according to McCullough, finally relented and one of the boats, with eight to ten men aboard, paddled off beyond the breakers and into the night. It headed west—toward Southeast Asia.

Meanwhile, McCullough had been periodically signaling with his flashlight as the craft treaded water at the lagoon's mouth. His light was getting dimmer and dimmer. Finally, at 2213, the *Nautilus* spotted a signal from *Lamb's Ark* and responded immediately. The men let out a roar of recognition. More than a few wept uncontrollably, too exhausted and elated to show any other emotion. The paddlers, finding renewed strength, dug in with all they had and it still took almost an hour to reach the submarines.

According to Peatross, who had a ringside seat high atop the conning tower of the *Nautilus*, "It was not until 2308 that the 72 exhausted Raiders in four rubber boats and a wooden outrigger canoe came alongside." (Lieutenant LeFrancois, who was weak from loss of blood from five bullet wounds and admittedly in a daze much of the second day, described the raft as being comprised of three rubber boats and two native outriggers.)

Peatross was shocked at the appearance of the survivors, particularly the battalion's commanding officer.

"As I watched Carlson come aboard, I was astounded at the change in his appearance," Peatross wrote. "He had always been somewhat lanky, but now he was gaunt—a walking skeleton. In the forty-three hours that had passed since I put him aboard the Company A boat for the trip to the beach, he seemed to have aged at least ten years."

Getting the seriously wounded aboard and down the hatch proved to be a delicate maneuver.

"I sat there utterly dazed; then somebody leaned heavily on my wounded shoulder and I was ready to fight again, this time either friend or foe," LeFrancois remembered. "I clambered aboard into the hands of gobs who got me down the hatch into a clean soft white bunk."

It took almost an hour to get everybody aboard the two submarines. There was no time to count noses. That would have to wait until they got back to Hawaii. Once everyone was aboard, the rubber boats were slashed and sent to the bottom along with the outrigger, which was loaded with many souvenirs.

Belowdecks, the feeling was one of utter relief. Most were too exhausted to engage in any celebration, however.

"When we finally got aboard ship the order was given to 'splice up the main brace' and everyone got a good shot of medicinal brandy," Private McCall remembered. He also remembered how completely wiped out everybody was. The men literally collapsed wherever they could, too tired to say anything at all. Their weak smiles communicated all that needed to be said.

"I didn't hear a sound from anyone," McCall said. "It was quieter than a mouse pissin' on a ball of cotton."

"Buck" Stidham, who had made it back to the *Argonaut* on Roosevelt's rubber boat earlier in the day, was so happy to see his comrades again that he didn't know whether to cheer or cry.

"We spent the day (August 18) submerged and feeling pretty bad for the Raiders who didn't make it back," Stidham said. "When they did get back that evening, it was definitely a moment for rejoicing as we greeted buddies we never expected to see again."

The final entry noted in the log of the *Nautilus* that day read: "2353— headed for Pearl Harbor."

Seventeen

"Surf Swimmers"

The first priority on the return trip to Pearl Harbor was to take care of the wounded. The most seriously wounded, including Pvt. Jess Hawkins and Lieutenant LeFrancois, remained with Dr. MacCracken aboard the *Nautilus* so that he could continue the treatment he had begun ashore. The other wounded were divided proportionately between MacCracken and Dr. Stigler, who had come out to the *Argonaut* the previous day.

An attempt was made to assign the Raiders to the same submarine they'd come out on, but they were hopelessly intermingled—and there wasn't time to sort them all out. It was imperative to get under way as soon as possible.

"As the men came aboard, we of course made a hasty accounting of names and numbers," Lieutenant Peatross said, "however, an accurate count at that time was impossible because of the mixing of troops between the two vessels and the fact that no single person had total knowledge of the killed, wounded, and missing. . . . There was no reason to think that anyone had been left ashore."

The wounded were placed in bunks reserved for submarine officers near the wardroom, which was turned into an operating room. The mess table became the operating table. Instruments were sterilized in a pan of boiling water in the small galley.

After having a bite to eat and resting for about an hour, Dr. Mac-Cracken got to work on the most seriously wounded, Private First Class Hawkins. Hawkins had been shot three times in the chest the night before while on guard duty at the departure beach. Two of the wounds were superficial, but the third required five hours of patchwork surgery before he could be declared stable. Had there not been a doctor available, he probably would have died.

Lieutenant LeFrancois was next. It took Dr. MacCracken almost two hours to remove the bullets from his right arm and shoulder.

"After my operation, I was drugged, and I felt that the air was suffocating me," LeFrancois said. "By special courtesy, a tube was installed from the ventilating system to my head, so that I could breathe to my heart's content."

Aboard the *Argonaut*, Dr. Stigler was almost as busy. Those with minor wounds or scrapes waited their turn at the end of the line. Many, like Sergeant Stidham, who noticed that a small wound in his forearm appeared to be infected, didn't even bother.

"When I entered [sickbay], Dr. Stigler was busy with several seriously wounded and looked like he hadn't slept in seventy-two hours," Stidham said. "I did a quick about face and left, since I didn't have the guts to hold up my little ouchy and say, 'Look, Doctor.'"

The submarines churned on, each on a different course, toward Hawaii, getting closer to home each day.

"The several days of relative inactivity on the return trip to Pearl Harbor served everyone well," Peatross wrote. "It gave us a chance to rest up, to soothe our jangled nerves, to reflect on our experiences on the raid, and to begin to think about what might come next."

The strains of "Anchors Aweigh" and "From the Halls of Montezuma" resonated throughout Pearl Harbor as the *Nautilus* slowly motored past Battleship Row on the morning of August 25 and again the following day when the *Argonaut* glided triumphantly past the giant warships to a crowded pier at the U.S. Submarine Base.

As each ship was about to enter the harbor, a call went out for all the Raiders to stop whatever they were doing and come topside. Photographs of the day revealed what a mangy, motley group they were. Unshaven and unwashed, many were wearing clothes given to them by navy personnel. A couple of Raiders were decked out in silk Japanese underwear they had captured on the raid. No two Raiders seemed to be wearing the same uniform—or any uniform at all. Some were in dungarees, others were in dyed-black khaki. Some wore a mixture of both. They were a sight to make a veteran drill instructor weep with shame.

"As we sailed up the entrance of Pearl Harbor, I noticed a broom mounted upside down on the conning tower of the *Nautilus*," Ben Carson said. "Every ship of the line in Pearl Harbor was turned out with formations on deck as we sailed by. I was asked to stand in the rear rank since I was outfitted in a navy work shirt and my own dyed black pants. I did not realize until much later that our return was the reason for the turnout."

Others who lined up on deck knew whom the greeting was for—and would never forget it.

"It was one of the most thrilling parts of my life," Dr. Stigler said. "Each ship that we passed gave us a salute. We must have heard the 'Marine Corps Hymn' ten times going through the channel."

Waiting on the dock was Admiral Nimitz, Marine general Harry Pickett, a Marine honor guard, and the Pacific Fleet Band. One more rendition of the "Marine Hymn" welcomed the Raiders as the *Nautilus* glided to a smooth stop alongside the dock. Lurking at the back of the crowd were a dozen members of the press and a few photographers snapping pictures of the arrival.

Also standing tall on the dock was the rest of the 2d Raider Battalion, including those fifty or so members of A and B Companies who had to be left behind because there wasn't room for them on the two submarines.

One of the latter, Pvt. Harry Reynolds of B Company, stood there with tears streaming down his face. Scuttlebutt had reached Hawaii that his best friend and boyhood pal, Pvt. Bob Maulding, was one of those killed on Makin and would not be coming back.

"I was just devastated," Reynolds recalled many years later. "Before he left [for Makin] he told me how much he loved his mother and sisters and that if he didn't come back how much he wanted me to tell them so for him. He had a premonition. It was scary. I learned a valuable lesson from that. For the rest of the war I never told anybody what I was thinking."

Commodore Haines presented Nimitz with a captured Japanese sword Carlson had given him. Nimitz later hung it on the wall of his office below another one that had been carried by one of the Japanese pilots shot down at Pearl Harbor. A captured Japanese flag, stained with the blood of the enemy, was sent to the Marine commandant, General Holcomb, by Jimmy Roosevelt to be presented to his father at the White House.

"Later, I learned that Pa put on a wonderful show of recoiling from the object and refusing to touch the evil banner," Roosevelt wrote.

Several of the Raiders came off Makin with souvenirs that were confiscated by the officers for "study" by the Marine Corps.

"When I came aboard the *Nautilus* for the return trip to Hawaii I had a Jap rifle with bayonet, a Jap pistol, a leather ammo belt, and a white Japanese sun helmet," Private McCall said. "All of them were later confiscated by battalion order so the souvenirs could be sent to Marine headquarters for study. But I suspect they are in someone's private collection.

"Of all the souvenirs I brought back, the best one of all was yours truly."

Nimitz was beaming as he came aboard the *Nautilus*. He saluted and shook hands all around. He was anxious to hear Carlson's full report. Any press conferences with the media would have to wait. The wounded were taken off first and transported by ambulances to the naval hospital. Then the rest of the Raiders trooped past the crowd to waiting trucks that took them to Camp Catlin and their first good night's sleep in almost three weeks. Haines and Carlson went off to give Nimitz a full briefing.

Nimitz had already been given a brief report on the Makin raid by Haines and Carlson a day after leaving Makin. The commodore broke radio silence to give Nimitz a terse accounting of the raid that he and Carlson had written on August 20 en route to Hawaii. The next day, August 21, Nimitz called in the press to deliver a short briefing on the Makin Raid. It was splashed across the front pages of newspapers throughout the United States and the world the following day, making instant heroes of Carlson and Jimmy Roosevelt.

The Nimitz communiqué to the press was only a few paragraphs and he did not entertain any questions. The number of Japanese killed on the raid was estimated at eighty. American casualties were described as "light" but no number was released to the press. Carlson, on August 20, had given Nimitz an unofficial figure of fourteen Raiders killed and buried on the island and a similar number wounded.

At the time, Carlson had no way of knowing the actual figures of American dead and missing because the two submarines carrying the survivors back to Hawaii were required to observe radio silence with each other. The final accounting had to be delayed until their return to Pearl, when a head count on both submarines could be conducted.

"One of our first acts after the *Argonaut* returned was to hold a muster of the survivors of the Makin raid for the purpose of resolving discrepancies in the count of the missing and the dead," said Lieutenant Peatross. "We still were not certain how many of those reported as missing in action had in fact been killed and vice versa, although on August 18, Carlson himself had gone over the battlefield and counted the dead."

In Carlson's first radio report to Nimitz just a day out of Makin, he said he had lost eleven men, including Captain Holtom, and Peatross's boat had suffered three killed for a total of fourteen. Either Carlson miscounted, which seems unlikely, or he had failed to find the other four bodies later declared as dead. The muster determined that thirty Raiders did not return from the raid. Before a man's status could be changed from missing to killed, at least two eyewitnesses had to testify conclusively that they had seen him killed.

By the evening of August 26, some twelve hours after the return of the *Argonaut*, Nimitz had a much clearer picture of what had actually taken place on Makin, including the surrender-note business. The official figure of American losses was set at thirty. Of that total, eighteen were determined to have been killed and the other twelve were listed as missing. These figures were to be kept strictly confidential for the time being. Also, there was to be no mention of the surrender-note episode. That was to be treated as if it had never happened.

Enemy losses, which would be released to the press, had grown significantly from the eighty originally given to Nimitz back on August 21. The new figures put the total of enemy dead at 350.

On the next day, August 27, and after getting a good night's rest, Carlson and Roosevelt held a joint press conference before a large media contingent that had been primed for a spectacular tale of adventure for nearly a week. The reporters, who had been provided the outline of the raid seven days earlier by Nimitz, were not disappointed. The press were more than ready to give the Makin Raid the same grand coverage they'd given the Doolittle Raid back in April. And that's precisely what they did.

New York Times war correspondent Robert Trumbull's report under the headline "Marines Wiped Out Japanese on Makin Isle in Hot Fighting" was typical of most of the battle reports of the day. Its rather lengthy one-sentence lead paragraph read:

Landing through the surf on the dark, moonless night of August 17, a specially trained force of the United States Marines fought through a screen of machine gunners, grenade throwers, and snipers who were strapped in the tops of palm trees to clean the Japanese out of Makin Island in the Gilberts, Lt. Col. Evans F. Carlson, commander, and Major James Roosevelt, second in command of the expedition, told correspondents here today.

Trumbull's account, which noted that Roosevelt was wearing a bandage on a finger that had been cut by coral, said that the Raiders wiped out a force of about 200 Japanese marines and reinforcements of about

150 more, figures that were said to be ten times the number of casualties suffered by the Americans. A multipage press release was passed out to the media before Carlson and Roosevelt met the media. It contained all the high points the navy and Marine Corps wanted emphasized.

Correspondent James F. Lowery of the *Honolulu Star-Bulletin* was a little more terse in his account of the Makin Raid, but it was just as riveting as Trumbull's.

"United States 'Kung Ho' marines—their memory of Wake still fresh—have completely leveled Makin island," Lowery wrote.

> There are but two Japanese left on that major island of the enemy-held Gilbert group to tell of the attack.
>
> The other 348, there before the "super mobile, super streamlined" marines struck August 17, are dead.
>
> Attacking on a dark moonless night, the marines destroyed all stores, three radio stations, and two enemy planes and withdrew with "light losses."
>
> It is a story of 40 hours of battle in which the marines and navy forces collaborated to completely eliminate a Japanese garrison of 200 men on the island and destroy 150 more on two boats in the lagoon.

Carlson, who did most of the talking at the press conference, said he "ascertained the losses of the enemy through my own survey and reports of the natives, who were very cooperative. There were only two out of the two hundred I could not account for."

Regarding American losses, Carlson said, "They were light and I can tell you we got ten Japanese for every American lost."

Roosevelt was asked by a writer from the *Los Angeles Times* if he managed to shoot down any Japs.

"Fired two shots at snipers," Roosevelt responded with a sheepish grin on his face.

"Would you call [the Raiders] some special name like 'Rough Riders?'" the writer asked Roosevelt.

"No," the president's son responded, "they're more like surf swimmers."

By the time Nimitz sent his official report to his boss in Washington, Admiral King, the Japanese losses had been pared down to between 100 and 150 men "at the cost of 30 of our Marine raiders killed in action and drowned."

There is nothing in Nimitz's report to King about the surrender-note incident, but because of the broadcast by Tokyo Rose, Nimitz almost certainly briefed King on the situation, just as Carlson had felt obliged to brief him.

En route to Pearl from Makin, Lieutenant Peatross interviewed many of the men on the *Nautilus* about the raid as preparation for his own after-action report. He was very anxious to hear Carlson's version of the surrender-note incident, but the Raider commander never brought it up.

"Although I wanted very much to hear about the outcome of the surrender offer, Carlson did not mention it in his briefing, and I sensed that it would be highly untactful of me to bring it up at the time," Peatross wrote. "I assumed that in due course we would have a critique and piece the entire thing together. However, Carlson immersed himself in the single-minded composition of his after-action report and thereafter obviously was not amenable to questions from junior officers or anyone else."

Peatross talked with Private McCall, who had gone on the surrender-note mission with Captain Coyte, and McCall confirmed that the incident had, in fact, taken place. Feeling that it might not be prudent to pursue the matter, Peatross decided to let it drop.

After a few days in Hawaii, Peatross was told by Carlson that Admiral Nimitz wanted to see him the next day. Peatross had no idea what the admiral wanted to talk about but guessed that it might concern the surrender note. The anxiety of a private meeting with the commander of the Pacific Fleet the next day caused Peatross, who had just been promoted to captain, to lose a much-needed good night's sleep.

"Why me?" Peatross asked himself en route to the meeting with Nimitz the next morning. "The only possible thing that I could think of was that he wanted to ask me about Carlson's surrender offer. The surrender note had already got back to Tokyo, and Tokyo Rose was making the most of it, having read it several times in her broadcasts. I couldn't figure out how the admiral could have found out about the surrender offer otherwise. I was reasonably certain that Carlson hadn't told him and almost as certain that the commodore hadn't either. Still, I couldn't be sure. However, if he really wanted to find out about the surrender, why ask me? Why not ask someone who had first-hand information? All I knew was what I had learned from [Sgt.] Lawson and [Pvt.] McCall."

Peatross needn't have worried. Nimitz immediately put him at ease with his calm manner and used the time to offer his personal congratulations on his role in the success of the Makin Raid. Carlson had apparently praised Peatross for his initiative on the raid and Nimitz merely wanted to second his congratulations to those already expressed by Carlson. Peatross was never asked about the surrender incident.

"I had never before in my life spent a more pleasant twenty minutes," a relieved Peatross later wrote. "Expecting to go through a pointed interrogation, then to be rushed in and out of the admiral's office, I instead had spent a thoroughly enjoyable time with a quiet, calm, and utterly unpretentious man who, in a very simple way, made me feel welcome from the very first moment. The meeting with Adm. Chester Nimitz was now the highlight of my young life."

Peatross would not revisit the surrender-note issue again until nearly fifty years later, when he began researching material prior to writing a book on the Raiders. He told those he interviewed that he felt honor bound to write the complete story of the Raiders, "to tell it the way it was and to present an honest, straightforward account of events and individuals—warts and all."

In his interviews with survivors, Peatross discovered that many Raiders either didn't know about the surrender issue or didn't want to believe that such a thing could have happened. "Marines don't surrender," more than a few replied when asked for their opinion, conveniently overlooking the fact that Marines had, in fact, surrendered at Wake Island and in the Philippines. There were some who were unwilling to be part of anything that might cast dispersions on either the name or reputation of Carlson, no matter what the evidence might show.

A surprising number of Raiders had never known about the surrender note and, in later years when the subject was brought up, immediately dismissed the idea as nothing more than scuttlebutt.

That feeling still exists today to some degree in the minds of those still living, despite the fact that the Marine Corps has admitted in writing that a surrender note was, in fact, written and delivered to the Japanese on Makin back in August of 1942.

Eighteen
"Peanuts, Popcorn, Navy Crosses"

A day after the press conference, Roosevelt was sent home to personally brief his father on the Makin mission at the White House. He brought with him a Japanese pistol and flag captured on Makin as souvenirs and a personal letter from Carlson to his father. The letter, dated August 27, 1942, is noteworthy not only for Carlson's praise of Jimmy Roosevelt's leadership but also for Carlson's unshakable faith in the Raider concept despite its obvious difficulties on the Makin Raid.

Dear Mr. President:

I can't tell you how happy I am to be able to send you this note by the hand of Jim.

Jim will give you full details of the raid on Makin Atoll, so I will omit them here except to refer to his own participation.

Naturally I was apprehensive about taking him along, but he was eager to go and I finally decided that this job would provide an admirable opportunity for his initial indoctrination in the mysteries of battle. I did not anticipate that the fighting would be as tough as it turned out to be. This deliberation was, of course, unknown to Jim.

Jim ran my command post during the engagement. He was as cool as the proverbial cucumber and kept the loose ends tied together without a hitch. Sniping was a problem, and the 6.5mm bullets of the Nips were zinging around throughout the morning of the 17th. Time and again I had to tell him to get into a sump hole and stay there so that I could be assured that my communications would continue to function, because he insisted on sticking his neck out to see how things were going. That night we were stuck on the beach. The next morning, when it was possible to get boats through the surf, I had to lay the law down in order to get him to go back to the sub so as to assure that at least one of us would be in a position to carry on with the battalion. I am recommending him for special commendation for his conduct and example. He does not know this yet.

It is a source of deep satisfaction to both of us to see our labors now receive general approbation. Jim and I knew we had the right formula, but it was so unorthodox that the opposition for months was virulent and persistent. I am urging him to convince headquarters while on this trip of the need for building more Raider battalions on this formula while we still have men available who are qualified to indicate the direction and pace.

As Jim will tell you, Admiral Nimitz's support has been consistent and wholehearted. We are both devoted to him.

The only improvement I found in the Japanese fighting technique over what I had seen in China was the perfection of their sniping. We'll lick this aspect too.

We are far from being boastful as a result of this raid. But it is true that this experience with the enemy has filled the men of this battalion with confidence. They know that in an even fight they can lick him hands down. And they have also learned that it is possible to outwit him. With it all, however, the men retain a spirit of humility that is reassuring. Perhaps the reason that most of those who participated "got religion." At our first meeting after our return the whole battalion sang the Doxology with a zest I have never seen or heard before.

We think of you often here and pray for your health and guidance.

With warm personal regards to Mrs. Roosevelt and you, I am,
Sincerely,
Evans Carlson

P.S. I am sending the flag which floated over Makin on our arrival. Jim and I want this to go to you from the Marine Corps, and he will pass it to you through General Holcomb.

The Makin Raid veterans were guests of the U.S. Navy at the swanky Royal Hawaiian Hotel, which had been leased by the navy as a rest area for submarine crews.

The stay at the Royal Hawaiian, which was one of the few hotels on Waikiki Beach at the time, was one continuous party for almost a week. The surviving veterans of the Makin Raid were feted like conquering heroes. Each of the survivors was presented with the submariner's Combat Patrol Pin, a unique honor in the long history of the U.S. Marine Corps.

Several of the submarine personnel set up stills on different floors of the hotel and a steady flow of moonshine was available night and day. So was the native drink of okolehao, known as oke to the American troops.

"The party at the Royal Hawaiian Hotel was a humdinger and a peedoodler," remembered Pvt. William McCall. "The booze came from the sub sailors and it was called torpedo juice. It was grain alcohol. You couldn't drink it, however, until you distilled the croton oil out of it à la M*A*S*H 4077 style. The oil was to prevent the sailors from drinking on duty, as it would give you a real bad case of the Alabama quick step.

"Taken internally it would take out feathers, guts, and all of your gastrointestinal system. The still was set in the head, near the bathtub. The tub was filled with lots of ice cubes and the copper coil was wound through the ice. It ran twenty-four hours a day."

Many of the Raiders, particularly those from the rural South, had experience with stills, but many others had to learn the dangers of drinking unfiltered moonshine the hard way.

"One guy couldn't wait," McCall said, "so he gulped a shot-glass full, croton oil and all. In no time at all he looked like he'd swallowed a flamethrower. It took a whole lot of well water to put that fire out."

Private Ben Carson, who was only six months past his nineteenth birthday at the time, remembers having a thoroughly good time during his brief stay at the Royal Hawaiian.

"One of the first things I noticed was a sign on the door of my hotel room that said the room rate was seventy-four dollars a day. My God, I thought, I could buy a car with that much money," said Carson, who was drawing a pay of twenty-one dollars a month as a "buckass" private (BAP) in the Marine Corps.

Carson was equally impressed with the chow.

"That was some mess hall—the food was great and sailors from the *Argonaut* and the *Nautilus* brought plenty of 'Pink Lady' to distill into consumable booze. The navy introduced fusel oil into the ethyl alcohol that drove the motors on the torpedoes so sailors would develop giant headaches if they drank it as booze. There are probably a dozen recognized ways to remove fusel oil, but the one representing the cheapest and fastest method was pouring 'Pink Lady' through a loaf of French bread which had both ends removed."

Many an unsuspecting Raider overestimated his ability to handle these homemade cocktails and paid the price the following morning with a combat-sized hangover.

Carson had a chance to meet up with his older brother, George, for the first time in two years. George Carson, who was a career navy man, had been stationed on the USS *Maryland* during the attack on Pearl Harbor. The *Maryland* had been spared severe damage back on December 7 because it was moored inboard of the USS *Oklahoma*, which was still capsized at its berth.

"My brother . . . tried to get me to promise to get out of the Raiders. 'You could get killed in that outfit,'" Carson said his brother told him. "I reminded him that the Raiders were well trained, but, even so, I promised to be careful. Two years later my brother died in an accidental explosion of a smoke canister on the deck of the *Maryland.*"

Most of the officers remained back at Camp Catlin, which gave the enlisted men free rein to live it up at the Royal Hawaiian. About the only time officers showed up was to bail out a wayward Raider, who may have ventured into town to sample one of those "wam-bam-scram" joints, as Lieutenant Peatross called them, and return him to the hotel.

Peatross was only too happy to see his men enjoying themselves. They had endured incredible hardships throughout the Makin mission. They had earned all the rest and relaxation they could handle. Peatross had been reminded of all those privations a couple of days earlier when he'd returned to the *Nautilus* to retrieve a book he had been reading on the trip.

"Although the *Nautilus* had been airing out for four days, the odor that hit me full force as I went aboard was the foulest I had ever smelled," Peatross wrote. "The concentrated stench of unwashed human bodies was incredible, and the very thought that we had actually lived aboard this submarine was unbelievable. After picking up the book from the wardroom, I went topside as quickly as possible, reaching fresh air just in time to avoid losing the contents of my stomach."

Meanwhile back at Camp Catlin, the other four companies of the 2d Raider Battalion were kept busy regaling some of the gullible press with accounts of a raid they had never been on.

"The media went into a frenzy trying to get stories about the raid on Makin," remembered Buck Stidham, who was one of those who did go on the raid. "Anybody that had a story to tell got quoted. Some of the tales were true, but most of it was pure baloney. Those of us who actually went on the raid, well, we just laughed as the reporters busily filled up their notebooks."

Over the years, the number of people who would claim to have been on the Makin Raid grew to a point where it was hard to know whom to believe. Some of that selective memory still exists today as those who remember the Raid are in their late seventies or early eighties.

"As you probably know," seventy-seven-year-old Ken McCullough, a bona fide veteran of the Raid, said in a 1999 interview, "If you took everyone's word who said they made the Makin Raid you would have enough people to fill an aircraft carrier."

Another veteran of the Raid, Dean Voight, spoke for many when he frankly admitted he had a difficult time being sure of just what happened on the Makin Raid.

"I only remember things I had fun at," Voight said in a 1999 interview, "so I don't remember much."

Carlson gave one of the best speeches (see Appendix Four) of his career on August 26 during a memorial service to the thirty men who failed to return from the Makin Raid. He delivered the eulogy from the porch of his billet at Camp Catlin. An American flag was pinned to the wall behind him as he took the podium. Most of the Raiders who had participated in the Makin Raid were off celebrating at the Royal Hawaiian Hotel, but there was a sea of cameras and news media present to capture the historic moment.

Dignitaries included Admiral Nimitz and many of his personal staff. The Fleet Band was also present for opening and closing musical numbers. It was a very solemn occasion, reminding many of a church service. It drew huge coverage in the United States, as did a similar speech he gave four months later after the Guadalcanal campaign (see Appendix Five).

The Makin Raid produced a plethora of heroes who were welcomed with loving arms by a nation still feeling the pain of the Pearl Harbor disaster. There were a total of twenty-three Navy Crosses and one Congressional Medal of Honor (see Appendix Three) awarded to the Makin Raiders, the latter posthumously given to Sgt. Clyde Thomason. Most of the officers on the Raid would receive Navy Crosses, among them Com-

modore Haines, Carlson, and Roosevelt, company commanders Coyte
and Plumley, the two doctors, Stigler and MacCracken, and platoon leaders Peatross, Elliot, and LeFrancois. The personnel office at navy headquarters was kept busy with a flurry of paperwork to secure medals and
citations for America's newest heroes.

Nimitz was so impressed by the resourcefulness and initiative of Lieutenant Peatross that he hurried along the paperwork recommending
him for the Navy Cross so that he could personally decorate him at the
earliest convenience. Peatross was the first to be decorated with the Navy
Cross by Nimitz on October 1 on the island of Espíritu Santo. The other
award winners, including Carlson himself, received their medals a few
months later, also on Espíritu Santo.

The generous dispensation of medals to the officers did not go un-
noticed by the enlisted men. Prior to one of the first Gung Ho meetings
held after their return to Hawaii, according to Private Carson, Pfc.
Clarence Healy got up before the officers arrived and, walking up and
down in front of the assembled crowd, called out, "Peanuts, popcorn,
Navy Crosses," just as if he was at the ballpark.

One week after returning to Pearl, the party was over for Carlson's
Raiders as the 2d Raider Battalion was alerted for a new assignment. Mes-
sengers were sent to the Royal Hawaiian Hotel to inform the Raiders that
buses would pick them up at 0900 the next morning to take them back
to Camp Catlin. Some of the men didn't want to leave. Others were so
hung over they were in no condition to leave.

The roundup also included the Honolulu jail, where several of the
Raiders were temporary guests of the local police, charged with the usual
misdemeanors servicemen were prone to commit during wartime, or
peacetime, for that matter.

Peatross remembered that two of his men failed to show up for
muster because they were locked up in a Honolulu brig, charged with
joyriding in a public vehicle. Peatross went down to bail out his men and
had to force himself not to smile or laugh out loud at some of the stories they told to explain why they had failed to report to base.

"While waiting by the highway that passed in front of Camp Catlin,
two raiders had watched the driver of a civilian trolley bus park his vehicle, take his coin changer, and go into the corner grocery store across
the street," Peatross later wrote. "Apparently reasoning that, as long as
the driver was in the store and the bus was not in use, it would be un-

patriotic for two of our nation's finest to be without transportation, so they took the trolley bus for their own personal use. After going about seven miles without mishap, they were stopped by the police and hauled off to jail."

Deals were made and some fines were paid. Eventually, all the Raiders were back at Camp Catlin, packing their bags for another adventure to another unknown destination.

The entire battalion sailed aboard the USS *Wharton* on September 6. The destination would be Espíritu Santo in the New Hebrides Islands, which, at the time, was the primary staging area for most reinforcements going to the southern Solomons–Guadalcanal. Here, they would continue their amphibious training and become part of the floating reserve of Adm. Richard Kelly Turner's Amphibious Task Force.

En route, the veterans of the Makin Raid were called upon to speak to the other men about what they had learned about Japanese tactics and techniques. One of the best speakers was Oscar Peatross, now a captain and commander of B Company.

"Accentuating the positive, I emphasized the importance of physical fitness, small-unit control, and automatic reaction when fired upon," Peatross said. "I stressed the role of our superior firepower over that of the Japanese. . . . I pointed out that the Japanese infantryman with his bolt-action rifle was no match for the Raider with his semiautomatic and automatic weapons."

The doctors gave lectures on jungle diseases, particularly malaria and jaundice, and warned against drinking unpurified water. The men began receiving a daily dosage of Atabrine, an antimalarial drug, a few days before landing.

On September 20, after fourteen days aboard ship, the Raiders arrived at Espíritu Santo, code-named "Base Button." The base was four thousand miles southwest of Hawaii and five hundred miles southeast of Guadalcanal. Peatross figured out that the 2d Raider Battalion had traveled more than fourteen thousand miles from its home base in San Diego in a little more than four months, "getting farther from home all the time and not a bit closer to Japan."

Nineteen

The Long Patrol

Base Button was in the early stages of development in September of 1942, and arriving units like the 2d Raider Battalion were expected to prepare their own billeting facilities, much as they had at Jacques Farm earlier in the year. The troops lived in pup tents for several days until barracks could be built. When finished, the campsite was named Camp Gung Ho.

During the first week at Espíritu Santo, the 1st and 2d Raider Battalions were directed to each transfer two officers and twenty-five enlisted men to nearby Samoa to help stock the formation of the 3d Raider Battalion. And, in early October, Headquarters, Marine Corps, ordered the immediate detachment of Major Roosevelt to San Diego, where he was to form the 4th Raider Battalion.

The 1st Marine Division, with the help of the 1st Raider Battalion, had carved out a perimeter around Henderson Field on nearby Guadalcanal in early August and had fought off every Japanese attempt to retake the island. Though the landing back on August 7 had been virtually unopposed, the American foothold on Guadalcanal, thanks to a steady stream of Japanese reinforcements, was still very much in doubt. In early October, Japanese forces on Guadalcanal numbered about 20,000, slightly less than the American total.

Those Marines and soldiers on Guadalcanal listened to radio broadcasts that emphasized the peril of the situation. "The shadows of a great conflict lie heavily over the Solomons—all that can be perceived is the magnitude of the stakes at issue," stated an editorial in the *New York Herald Tribune* on October 16.

That same day, when a reporter asked Secretary of the Navy Frank Knox if the Americans could hold Guadalcanal, Knox was less than optimistic.

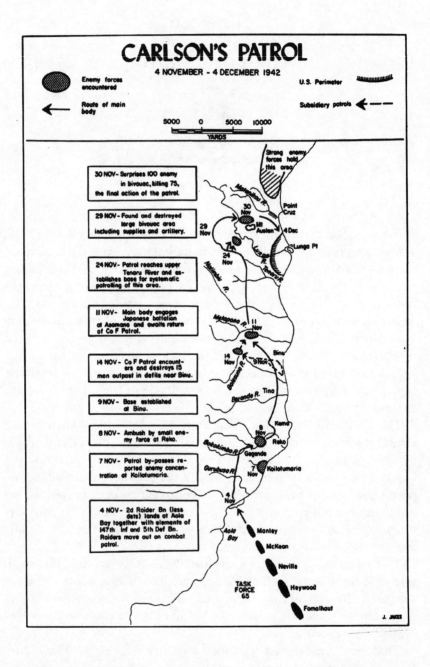

CARLSON'S PATROL
4 NOVEMBER - 4 DECEMBER 1942

Enemy forces encountered

Route of main body

U.S. Perimeter

Subsidiary patrols

5000   0   5000   10000
YARDS

Strong enemy forces hold this area

30 NOV- Surprises 100 enemy in bivouac, killing 75, the final action of the patrol.

29 NOV- Found and destroyed large bivouac area including supplies and artillery.

24 NOV- Patrol reaches upper Tenaru River and establishes base for systematic patrolling of this area.

11 NOV- Main body engages Japanese battalion at Asamana and awaits return of Co F Patrol.

14 NOV- Co F Patrol encounters and destroys 15 men outpost in defile near Binu.

9 NOV- Base established at Binu.

8 NOV- Ambush by small enemy force at Reko.

7 NOV- Patrol by-passes reported enemy concentration at Koilotumaria.

4 NOV- 2d Raider Bn (less dets) lands at Aola Bay together with elements of 147th Inf and 5th Def Bn. Raiders move out on combat patrol.

Matanikau R.
Point Cruz
30 Nov
Mt Austen
4 Dec
Lunga Pt
29 Nov
Lunga R.
Tenaru R.
7 Nov
24 Nov
Nalimbiu R.
Malapono R.
11 Nov
14 Nov
9 Nov
Binu
Bokokimbo R.
Balesuna R.
Berande R.   Tina
Gurubusa R.
Kema
8 Nov
Reko
Gegende
7 Nov
Koilotumaria
4 Nov

Aola Bay
Manley
McKean
Neville
Heywood
Fomalhaut

TASK FORCE 65

J. JAKES

"I certainly hope so and expect so," Knox said. "I will not make any predictions, but every man will give a good account of himself. What I am trying to say is that there is a good stiff fight going on. Everybody hopes we can hold on."

Carlson wasted little time in letting the Marine Corps know that he and his battalion were ready and anxious for action on Guadalcanal. He traveled to the island to meet with 1st Marine Division commander Gen. Archie Vandegrift and had met with Adm. Chester Nimitz and Adm. Richmond Kelly Turner when the two visited Espíritu Santo in late September.

Peatross also had a meeting with Nimitz on October 1 aboard the USS *McCawley*, Admiral Turner's flagship, which was anchored at Espíritu Santo. Carlson told Peatross early that morning that he, Peatross, was to represent the battalion in a small ceremony at 1100. Peatross wasn't told until he boarded the ship that he was to receive the Navy Cross for his leadership on the Makin Raid from Nimitz himself. The other Navy Cross winners from the Makin Raid would receive their medals several months later.

During October, Carlson made two more trips to Guadalcanal to plead his unit's case for any piece of the fighting going on there. The second visit paid off. The 2d Raider Battalion was given the assignment of providing security for naval construction units while they landed the personnel and equipment required to build an airfield at a place called Aola Bay, forty miles east of the defensive position around Henderson Field. The Raiders would be relieved by army units after two or three days and return to Espíritu Santo.

Carlson would take only two of his companies (C and E) on the mission but cautioned the other four to be prepared to move on six hours' notice. If Carlson was disappointed at this rather tame assignment, he didn't let on. He had gotten his foot in the door at Guadalcanal and for now, that was all that mattered to him.

On October 31, the battalion command group along with Companies C and E sailed to Guadalcanal, where they were scheduled to land in the early-morning hours of November 3. Heavy rain postponed the landing one day, and the Raiders landed unopposed the next. They were relieved the following day, November 5, by the Army's 1st Battalion, 147th Infantry.

Fate then intervened to extend the Raiders' mission. Just before they were to climb aboard troopships for a return to Espíritu Santo, General

Vandegrift issued orders for them to march overland to the west to cut off any Japanese who might try to escape in their direction. Vandegrift's order was delivered to Carlson by airplane drop. Meanwhile, the two troop transports were to return to Espíritu Santo, pick up three more Raider companies (B, D, and F), and return to Guadalcanal, where they would join their battalion.

Carlson had gotten just what he wanted, another chance to show how good his battalion was. Or maybe it was a chance to atone for the mistakes made on the Makin Raid. He smiled broadly at the prospect.

Carlson huddled with his officers and senior NCOs the night of November 5 to roughly map out the course of action. He would leave a small party at Aola Bay to resupply the column with food every four days, transporting the rations by landing craft to a prearranged point on the coast. There a patrol with carriers would meet the boat and man-pack the supplies inland to the patrol base. The three additional companies in his battalion would join up with him at one of these prearranged points.

At daylight on November 6, Carlson and his command group, two Raider companies, and a group of native scouts and carriers under Maj. John Mather of the Australian army, set out on a march—later dubbed the "long patrol"—that wouldn't stop until December 4. Carlson pushed his battalion all the way, often moving ahead of the main body to speed up the march.

The terrain on Guadalcanal was a lot different from Makin. Guadalcanal was covered by a dark, deep jungle with a damp, rotting smell. Tree roots, branches, and grasping vines slowed progress to a crawl in places. The rivers ran deep and fast, especially after heavy rains. The place was crawling with six-inch land crabs and foot-long lizards.

For a month their food consisted of raisins, tea, bacon, salt, sugar, and rice. There were all kinds of rice, polished rice, unpolished, coarse Japanese rice, boiled rice, fried rice, raw rice, rice mixed with anything available, and rice with rice.

"To this day I refuse to eat any rice," Pvt. Ben Carson said many years later.

Before the march was over, 225 men came down with malaria, dengue fever, dysentery, ringworm, and other maladies the doctors called jungle rot. Yet Carlson and his men never wavered.

Carlson moved his force along jungle trails to the west on a three-day hike to a small village called Binu, located ten miles upriver from the coast. He selected Binu as a base camp primarily because it was located only about three miles southeast of the enemy force entrapped near Metapona, which placed the Raiders in position to block the movement of any escapees to the east and south. Also, Binu was the last inhabited village between the Balasuna River and the 1st Marine Division perimeter and could provide a source of native carriers as well as information on enemy activities in recent weeks.

Meanwhile, three more companies of Raiders (B, D, and F) had landed at Aola Bay on November 8. They received orders to move by landing craft the next day fifteen miles westward along the coast to Tasimboko, where guides would be waiting to lead them the next day, November 10, to Binu.

Early the next morning, the three Raider companies set out to find Carlson at Binu. The maps they carried, they quickly discovered, were of little help.

"As our maps were grossly inaccurate with almost no topographical detail, we probably would never have made it to Binu in one day, if at all, had it not been for our native guides," Captain Peatross said.

By early afternoon, Peatross reported in to Carlson at Binu. There had been only one casualty when a native guide, operating from the point, was wounded in the leg.

Carlson briefed the newly arrived Raider companies on the battalion's new mission, which was to conduct aggressive patrols on the division perimeter, adding that he didn't know how far or for how long they would be out. A patrol earlier that day had made contact with the 2d Battalion, 7th Marines, and confirmed that an enemy force of about 3,000 had escaped from the American ring encircling them nearby on the Metapona River. They were hungry and tired, and probably dispirited now that they had orders to retrace their steps back to the western side of the perimeter. But they were still a formidable force.

Carlson was determined to patrol the entire division perimeter so that General Vandegrift could have an accurate and detailed enemy situation report to pass on to the army commander, Gen. Alexander Patch, when the latter took over in December.

"My plan of operation is to fan out strong combat patrols to search for the enemy, each patrol reporting to the battalion CP by radio contact every two hours," Carlson told his officers. "Once contact is made, I will concentrate the patrols as needed to destroy the enemy. As the enemy is cleared from our front, I plan to move the base forward and repeat the tactical cycle. One company will be retained at the base to provide security."

Vandegrift had already approved of Carlson's plan and also gave him permission to bring his final company (A) to Guadalcanal from Espíritu Santo.

The next day, November 11, the battalion fanned out to look for the enemy. B Company, under Captain Peatross, remained behind as base security; C Company, under Capt. Hal Throneson, patrolled to the west toward the division perimeter; E Company, under Capt. Dick Washburn, moved north toward the sea and then west to reconnoiter a trail recently cut by native scouts; D Company, under Capt. Charles McAuliffe, moved on a parallel course to E Company; and F Company, under Capt. Bill Schwerin, headed north. D Company was only a platoon at this point because Carlson had used most of its manpower to fill out the remaining companies prior to departing Espíritu Santo.

Besides providing base security, B Company was also required to have ready one reinforced rifle platoon to rush to any of the patrols should they run into trouble.

Shortly after 1000, C Company radioed base camp that it was pinned down by an enemy force estimated to be a reinforced company armed with rifles, automatic rifles, machine guns, mortars, and 20mm guns. Carlson ordered D and E Companies to move on the enemy force from the north. Also thrown into the fray was an "alert platoon" from B Company.

At around 1130, E Company radioed that it had encountered about two enemy companies.

"As only an occasional message came into the battalion command post, our picture of the overall situation was vague, as it usually is in the heat of battle," Peatross said. "Sensing the battlefield noises, however, it sounded as though Company D was receiving the worst of it and was being pounded heavily by enemy mortars."

About two hours later, a haggard D Company commander, Captain McAuliffe, and nine of his men unexpectedly stumbled into base camp.

"To a man, they reminded me of the Raiders we had picked up at the mouth of the lagoon on the second night of the Makin Raid," Peatross said. "I accompanied Mac to the battalion command post and listened as he reported to Carlson that, as far as he knew and except for the men who were with him, his company had been annihilated."

McAuliffe had been with his point squad when he was pinned down and cut off from the rest of his company. Two of his men had been killed. Carlson tried to maintain a calm demeanor, but inside he was furious. He quickly ordered Peatross to take a platoon and find the rest of D Company. Moments later, however, the rest of the skeleton company began straggling in to the base camp. In those few moments, Carlson had relieved McAuliffe as company commander for what he later described in his after-action report as a "total ineptitude for leadership in battle."

Carlson took Company F and rushed out to see what was happening to C Company. According to Carlson's after-action report, he found C Company commander Captain Throneson "disorganized" and in "a daze." The company had five men killed. Several days later, Carlson would relieve Throneson for demonstrating what he called "marked ineptitude and incompetency in action."

Company E also had an interesting day on November 11. The lead platoon, commanded by Carlson's son, Lt. Evans C. Carlson, caught an enemy patrol by surprise at a river crossing and inflicted heavy casualties. Carlson later received a Silver Star for his action. When the enemy brought up reinforcements, however, E Company commander Captain Washburn, unable to contact base camp by radio, decided on his own to withdraw back to the battalion command post. During a night disengagement, two of his men were killed and a third died from wounds the following day.

The Raiders had suffered ten killed on their first day of active patrolling on November 11 and had one of its company commanders relieved for "ineptitude." Carlson was bitterly disappointed in the performance of his Raiders but tried hard not to show it.

Carlson had decided to move his command post from Binu to the empty village of Asamana on the Metapona River. Asamana was a little farther west toward the 1st Marine Division perimeter and a little closer to where he thought the enemy was hiding.

"Upon occupying Asamana, we found tacked to the trees near the center of the village small signs in Japanese assigning areas to various companies—at least enough to make up a battalion," Peatross wrote. "In all probability this was the designated assembly area for the enemy troops who had broken out of the encirclement near Metapona, but having reached it first, all we had to do was wait for the enemy to come to us, which it seemed they were determined to do."

The Raiders watched and waited, picking off a stray Japanese soldier or two who wandered into the village obviously believing it was still occupied by their troops.

While digging foxholes that first night, the Raiders suddenly discovered they were not alone in the village.

"Selecting a promising site, I set to digging with a will, if not great enthusiasm," Peatross wrote many years later. "After excavating only eight inches or so of the muddy earth, my entrenching tool encountered something firm but certainly not a rock. Thinking that I had come upon some long-abandoned household item, I probed around in the clammy earth with my fingers to determine what I had uncovered. Suddenly to my great surprise and no little revulsion my fingers were tracing out the unmistakable features of a human head: chin, lips, nose, eye sockets. The obstacle to my digging was the recently buried corpse of a Japanese soldier."

Trying another site to dig, Peatross found the same thing.

"The entire mud floor of our hut was lined with bodies—literally a Japanese military cemetery. If our hut were a random sample, then the estimate of 120 killed the day before would have been very conservative," Peatross said.

The next day, November 13, the Raiders called in artillery fire on a massed column of enemy soldiers spotted advancing on their position. Some of the shells nearly hit Captain Throneson's C Company, which was moving up to support the base at Asamana. Throneson was visibly upset and let Colonel Carlson know about it. After resting up the next day, the battalion hiked back to its old base camp at Binu, where a new supply of rations had arrived.

"Each man received a cake of lye soap, which we needed badly," Peatross remembered. "Although I had been soaked in the river and drenched with rain several times since spending the night with the dead Japanese, my clothes still reeked of the sickeningly sweetish odor of decaying flesh, and the opportunity to bathe was most welcome. After posting security, one company at a time went into the river and washed up."

Later that night at an operations briefing, Peatross noticed that C Company commander Captain Throneson was conspicuously absent. Apparently Throneson, who had had several run-ins with Carlson both at Espíritu Santo and on Guadalcanal, had been "disrespectful" to his commander and the latter had relieved him on the spot.

Peatross took strong exception to the relief of Throneson, particularly the strong wording of the latter's fitness report, filed later by Carlson. If

Throneson had been inept back on November 11, Peatross wondered, why did he wait three more days to relieve him?

"Carlson [alleged] that Throneson lost control of his company and failed to maintain contact with the enemy as ordered and implies that the company was held up for four hours by a handful of snipers," Peatross wrote. "However, if these be grounds for the summary relief of a commander, then Carlson should have been relieved by Commodore Haines on the first day at Makin. There Carlson had permitted his two companies to be held up for well over four hours by a dozen or so snipers. . . . But Carlson was no Haines, and unfortunately another good officer joined the ever-growing list of those who had come a cropper of Evans Fordyce Carlson."

The battalion moved back to its base at Asamana and increased its patrolling to the west and south toward Mount Austen, which overlooked the 1st Marine Division perimeter. The patrols were to destroy enemy bases and seek out and destroy enemy artillery pieces, called "Pistol Petes" by the Marines, which had been delivering harassing fire on Henderson Field for weeks.

A patrol from F Company, under Lt. James Jacobson, surprised a fifteen-man enemy contingent that had stopped to eat. The patrol killed all fifteen without any casualties of their own, earning Jacobson a Silver Star.

Most of the patrols were uneventful. The Raiders found the jungle to be a bigger hassle than the enemy.

Private Ben Carson remembers climbing in and out of rivers for hours. Not that he minded. The cool waters were refreshing and helped wash away the sweat and stench of constant patrolling.

"While wading through a stream I reached down and scooped a handful of water to my mouth," Carson said. "Dr. Stigler was right behind me and he gave me hell for drinking river water. 'Use your purification tablets,' he told me."

A few minutes later, as the patrol moved farther upstream, Carson came upon two dead Japanese soldiers, badly bloated and lying by the riverbank.

"Hey, Doc," Carson whispered back to Stigler. "Think your pills will help these guys?"

Over the next week, the men conducted short patrols and returned to base camp to attend to their sore feet. Many had blisters and jungle rot of some kind. A few had to be evacuated because of malaria and jaundice. On November 25, A Company arrived from Espíritu Santo, giving Carlson a full battalion on Guadalcanal for the first time.

On the twenty-fifth, a squad patrol from B Company discovered a cache of about one hundred weapons in an old Japanese bivouac area about two miles south of Henderson Field. Captain Peatross rushed up to the site to see for himself.

"The rifles were in stacks of four, as if a company had halted, dressed ranks, stacked arms, and fallen out to take a break from which it never returned," Peatross said. Many of the rifles were given to the native guides, which proved to be a great source of pride.

The base camp moved once again, to the upper reaches of the Tenaru River and even closer to the division perimeter.

On November 28, a patrol headed by Captain Schwerin located an artillery position near the Tenaru River. There was no gun at the site, but there was a quantity of 75mm ammunition. Also, a well-traveled trail led westward toward Mount Austen. Two days later, using ropes to scale up and down some ridges, a patrol found a 75mm mountain gun and a 37mm antitank gun. The Raiders dismembered both weapons, scattering parts along the ridges.

"Both were in excellent condition and obviously well maintained," Peatross said. "I could not help but wonder at and admire the Herculean effort it must have taken to move it and its smaller companion from the coast through some of the most rugged terrain on Guadalcanal."

Not too far away, a six-man squad from F Company, under Cpl. John Yancey, had surprised a group of almost a hundred enemy soldiers seeking cover from the pouring rain under makeshift shelters. Most of the Japanese soldiers were killed in their shelters and many others were picked off trying to flee the scene. Carlson called Yancey's actions "the most spectacular of any of our engagements," and heartily recommended him for the Navy Cross.

The enemy bivouac area may have been a rest area or hospital site. Two days later, a patrol from B Company came upon a group of ten enemy soldiers sitting around a small fire on a large sand spit that jutted out into the river. All were killed in a single burst of fire.

"They were a pitiful sight," Captain Peatross said of the enemy troops killed during the last few days of the patrol, "emaciated beyond words, pale and sickly looking; one had a crutch and another had a crude homemade splint on his leg. Their uniforms were in rags, and although each had a rifle, not one had a full clip of ammunition."

Meanwhile, Carlson had been given orders by General Vandegrift to terminate his activities and begin returning to the division perimeter on December 3. He decided to have his battalion enter the perimeter from two directions. Companies C, D, and E, under Captain Washburn, would proceed down the Tenaru River and enter near the coast, while the other three companies, led by Carlson, would complete the sweep over Mount Austen and enter from the southwest, thus completing a full circuit of the perimeter.

Carlson, of course, picked the more dangerous route for himself.

"A patrol has just reported to me that on top of Mount Austen, in a spiderweb of ridges, is a very strong Jap position," Carlson told his men. "The Jap position is unoccupied. If we get up there in a hurry, we can take those positions; we can relieve the pressure on Henderson Field. We can find out how strong the enemy is there. This will help our command to make a more accurate estimate of the situation. It may mean cutting down the time it will take to finish up Guadalcanal. It would be a good thing, wouldn't it? We're going to do it because it's important, because we're fitted to do it and in a position to do it."

It was also the hard way to enter the perimeter.

Within fifteen minutes after A Company, led by Capt. Bert Gary, reached the crest of Mount Austen, an enemy patrol was spotted. Giving chase, Lt. Jack Miller, GySgt. Victor "Transport" Magahakian, and two others were seriously wounded.

Miller was wounded by an American-made Thompson submachine gun, perhaps one captured from the 2d Raiders following the Makin Raid. Peatross found the whole situation "eerie."

"Jack Miller had been slated to take the 2d Platoon of Company A to Makin," Peatross said, "but just before we left he broke an arm and, much to his disappointment, had to be left behind. Now less than four months later he was wounded by a weapon that we might have lost on Makin."

Peatross had another eerie moment a little while later when he went to examine a thought-to-be dead Japanese soldier for intelligence information. The soldier suddenly jumped to his feet and grabbed for his rifle. Colonel Carlson spotted the action and yelled to Peatross to "shoot the bastard."

"I whirled about [and] brought up my shotgun and squeezed the trigger just as he was bringing his rifle to bear on me," Peatross said. "The impact of the buckshot spun him about and dropped him with his head resting a few inches from my boots, his face up, and his eyes open and focused on me."

Peatross searched the body and came across a picture of what he took to be his wife and children. It gave him great sadness.

"For the very first time I saw my 'enemy' not as a ravening beast but as another human being," Peatross said, "and I felt sorry for him and his loved ones but not for his country, not for the political system that brought him to this end."

The next morning, December 4, B Company took the point for the climb down Mount Austen. They hadn't gone a hundred yards when a Japanese machine gun opened fire, killing the first two men and wounding a third. Private First Class Cyrill Matelski led a three-man fire team to seek out and destroy the gun.

"We all three saw someone in a GI helmet," recalled fire-team member Ben Carson. "Matelski hollered, 'Ahoy Raider,' [but] it was a Jap in the American helmet and that son-of-a-bitch dropped Matelski with a shot right between the eyes."

Matelski and Carson were buddies from the Makin Raid and had spent a great deal of time together at the week-long party at the Royal Hawaiian Hotel when they returned to Pearl Harbor.

The machine gun was finally silenced by Cpl. Orin Croft, who crawled to within fifty yards of the shooter and blew him away with a BAR, which earned him a Silver Star.

F Company took the lead as B Company stopped to bury its three dead. The wounded man, Pvt. Stuyvesant Van Buren, was carried past Peatross near the burial site. "Captain, how am I doing now?" Van Buren asked, referring to the time he and a buddy had appropriated a trolley bus and driven it to Honolulu a few days prior to shipping out to Espíritu Santo. After bailing him out of jail, Peatross had promised him a promotion if he behaved himself for the next three months.

"Hold on to your stretcher," Peatross told him. "It's all downhill from here." Van Buren could not hold on, however. He died of his wounds in the division hospital the next day.

Carlson was concerned about the condition of Lt. Jack Miller, who had been wounded the day before. Despite constant care by two doctors, he appeared to be worsening by the minute. Finally, halfway down the north slope of Mount Austen and within site of the division perimeter, he died.

Carlson hiked back up the trail to give Miller a burial service. He took out a small American flag and put it on Miller's body and said a prayer from his Bible. "Father," he said, "accept this body of Jack Miller to Thine own. . . .Thou knowest he knew the reasons for which he fought. Give him peace. Amen." Miller was later awarded the Navy Cross.

Without further enemy contact, the three companies entered the division perimeter by midafternoon. The Raiders hiked another eight miles to their bivouac area, marching past the other Marine veterans along the way.

"It was a thrill to see them on the edge of the road, waving as we passed by, and it made us feel pretty important," Peatross said.

During their month-long patrol, the Raiders had hiked some 150 miles to cross a straight-line distance of 30 to 40 miles, fought several battles of varying size, killed 488 Japanese soldiers, and captured and destroyed large amounts of equipment and ammunition. The Raiders earned five Navy Crosses.

The losses were 16 killed and 19 wounded. Nonbattle losses totaled 225, which included 125 from malaria, 71 from ringworm or jungle rot, and 29 from of dysentery. None of those who survived the "Long Patrol" came away completely healthy.

Companies C and F had landed at Aola Bay with 133 officers and men each. They entered the perimeter on December 4 with a combined total of 57 Marines, barely one-fifth their original strength. The other four companies suffered similar attrition.

Twenty

End of the Raiders

They say that the Raiders
Are coming to Tulagi
But Colonel Carlson says no;
It isn't the season.
But that's not the reason.
They're in Hollywood
Making *Gung Ho!*
    —Marine Raiders' sung to the tune of the song "Bless 'Em All."

The 2d Raider Battalion became the second Marine outfit in the war to earn a Presidential Unit Citation (see Appendix Six), for their remarkable achievements on the "long patrol." President Roosevelt had cited the Marine Force at Wake Island the previous January for its gallant two-week stand against the Japanese before being forced to surrender on December 23.

Carlson would earn his third Navy Cross at Guadalcanal for his "long patrol" behind enemy lines but the publicity he and his unit engendered, which was viewed by many of the Marine Corps brass as self-serving, may have signaled the beginning of the end for both the Raider concept and Carlson's own career as a commander.

The regular Marine Corps had grown increasingly weary of the publicity surrounding Carlson's exploits. They had grown tired and disgusted with what they perceived as a glory hound. A photograph of Carlson sitting on the hood of his jeep talking to reporters, one of whom was the famed journalist Richard Tregaskis, after his month-long march on Guadalcanal, was plastered in every newspaper in America. Film of the event also ran in every theater in the country.

The print media was particularly receptive to Carlson's charm. Carlson's friend from his early days in China, pro-Communist writer Agnes Smedley, lionized the leader of the 2d Raider Battalion to millions of readers in America when she wrote:

> Carlson is one of those dangerous men of lean and hungry look. He's a throwback from our own distant revolutionary past—a mixture of Tom Paine, John Brown—with a touch of Lincoln. But all of him is New England—craggy and grim in appearance, yet kindly and philosophical.

Smedley's article praised the 2d Raider Battalion for its success as a guerrilla unit in Guadalcanal, where it was credited with killing an estimated 480 to 800 Japanese while losing only sixteen men.

"More significant," Smedley wrote, "was the battalion's lack of a single mental casualty at a time when our South Pacific hospitals were filled with mental crack-ups because men did not know why they were called upon to endure indescribable suffering and perhaps die in a war caused by God knows what."

The continuing publicity around Carlson's Raiders exasperated 1st Marine Division commander Alexander Vandegrift, whose unit had been slogging away on Guadalcanal since August 7, yet appeared to take a backseat to the more colorful and controversial 2d Raiders. Carlson's march even seemed to overshadow a brilliant performance by the 1st Raider Battalion in mid-September, one that probably saved Guadalcanal from being retaken by the Japanese. That action had earned its leader, Lt. Col. Merritt Edson, a Congressional Medal of Honor and a promotion to full colonel. Vandegrift would also be awarded the Medal of Honor before moving on to become commandant of the Marine Corps the following year.

By early 1943, word within the Marine Corps had gone back and forth from Washington to the Pacific that something had to be done with Carlson's Raiders. They were being made too much of. It was getting so that people in the States thought of Carlson's Raiders instead of the Marine Corps. There was too much publicity, too many editorials, and too many radio speeches. It seemed that without "Gung Ho" no Marine outfit could be any good.

Carlson was the man *New York Times* military editor Hanson W. Baldwin was probably thinking of when he wrote that Marines have a "tendency to move into publicity vacuums."

Of course, nothing official was said or done by the Marine Corps brass about Carlson or the Raiders for fear that it might draw the wrath of President Roosevelt, who still considered them his "pet" outfit. But the envy and paranoia were palpable. Remarks were overheard in high places that the Raiders were nothing but arrogant prima donnas and a bunch of publicity hounds. The widely acclaimed "Gung Ho boys" of Evans Carlson were not very popular with their brother Marines either. The "ordinary" Marines, if such a description could be made, did not agree that the Raiders deserved to be singled out as exceptional.

Even the Raiders' colorful motto of "Gung Ho" came under criticism. The grunts on Guadalcanal sneered at the colorful epithet. If the Marine Corps's own slogan of "Semper Fidelis" was often interpreted to mean "I got mine, how'd you make out?" the Raider's Chinese expression of "Gung Ho" was taken to really mean, "Which way's the photographer?"

The general staff of the Marine Corps had come to the conclusion that more than a firm hand and a watchful eye were needed to keep this group in their place.

More and more, the Marine brass began to realize that merely keeping an eye on Carlson and the Raiders was not enough. Many felt they had to be stopped if the Corps hoped to survive after the war as a separate fighting force with all its supporting air and artillery. Some felt the postwar Marine Corps would consist only of a regiment or two of commandos.

Carlson saw it coming, of course. As President Roosevelt's attention was diverted to other operations both in Europe and the Pacific as the war heated up, pressure against Carlson by the Marine establishment became more overt. The Raiders were denied many of the creature comforts given other units that were pulled off the line, things like showers, movies, post exchange privileges, and even lumber to improve their campsites. Carlson refused to make an issue of these deprivations because it might be inferred that he was once again asking for special favors. His men, who had always been loyal to him, began to grumble behind his back. Some turned on him, blaming him for shortages that did not seem to befall other units.

In February of 1943, Carlson addressed his men on the first anniversary of the unit's formation and found it necessary to remind them and himself what the Raiders were all about. Carlson realized that all the values he held dear were under assault from without and within. It was a pep talk that sounded more like a good-bye.

Carlson called his men "pioneers," who would look back on their military service with great pride.

"Possibly there are those among you who do not realize how far you have come and what you have accomplished," he said. "Our goal was to create and perfect a cohesive, smooth-functioning team which, by virtue of its harmony of action, unity of purpose, and its invincible determination, would be able to outpoint the enemy on every count.

"What were the requisites? First, the quality of leadership. Leaders must invariably be professionally competent; they must be honest, especially honest intellectually, admitting their mistakes when they make them and endeavoring to correct them. It was necessary that officers live close to their men, studying them, encouraging them, and teaching them not only military technique and maneuvers but basic ethical doctrines as well. They must cheerfully and willingly forego those superficial privileges which ordinarily insulate officers from their men and impair mutual sympathy and understanding. They must share the hardships and privations of those they lead and prove by their character and ability their qualifications for leadership. Only in this way could full confidence be engendered and a harmony of spirit prevail. The basis of leadership is merit.

"Most important, though, was the development of what we call the Gung Ho spirit: our ability to cooperate—work together," he told his troops. "Not only was it imperative to understand this spirit; it was even more imperative to apply it to daily actions no matter how unimportant they might seem. This called for self-discipline and implicit belief in the doctrine of helping the other fellow. Followed through to its ultimate end it would mean that each, while helping the other fellow, would in turn be helped by him.

"It was in the matter of Gung Ho that we made our slowest progress, though progress we have made. We were handicapped by our native background, that background in which greed and rugged individualism predominated. Human beings are creatures of habit. Human nature does not change its coat without a struggle. But Rome wasn't built in a day. The important thing was for each individual to have the desire to help the other fellow, the desire to achieve that mastery over his mind, his body, and his desires that he might succeed in disciplining himself. This means tolerance of ideas, tolerance of personal eccentricities, the sweeping away of personal prejudices, concentration on an effort to see the good in human beings of all types and persuasions.

What a task; what a task! As I say, we have made progress, great progress, but we still have a long way to go before we attain that degree of perfection which will rid this outfit of petty friction and will make us a living harmonious entity.

"Finally, it was necessary to the success of this military pattern of ours that individuals understand the reasons for which they fight and offer themselves for sacrifice. Hope for glory will carry some men a long way in battle; pride in the outfit and the desire not to let your buddies down is an even more potent force; but the force which impels men to carry on when the going is tough and victory appears to be remote is a deep spiritual conviction in the righteousness of the cause for which he fights and in the belief that victory will bring an improved social pattern wherein his loved ones and the loved ones of future generations will enjoy a greater measure of happiness and well- being than was his lot. And so it has been an unfailing policy in this organization to articulate for you and constantly to remind you of the reasons why we endure and fight and sacrifice."

Carlson then got personal, giving the men a hint of the pressures he had been under from his superiors.

"Do you suppose these past months since we first came together have been without discouragement for me?" he asked. "I hesitate to tell you how low my spirits have been at times, or how thin my faith has worn. But never has it been completely extinguished. Many of you have been a great trial to me, both officers and men. But always, even in the darkest moments, my faith in your ultimate ability to master yourselves, my faith in your desire to do the right thing, has remained with me."

Carlson also addressed the grumblings he had heard about all the hardships they were facing compared to those back in the States who were living the life of ease.

"Yes, I know what you are thinking," Carlson said, looking straight at his men. "There are men back home who serve in places of safety and where conditions are more comfortable. What a hell of a war effort we would make if each jockeyed with the other for the soft jobs! We must be honest with ourselves and our convictions. And remember this, the right to determine the pattern of life we shall have in our country after the war belongs to those who have had the courage to suffer pain and privation and who have persistently offered themselves for sacrifice. It belongs to such as you. Our job, yours and mine, is to see this thing through. By so doing we raise ourselves to be peers among men. Ours is the satisfaction of having done the job. No one, nothing, can ever rob us of this achievement.

"Remember, too, that those who serve in factories and offices and on the farm back home are also making essential contributions to the war effort. We on the firing line could not do our job without their uncompromising effort to produce and transport to us the means with which to fight. There is such a thing as division of labor in war as well as in peacetime production. Each contributes according to his ability and his talent; each receives according to his needs. Gung Ho is the watchword for not only this battalion, but for all units of the armed services and for all those who labor on the home front.

"Our contribution is to fight and win battles. In your ability and willingness to continue to make this sublime contribution I have the fullest confidence. May that Supreme Being who has guided us with such infinite wisdom in the past continue to watch over, protect, and guide you, bringing us to victory and a richer fulfillment of life's obligations."

During March of 1943, when his unit was shuffled from Wellington, New Zealand, to Espíritu Santo, Carlson felt he was fighting for the life of his battalion against enormous and ever-increasing odds. Jimmy Roosevelt had been sent home the previous October to organize a 4th Raider Battalion. The link Carlson had with the president was gone and he would never get it back. The 3d Raider Battalion had been formed in September under Lt. Col. Harry B. Liversedge and was now awaiting assignment in the South Pacific.

The coup de grace occurred in mid-March, when the 1st Marine Raider Regiment was organized on Espíritu Santo. Liversedge was named commanding officer and Carlson was made executive officer. A week later, Lt. Col. Alan Shapley took over command of the 2d Raiders. He was an orthodox line officer who had earned a Navy Cross on board the *Arizona* during the attack on Pearl Harbor on December 7. He let it be known that he felt the Makin Raid had been a "fiasco" and that he had no interest in "Gung Ho."

Carlson couldn't help but get the message. It was payback time. He was being kicked upstairs to a position where he could no longer generate any more publicity. With the war speeding up and millions of men now in uniform on two fronts, Carlson could no longer count on any special treatment from the commander-in-chief. He had been firmly shoved aside and there wasn't anything he could do about it.

Carlson was never again allowed to have direct command of men. He would later participate in operations at Tarawa, Kwajalein, and Saipan but only as a staff officer, a planner, or an inspector. He would never be a commander again. His career as a military leader of men was over. He would see other officers promoted rapidly but not himself. In his eyes, he was finished. The Marine brass had won. His career was over.

Carlson was ordered back to San Diego in the early summer of 1943 for a two-month hospital rest from the effects of malaria, jaundice, and nervous exhaustion. He knew that his days with the Raiders were over.

He met with Marine commandant General Holcomb and with Gen. William J. Donovan of the Office of Strategic Services (OSS) in Washington, to see if he could be of service in some capacity. A top-secret job was allegedly offered to him by Donovan. The job, which apparently involved the assassination of a public figure in the Far East, was repugnant to him and he declined to have anything to do with it.

"I'd rather go back to the Pacific," he told a friend, "and get a good clean bullet right in the heart."

In July of his convalescent leave, Carlson met Lucien Hubbard, a journalist and screenwriter who was seeking approval of a script for a movie on Carlson's Raiders to be called *Gung Ho!* The script was based on a story written by Raider lieutenant Wilfred LeFrancois, which was eventually published in the *Saturday Evening Post* in December. Walter Wanger, one of Hollywood's most progressive and thoughtful producers, was to make it. Carlson, LeFrancois, and Sgt. Victor "Transport" Maghakian agreed to act as technical advisors.

Later that year, when filming began near Oceanside, California, and on San Clemente Island off the coast of southern California, Carlson rebelled against staying in a hotel room when most of the cast, which utilized Mexicans as Japanese soldiers, were given bunks in a temporary building. He convinced the director that everyone should move to the temporary facility in the spirit of "Gung Ho."

The movie starred Randolph Scott as Colonel Carlson. It also featured Noah Beery, Jr., Alan Curtis, J. Carrol Naish, Grace McDonald, Rod Cameron, and Robert Mitchum. It was a smash hit and was responsible for selling millions of dollars in war bonds. Promoted more as a documentary than a feature film, it served as a great recruiting tool for the Marine Corps. It was a propaganda film of the first order, heavy on fiction and light on facts. Seven of the Marines in the cast were actually on the Makin Raid. The critics loved the movie.

"It possessed all the elements of suspense, of sudden and concentrated action, and of heroic accomplishment against odds," Bosley Crowther of the *New York Times* wrote after its official opening in January of 1944. "It also possessed the further virtue of being a carefully calculated affair in which personal ingenuity was encouraged—a feature upon which Hollywood dotes. So it is not in the least surprising that Walter Wanger and Director Ray Enright have found inspiration in it for a sizzling war film entitled *Gung Ho!* If—as one might suspect at moments—they have gilded the lily just a bit, if they have touched up the desperado aspects with a dash of Hollywood coloring here and there, it is not necessarily misleading. . . .The fighting on the island is as hot and lurid as any that we've seen. As a matter of fact, the stabbing and the sticking go on ad nauseam. *Gung Ho!* is for folks with strong stomachs and a taste for the submachine gun."

The *Los Angeles Times* called the movie "as close to the real thing as you are likely to get" but found fault with one element of the story line.

"The story hews to the documentary line throughout, there being little in the way of 'plot' to distract either the men or us from the work," reviewer Philip K. Scheuer wrote. "They couldn't resist bringing in one of those typical movie feuds, however—this one between Noah Beery, Jr. and David Bruce, half-brothers in love with the same girl, Grace McDonald. You will note it and forget it."

The *New York Herald Tribune* said Carlson's role as technical advisor gave the movie immense credibility.

"[Carlson] had under his jurisdiction the same number of troops as made his actual raid," the reviewer wrote. "He coached these sea soldiers for their mock assault on a fabricated Makin near Oceanside, California, precisely as he had instructed his own raiders in August 1942. He worked side by side with Ray Enright, director, through production, and served Scott as model for the actor's Carlson role. He proved an affable, humorous sort of warrior, whose voice in ordinary conversation was so soft and low as to be almost inaudible. A pipe smoker, he liked to finger a smoked-out briar while giving his battle instructions to the 200 Marines from Camp Pendleton who reenacted the Makin raid in *Gung Ho.*"

Life magazine called the movie a "moving and, for the most part, faithful" depiction of the 2d Marine Raider Battalion's attack on Makin.

"In many respects [it is] the most literal war movie yet produced, it presents the most factual and intelligent sequence on a segment of Central Pacific fighting yet seen. *Gung Ho!* has no plot in the usual Hollywood interpretation. It is merely a report on the achievement of a gallant Marine battalion. It has no star in the individual sense, for its hero is a group of men. It is remarkably free of clichés which invalidate most war movies. But even more important, it is done with such clarity that even the most ignorant can follow the battle pattern with ease."

Though it was a huge hit on the home front, it was universally panned by the Makin Raiders who later saw it.

"It was pure Hollywood," Ben Carson said. "There was one scene where the Raiders were painting an American flag on the top of a building. Like we carried buckets of red, white, and blue paint with us on the raid."

Carson said he nearly walked out on the movie when he first saw it. He felt belittled and embarrassed.

Buck Stidham felt pretty much the same way.

"It wasn't very accurate at all," Stidham said. "They had a love interest and we didn't have time for that. It was pure Hollywood."

Brian Quirk broke out in laughter when he saw the movie because it was so far from the truth.

"It didn't show how and why the landing was so disorganized and how the motors didn't work," Quirk said. "They had a character in there of a former fighter called 'Pig Iron' (played by Mitchum). Well, there was a 'Pig Iron' in our outfit but he didn't go on the raid. He got his nickname from carrying the heavy base plate of a 60mm mortar. No, I wouldn't say the movie was very accurate at all."

One man who thoroughly enjoyed the movie was Carlson's father, Tom. Tom Carlson wrote a letter of appreciation to Randolph Scott and a long missive to his son to express how proud he was of the film.

"The picture is a highly creditable production," Tom Carlson wrote his son. "It is thoroughly done from beginning to end and carries out the spirit of your training with which, of course, I am familiar, with a graphic definiteness that makes the whole thing immediately real.

"Some war stuff is apt to be a bit revolting, but there was nothing of that in the film. There are bloody moments but the impression is one of convincingness. If men must go to war, better this thorough and intelligent training and this quick and final way.

"But the overshadowing presence in the picture is the man who represents you. Randolph Scott as Colonel Thorwald is a gripping representation of your spirit and bearing.

"I was deeply moved by his likeness to you in quiet authority, in the kindness of his speech, with a driving purpose through tough training not only to win a war but to save the men themselves as far as possible. He is not unlike you in face, figure, and bearing and carries a quiet confidence that truly represents an inspiring leader. I would like to know him."

After sitting around in a staff job with the 4th Marine Division at Camp Pendleton, Carlson wanted desperately to get back into the action. He volunteered to join the 2d Division as an observer in November of 1943 just before the assault on Tarawa. He went ashore in the same boat as regimental commander Col. David Shoup. Shoup, a Medal of Honor winner who would later become Marine commandant, was impressed by Carlson's courage and is credited with the famous one-liner about the old Raider: "He may be red, but he isn't yellow."

Tarawa was one of the biggest slaughters of World War II. The Marines virtually wiped out a Japanese garrison estimated at between 4,000 and 5,000 men. They took only 146 prisoners. Only 17 were Japanese. The others were Korean laborers. The Marines suffered 3,300 casualties and the ratio of dead to wounded—almost one to two—was reported to be the highest of any battle in the entire war.

Carlson dashed about Tarawa through murderous fire almost as if he had a death wish. Some thought he did.

Although not physically wounded, Carlson would feel the stings from comments uttered by an old foe, Merritt Edson. Edson, who was the assistant division commander of the 2d Marines at Tarawa and who had long harbored a grudge against Carlson from the former's days as commander of the 1st Raider Battalion, objected strongly to a photo that appeared in the *Marine Corps Gazette* of himself, Shoup, and Carlson as the "leaders of the assault" at Tarawa.

Edson took advantage of his position as a director of the *Gazette* to write to the editor and call his attention to the fact that division commander Gen. Julian C. Smith deserved the lion's share of any credit at Tarawa and that Carlson was just an observer. Edson thought it "very unfortunate that an official Marine Corps publication should have carried the impression conveyed by the public press that [Carlson] was in any way connected with the planning or direction of this operation."

It was true that Carlson had been merely an observer, but he had also performed valuable services in the course of the battle, a fact Edson conveniently ignored.

In January of 1944, Carlson could only watch helplessly as his beloved Raiders were disbanded as a specially designated outfit and his men dispersed among other regular Marine battalions. It hurt worse than taking a bullet to the heart.

Carlson was badly wounded in the right arm and left thigh the following June as an observer on Saipan. While recuperating in San Diego, he was visited by President and Mrs. Roosevelt. The latter referred to him as General Carlson in her column, creating a flurry of activity among his admirers who claimed that with his record he should have been given general's stars long ago. It wasn't until March of 1945 that he was finally promoted to full colonel, far behind his contemporaries. His former deputy, Jimmy Roosevelt, had been promoted to full colonel back in April of 1944, eleven months before his old boss.

When Carlson was retired "for wounds and disability" in the summer of 1946, he was promoted to brigadier general. It was an automatic promotion given to men who had received high battle honors such as the Navy Cross. Jimmy Roosevelt also retired as a brigadier general.

His body worn out and his health deteriorating, Carlson tried to keep up with events of the day but it was a struggle. He was helping on a book about his life in the spring of 1946 when he received some stunning news from the Japanese War Crimes trial currently going on at Guam. According to an Associated Press dispatch dated May 22, 1946, nine U.S. Marines—all from Carlson's Raiders—had been beheaded on Kwajalein Island on October 16, 1942, after having been captured two months earlier on Makin Atoll.

It was the first time Carlson or anybody else had known that there were Raiders accidentally left behind on Makin—nine of them, according to the reports from Guam. Carlson, who was confined to bed because of his serious heart problems, was shaken to his very core by the news, but he managed to summon up the strength and fortitude to respond in writing:

You have my account of what happened at Makin. You have also interrogated numerous Raiders who have also participated in that raid. My official report contained the basic facts as I knew them. You remember that there were 12 men whom I reported as "missing." Of this number 5 were the crew of the rescue boat which was strafed by Japanese planes on the morning of the 18th of August. None of the 12 were seen by the 70 of us who spent the second day on the island. I was the last Marine to leave the beach, when we attempted the evacuation on the night of the 17th of August, and when we succeeded in getting away on the night of the 18th.

There can be no question about the 18 that were killed in action, for I checked their bodies. The 12 "missing" were presumed to have been lost in the surf during the first night attempt at evacuation and during the strafing of the boat the following morning.

It is entirely possible that some or all of the 12 whom we listed as "missing"' men had reached the shore of an adjacent island or the southern tip of Butaritari. This is the only explanation I can offer for the AP dispatch from Guam. If I had had knowledge that any Raiders remained on the island at the time we left, I would either have evacuated them or remained with them.

Carlson's health had not been good since the injuries he suffered on Saipan in June of 1944. In June of 1945 he underwent another operation on his injured right arm. He had endured a bone-graft operation during which a piece of his shin was placed in his right arm. The bones were not knitting together as they should and he was in a great deal of pain.

Now living in Escondido, California, he tried not to let his physical difficulties keep him from thinking of the future. He considered teaching jobs at the California Institute of Technology and Occidental College. Some of his friends, including Jimmy Roosevelt, encouraged him to enter the 1946 Democratic primaries for the U.S. Senate from California. He was reluctant to pursue such a lofty goal, however, and declined.

He knew he would have been a hard sell as a politician. He was much too rigid in his beliefs. He told his supporters that he wouldn't make deals or play the game of compromise and deceit. He was strongly pro-labor, anti–big business, opposed to America's support of Chiang Kai-shek against the Chinese Communists, and in favor of America sharing its atomic discoveries with the world. On these principles he was totally inflexible.

Concerned with what others in the Marine Corps might think about him using his military position for political purposes, he wrote a personal and confidential letter to Marine commandant Alexander A. Vandegrift in late July of 1945 in which he poured his heart out.

He told Vandegrift that he was being pushed to run for the U.S. Senate in California and assured the general that he would never engage in any politics while wearing a Marine Corps uniform. He asked for advice concerning when he should put himself on the inactive list should he decide to run. (See Appendix Seven.)

Vandegrift wrote back on August 11, just two days after the United States had dropped a second atomic bomb on Nagasaki. His letter was short and personal.

> With regard to the time for going on the inactive list, I would say this: Now that the war is over, to all intents and purposes, the need for men is not as great as it was some months ago. If at the end of your hospitalization you intend to do anything in a political way relative to making contacts or otherwise towards your candidacy, I think it would be better that you go on the inactive list at that time. Should though you not intend to do this and the needs for the Marine Corps require your services, I think it better that you wait until you file for election.

Vandegrift ended the letter with an interesting final sentence.

> I imagine you will have rather stiff competition in California, but personally I wish you all the luck in the world.

Carlson's health began to fade badly by the end of 1945 after he flew to New York to speak before the American Veterans Committee on Atomic Energy at Madison Square Garden. After flying back across the country, he gave speeches in San Francisco, San Diego, Bakersfield, and Los Angeles.

The grueling round trip took its toll. Carlson experienced chest pains but linked the symptoms to his war wounds or a chest cold. He had his first heart attack a few days before Christmas. His doctors told him he must have complete bed rest for at least six months or he might not live.

"I've fallen apart like a one-horse shay," he told a friend.

After more than a year of convalescence at his new home near Portland, Oregon, Carlson died on May 27, 1947, just three months after his fifty-first birthday. As he requested, he was buried with full military honors at Arlington National Cemetery outside Washington, D.C., but only after one last humiliation by the Marine Corps bureaucracy.

The Marine Corps informed Carlson's widow, Peggy, that burial at Arlington was fine with them but then told her that there were no government funds available to transport the general's body from Portland, Oregon, to Washington, D.C. Apparently, Carlson had died virtually penniless.

Jimmy Roosevelt immediately contacted Marine Corps Headquarters and was told by the commandant, General Vandegrift, that the Marine Corps would gladly give to the general a full military funeral and make all necessary arrangements at Arlington, but that it was simply impossible under government regulations for the Marine Corps to arrange for the transportation of the body to Washington, or to advance any funds to his widow.

Roosevelt was outraged. He and six of his friends quickly raised $812.95 and wired it to Peggy Carlson, which proved sufficient to enable her to pay for the shipment of her husband's body to Washington with enough left over to cover a good part of her own personal expenses.

Many of the mourners at Carlson's funeral were his friends from outside the military. Cards and letters of condolence came from around the world.

Madam Sun Yat-sen, widow of the founder of the Chinese Republic, sent her condolences to Peggy Carlson in a cable to the Committee for a Democratic Far Eastern Policy of which Carlson was chairman. It read:

> Deeply grieved over General Carlson's untimely death, which is a great loss to the world democratic cause. The Chinese people will continue to battle against world fascism and the enemies of the progress of mankind. We shall continue to struggle so that the global peoples' victory to which he dedicated his life, and for which millions were sacrificed, will be accomplished.

The media covered Carlson's funeral as it had his life, treating him as one of America's greatest war heroes. Other than General Vandegrift, however, few of his military contemporaries bothered to attend the funeral. Evans junior, then a captain heading off to flight school, remembers the general being gracious to his father.

"[Vandegrift] was greatly moved at the funeral. He and I both shed some tears," Evans junior recalled. "The general made a major point of seeking me out to spend some time with me. He knew very well what my father had done during our patrol on Guadalcanal and how it took the pressure off his troops. He was very appreciative."

(Evans junior would win a second Silver Star in Korea as an aviator. He retired from the Marine Corps in 1967 as a full colonel and lives in South Carolina.)

However, there were no other glowing tributes from anyone else in the Marine Corps. His longtime rival and fellow New Englander, Merritt Edson, refused to chair a memorial service for him, saying, "I have never been nor am I now an ardent admirer of General Carlson's. Although I respected his bravery as an individual, I have never agreed with the doctrines and policies which he espoused."

After the war, Edson was an instrumental figure in efforts to preserve the Marine Corps as a separate military entity in the face of President Truman's drive to unify the services. He waged a fierce campaign in the halls of Congress, in the media, and in public appearances across the nation. Finally, as Carlson had done a decade earlier, Edson demonstrated the courage of his convictions by resigning his commission in order to testify publicly before committees of both houses of Congress. The effort paid off as his beloved Corps survived as a separate force.

Like Carlson, Edson paid a price for his convictions. Despondent over personal matters, Edson took his own life in 1955. He was only fifty-eight.

Jimmy Roosevelt, who retained the rank of brigadier general in the Marine Corps reserve, became active in California politics after the war. His political instincts were nothing like his father's, however. He was involved in a "Democrats for Eisenhower" movement in 1948, which enraged President Truman so much that when Roosevelt ran for governor of California in 1950, Truman refused to endorse him despite ardent pleadings from his mother, Eleanor Roosevelt. Jimmy Roosevelt lost to incumbent Earl Warren. Four years later, Roosevelt was elected to Congress from California's 26th District and served until 1965, when he lost to Sam Yorty in a bid for mayor of Los Angeles. He died in 1991 at the age of eighty-three.

History has been much kinder to members of the 1st Raider Battalion than it has to those from the 2d. A total of 111 U.S. Navy ships have been named for U.S. Marine heroes of World War II. Twenty-seven (26 percent) were named for U.S. Marine Raiders—21 from the 1st Raiders, including its commander Merritt Edson, two to navy personnel serving with the 1st Raiders, one from the 3d Raiders, and five from the 2d Raiders.

The five men honored from the 2d Raider Battalion include two who were killed on the Makin Raid, Sgt. Dallas H. Cook and Sgt. Clyde Thomason. The USS *Cook* (APD-130) was a high-speed transport, while the USS *Thomason* (DE-203) was a destroyer escort. The others were named after Lt. Jack Miller (DE 410) and Pvt. Joseph M. Auman (APD-117), who were both killed on Guadalcanal, and Lt. Col. Joseph P. McCaffery (DD-860), who was killed on Bougainville. Cook, Miller, Auman, and McCaffery won the Navy Cross while Thomason received the Medal of Honor.

No navy ship was ever named in honor of Evans Fordyce Carlson, despite the fact that he earned three Navy Crosses during his career.

Twenty-One
A Piece of Folly?

So, the question remains: Was the attack on Makin Atoll one of the greatest commando raids by American forces in World War II or was it a piece of folly? Arguments have been made on both sides of the question over the years. The evidence, gathered over more than half a century, seems to support the latter conclusion.

The fact that a raid of this type, that is using submarines, was never again attempted strongly suggests that military planners of the day viewed such an enterprise as unfeasible.

Cynics decried the raid, claiming that it made absolutely no sense to spend so much time and effort putting a couple of hundred Marines ashore on an island of such little importance—and one that they had no intention of keeping. The operation was a waste of manpower and resources that could have been put to better use elsewhere.

Critics claim that the operation was thrown together in great haste with little rehearsal and then undertaken with the flimsiest of intelligence. A comparison can be drawn with the Doolittle Raid over Japan four months earlier. There were terrible risks involved in both missions, including the possible annihilation of all the forces involved.

But, one must consider the psychological tenor of the times. A frightened America desperately needed good news from the Pacific. The American people needed reasons to have hope and to hold their heads high. They needed victories and heroes, and with the help of a cooperative media, they got both. Or did they?

The first reports of the Makin Raid acclaimed it as a great "victory" and a "brilliant" exploit by the U.S. Navy and Marine Corps public relations machinery. Medals were awarded all around. The Raiders and

"Gung Ho" were on everybody's lips back home. They became great recruiting tools for the Marine Corps. For a time, Carlson and Jimmy Roosevelt became household names as two of America's greatest heroes.

Those who took part in the raid were and still are loath to criticize it
even in hindsight, when the evidence clearly shows that they were fortunate to avoid losing most, if not all, of the raiding party.

Brian Quirk, one of the survivors of the raid, cites the report that Admiral Nimitz sent to his boss, Admiral King, as evidence that the Raiders
accomplished their primary mission at Makin. They were to create a diversion to confuse the Japanese and perhaps divert any reinforcements
they planned on sending to Guadalcanal. Nimitz, while admitting that
"the losses were somewhat larger than they should have been," told King
that the goals of the expedition were achieved. Considerable damage was
inflicted on the Japanese, he said, and at a crucial time in the Solomon
Islands operations the Japanese were forced to divert men, ships, and
planning to the relief of Makin Island.

"Coming from Nimitz, that's good enough for me," Quirk said in a
1999 interview.

Commodore Haines, the overall commander of the Makin Raid, told
reporters in Hawaii just after returning from the raid that he believed
that the Raider action had forced the Japanese to divert a task force of
carriers, transports, and destroyers headed for Guadalcanal to the
Gilberts, thus achieving the primary objective of the mission.

That argument appears to be wishful thinking.

Most experts doubt that any Japanese forces were diverted from
Guadalcanal. On the contrary, quite a few military historians claim the
Makin Raid served in the long run only to convince the Japanese to
strengthen their defenses elsewhere in the Gilberts, particularly at
Tarawa. When the Marines landed at Tarawa, a scant ninety miles south
of Makin, in the fall of 1943, they walked into a terrible hail of fire. In
seventy-six hours of ghastly bloodletting, U.S. forces lost 3,056 killed,
wounded, and missing, about 33 percent of the attacking force. Just
over 1,000 Marines were killed. Carlson, who was along as an observer,
overheard conversations claiming that the reason the island was so
heavily defended was because of his raid on nearby Makin fifteen
months earlier.

Marine general Holland "Howlin' Mad" Smith, who had nothing to
do with the planning for the Makin Raid, was blunt in his assessment of
the operation, one he later said he "deplored" from the beginning.

"Carlson's raid was a spectacular performance but it was also a piece of folly," Smith wrote a few years after the war. "The raid had no useful military purpose and served only to alert the Japanese to our intentions in the Gilberts."

Though complimentary to the Raiders themselves, calling them the "elite of toughness," Smith dismissed the Makin Raid as "almost useless."

Historian Jasper Holmes, who was a naval submarine intelligence officer at the time, wrote, "It is doubtful that any Japanese forces were diverted from Guadalcanal. In the long run [the Makin Raid] served only to convince the Japanese to strengthen their defenses in the Gilberts."

Another historian, Clay Blair, Jr., who was a submarine officer during the war, pulled no punches in giving his opinion of the value of the operation.

"Everything was thrown together in great haste. Debarkation was a fiasco even though they had rehearsed at Pearl," Blair wrote. "Seas swamped rubber boats, drowning most of the outboard motors. The few boats that ran towed the others. Carlson lost sight of his 'flag boat' and had to go ashore in someone else's. Raiders got ashore in a helter-skelter fashion and received a warmer-than-expected welcome. Communications between the Marines and subs was primitive and sporadic."

The official Marine Corps position on the raid now admits that it had limited success, if any at all.

"The raid itself had mixed results," the Marine Corps wrote in a 1995 commemorative series called *From Makin to Bougainville*. "Reports painted it as a great victory and it boosted morale on the home front. Many believed it achieved its original goal of diverting forces from Guadalcanal, but the Japanese had immediately guessed the size and purpose of the operation and had not let it alter their plans for the Solomons. However, it did cause the enemy to worry about the potential for other such raids on rear area installations. On the negative side, that threat may have played a part in the subsequent Japanese decision to fortify heavily places like Tarawa Atoll, the scene of a costly amphibious assault later in the war. At the tactical level, the 2d Raiders had proven themselves in direct combat with the enemy. Their greatest difficulties had involved rough seas and poor equipment; bravery could not fix those limitations. Despite the trumpeted success of the operation, the navy never again attempted to use submarines to conduct raids behind enemy lines."

Tokyo dismissed the Makin Raid as "a puny attempt" to pin down their forces while the Americans invaded the Solomons. The revelation of the

Gilberts' vulnerability was something of a shock, however. It was now plain to the Japanese that unless these outlying islands were fortified and garrisoned in strength they might easily fall into American hands and serve as bases for a thrust into the neighboring Marshalls. The Japanese moved quickly to see that didn't happen.

Admiral Matone Ugaki, Yamamoto's chief of staff, wrote in his diary a few days after the Makin Raid that the Americans "will make surprise attacks on other islands in this way, and we must never relax."

Pinprick raids may be good for morale, another historian declared, and sometimes offer useful practice but they can also anger and alert the enemy or backfire in other ways. The Makin operation was completely unnecessary and was not repeated elsewhere.

Although no one has ever questioned Carlson's bravery under fire, some of his junior officers, notably Peatross, were critical of his leadership and decision making, especially the attempt to surrender to a nonexistent enemy. Peatross thought that Carlson suffered from inertia on Makin, losing his aggressiveness and ability to think clearly in a crisis situation.

"It is difficult to understand why Carlson, a seasoned combat commander and an experienced intelligence officer, was not more aggressive in carrying out his mission and persisted in overestimating the enemy's strength or, even worse, underrating his own," Peatross wrote many years later.

"As [Carlson] walked along the battle line and talked with his Raiders, he saw with his own eyes the enemy dead strewn about the battlefield, and heard with his own ears the marked diminution in the volume and variety of enemy fire until all that remained was intermittent sniper fire, Carlson should have realized long since that the prize was his for the taking. But he didn't."

Peatross was also quick to point out that Carlson had many political enemies at the time of the raid and after all the positive publicity it received, they were only too happy to find as much fault with him as they could.

"Many senior Marine Corps officers of this era were politically very conservative and considered Carlson to be a Bolshevik," Peatross wrote. "His book *Twin Stars of China,* extolling the Chinese Communist Party and its leaders, and his close association with President Roosevelt and the flock of closet communists and salon socialists that gathered under the banner of the New Deal, did nothing to dissuade them from this conviction. They had opposed Carlson's efforts to form a raider unit, and now as they saw him and his unit thrust most favorably into the national spotlight, they began a campaign of criticism that continued almost unabated until the Raider battalions disappeared from the U.S. Marine Corps tables of organization and Evans F. Carlson was dead.

"The major and most enduring criticism that we heard was that the Makin raid was poorly conceived and wasteful of men and material. A later variation on this central theme argued that our raid was the proximate cause of our heavy casualties at Tarawa in November 1943, by inducing the massive reinforcement of Japanese positions in the Gilbert Islands. It is tempting to dismiss these criticisms outright as 'sour grapes' or 'professional jealousy' and [be] done with them; for their target was not so much the raid as it was Carlson. I daresay that had almost any other lieutenant colonel in the Marine Corps been in command at Makin, there would not have been so much as a whisper of criticism."

Furthermore, Peatross asserts that if there is to be criticism of the concept of the Makin Raid and the consequences it spawned, it should be directed at Nimitz, not Carlson.

"The raid on Makin was conceived at [Nimitz's] headquarters, by his staff, and at his direction," Peatross wrote. "From the beginning it was designed as a strategic diversion with the primary objective of fooling the enemy as to our actual intentions in the Central Pacific and inducing him to divert forces that otherwise might be used to reinforce the Guadalcanal area. . . . Since Admiral Nimitz was satisfied with the results of the raid, we well might ask: 'Where's the beef?'"

Admiral Nimitz was indeed satisfied with the raid but did take Carlson to task in his report to Washington in one important area. He criticized Carlson for not acting aggressively enough:

"The old story in war of the importance of the offensive was again demonstrated," Nimitz wrote. "On the afternoon of August 17, had the raiding force sent out reconnaissance patrols and pushed forward instead of withdrawing, they would have discovered that the apparent heavy resistance was the fire of only a handful of men fighting to the death. They could have destroyed installations on the island and reembarked at their leisure, probably saving most of the loss of life from drowning and from strafing by planes on 18 August."

Another criticism leveled by Nimitz at Carlson was the latter's overreliance on intelligence information given to him by the natives. It was noted as point number 29 and titled "Native reports should be considered with suspicion."

"The Japanese may have deliberately spread the rumor of reinforcements in order to influence the decisions of the raider commander. Active patrols would have given him sound information as to the location and strength of the enemy," Nimitz wrote.

Although there is no mention of the surrender note in the report, Nimitz may have hinted at it when he chided Carlson for exhibiting what could only be called a panic attack:

"The night of August 17 . . . emphasizes the truth that is as old as the military profession: No matter how bad your own situation may appear to be, there is always the possibility that the situation of the enemy is much worse. To this might be added another truth, that a few resolute men seem like battalions."

Twenty-Two
Many Questions, Few Answers

Some fifty-eight years after the Makin Raid the only certainty concerning American casualties is that thirty Raiders out of a force of 219 did not return.

Of the thirty Raiders who failed to return following the raid, nineteen were finally discovered in a mass grave on the main island of Butaritari in December of 1999. After an exhaustive year of DNA testing by military specialist from Hawaii, the nineteen were positively identified in December of 2000 (see Appendix One).

Of the remaining eleven men who failed to return, five (Sgt. Robert Allard, Sgt. Dallas Cook, Pvt. John Kerns, Pfc. Richard Olbert, and Pvt. Donald Roberton) were originally listed as "probably killed" when witnesses saw their rubber boat strafed and sunk by Japanese planes on the morning of the second day. That belief was attested to by witnesses on the shore and the periscope operator on the *Nautilus*. Though no one ever reported seeing these five men again on the island, one of them, Sergeant Allard, was said to have negotiated the surrender of nine remaining Raiders on Butaritari a day after Japanese reinforcements arrived on the island. If Allard had survived the attack by the Japanese plane and allegedly swum to safety ashore, isn't it possible that the other four men in his boat did the same?

Brian Quirk, who knew all five of the men in the rescue boat very well, says that all of these men were great athletes and great swimmers.

"They could have drifted down the island with the tide and landed at the southwestern tip of Butaritari or another nearby island. It could have happened," Quirk said.

Quirk also took exception to reports that any Raiders were "left behind" by their comrades. "They were accidentally lost either on land or

in the water," he said. "There is a clear distinction between being left behind or accidentally lost."

A large force of Japanese marines landed on Butaritari on August 19,
the day after the Raiders left. Over the next several days, according to
testimony given at the war crimes trial in 1946, they took into custody
nine Raiders they found on the island. A German priest, Friar Dur-
rheimer, claimed he helped negotiate the surrender for Sergeant Allard,
the ranking member of the remaining Raiders. The Japanese reinforcements also found the surrender note on the dead body of a
Japanese soldier. The note, which had an illegible signature, was passed
up through channels and finally given to the notorious Tokyo Rose, who
gave it great exposure on her radio show.

The nine Raider captives were shipped to Kwajalein within a few days,
where they initially received good care at the hands of curious Japanese.
Testimony at the war crimes trial in 1946 revealed that the Japanese fre-
quently gave them candy and cigarettes and joshed with them about the
sights they would see in Tokyo. For six weeks, the Raiders had no reason
to doubt the good faith of their captors.

But in early October, VAdm. Koso Abe, the commander of the Marshall Island bases, became impatient over the delay in moving them out.
After a brief conference with another admiral from Truk, Abe summarily ordered the men executed, allegedly because they had become "an
administrative nuisance."

At his trial, Abe said he was acting on orders from above. Some believe that the Japanese hierarchy had become incensed over what they
viewed as Raider trickery in having written a surrender note and then
killed the messenger. They decided to make an example of them.

The onerous task of executing the Raiders fell on the shoulders of
Capt. Yoshio Obara, the Kwajalein garrison commander. Obara, who had
two brothers in America and nephews in the U.S. Army, protested ve-
hemently against the inhuman and illegal order, but Abe remained
adamant. Obara was unable to find a single volunteer executioner and
at last detailed four officers, who reluctantly obeyed. Dubious homage
was accorded the doomed men when Obara selected a date for the execution that coincided with Japan's annual memorial to departed heroes,
the Yasukuni Shrine Festival. On October 16, the nine Raiders were led
to a large grave and ceremoniously beheaded in the presence of the
sadistic Abe.

After the burial, Obara's men allegedly placed flowers on the grave
and considered the incident closed. But a Marshallese native, Lajena

Lokot, had witnessed the execution from a hiding place in the bushes and testified against the principals at the war crimes trial. Lokot, who was employed in the Japanese officer's kitchen on Kwajalein, testified that one day he was ordered to take a table to an isolated spot some distance from the cantonment. Curious as to why the table was needed at such an out-of-the-way spot, he decided to stay and see what happened. Hiding in some nearby bushes, he watched as the Japanese brought up the Americans and witnessed the beheading of the first man before fleeing in terror.

Lokot's testimony was followed by that of Capt. Hiyoski Koichi, who also said he witnessed the executions. Abe claimed he was acting under orders from his superiors in Tokyo to carry out the executions but could not identify the person who issued the order.

"Captain Obara [said] it was quite unbearable to execute the prisoners and he wanted them to be sent home [to Japan] as he had previous prisoners," Abe testified. "I sympathized with the prisoners and also wanted them sent home, but I had been ordered by Central Authorities and there was nothing I could do but obey, and ordered the executions."

Even though the bodies were never found, Admiral Abe was convicted by a court of allied officers for violating "the law and custom of war and the moral standards of civilized society." He was hanged at Guam on June 19, 1947. Captain Obara received a ten-year prison sentence. He was paroled in December of 1951. A third defendant, Lt. Comdr. Hisakichi Maika, was sentenced to five years in prison and was paroled in April of 1950.

The identity of those Raiders who were so brutally executed remains a mystery. Their graves have never been found. Many believe Allard had to be one of them. But who were the others?" Instead of nine victims, could there have been as many as eleven, the number carried as missing?

Sergeant McCullough, who was among the last to leave Makin the night of August 18, believes that some, if not all, of the missing men could have been on that rubber boat that broke away from the outrigger. That would seem unlikely, however, because Lieutenant Peatross counted seventy-two men coming out on the final night, approximately the number in Carlson's party.

"They pulled away from us and that is the last I saw of them," McCullough insisted in a 1999 interview. "I think they got lost and went back to the island. This may be wrong but until someone proves me wrong, I will believe this is what happened. I have read a good many reports on leaving the men on the island. Every one of the Marines knew we were going to leave that evening after I got the subs to come around to the other side. I know this for sure. We didn't leave anybody behind on the island. We made a thorough search before getting on the boats. The island was too small to miss anyone."

In 1999, a member of the Raider Association, Don Harn, wrote the American Embassy in Japan seeking the identity of the Raiders who had been executed on Kwajalein fifty-seven years earlier. The reply was disheartening.

> We very much regret to inform you that no records have been kept with respect to the fate of the 12 [sic] U.S. Marines who were captured by Japanese forces on Makin Island and then transferred to Kwajalein Island.
> All American POWs captured by Japanese forces in the last war (including those who died in POW camps) were given "Prisoner Name Tags" for individual identification. All of these tags were handed over to the U.S. government by the Japanese government on May 31st, 1955, via the American Embassy in Tokyo.

So, if all this is true, of the thirty men who failed to return, 19 were killed and left for burial by the natives on the island, nine were left behind only to be captured and executed, and two remain missing and presumed drowned. Each of these alleged facts comes with its own set of questions, however.

The first priority in unraveling this long-standing mystery has been to try to identify the Raiders allegedly buried on Butaritari Island. That was first attempted on November 21, 1943, when Jimmy Roosevelt, then a lieutenant colonel and assigned as an observer with the army's 27th Infantry Division, went ashore on Butaritari when the division landed at Makin. His specific mission was to locate the graves of the nineteen Raiders believed to be buried there and facilitate the removal of the bodies back to the United States.

Carlson's biographer, Michael Blankfort, said that when Roosevelt landed, he sought out the native police chief, Joe Miller, the man who had been given fifty dollars by Carlson to provide the Raiders with a Christian burial. Miller reportedly brought Roosevelt to a burial site and showed him some graves.

"The graves had been well cared for; they had little headstones and palm fronds and a few flowers over them. 'It be done,' Miller told Roosevelt," according to Blankfort.

Peatross, in his history of the Raiders, said the final resting place for the nineteen Raiders on Butaritari Island was a mass grave, though he didn't say how he knew this.

General Holland Smith, the overall commander of the Makin-Tarawa operation in late 1943, mentions in his book *Coral and Brass* that Roosevelt went ashore with the regimental commander and was with him when the latter was killed by a sniper's bullet. Smith severely criticized the slow progress of the army troops on Butaritari and the fact that Roosevelt received a Silver Star for his part in the Makin operation, "which consisted of being present."

"Had the matter been referred to me, a courtesy which should have been extended to the Commanding General," Smith later wrote, "I would have strongly disapproved the recommendation. Jimmy Roosevelt proved himself a competent and courageous Marine on many occasions, but I always wondered how he felt about that decoration."

In any event, Roosevelt, in a top secret report to his superiors late in 1943, allegedly determined that the bodies of the Raiders were "nonrecoverable." Why that was so, and why he didn't at least bring back the dog tags, remains a mystery. Why Carlson didn't initially retrieve the dog tags, which in those days included a thumbprint, is another mystery that may never be solved. The Marine Corps has been unable to find a record of Roosevelt's 1943 report, if, in fact, one ever existed.

It was theorized by some that there was no grave site on Butaritari for the fallen Raiders and that the bodies were burned by the Japanese when they arrived on the island with reinforcements on August 19, 1942. It was further alleged by some that the native police chief, Joe Miller, took the fifty dollars Colonel Carlson gave him as an incentive but had no intention of burying the bodies because he didn't want to be viewed as a collaborator by the Japanese when they returned. And Miller knew damn well the Japs would be back in force in a matter of days.

"There were almost 200 dead (and stinking) Japs laying all over Makin when the Japs came down from Kwajalein," wrote Francis Hepburn, a former member of the 4th Raider Battalion and a unit historian who remains active with the Raider newsletter. "There were 18 or 20 Raiders in the group. The Japs had no means of refrigerating this mess; their only recourse was to cremate, Americans and Japs alike. Cremation is customary in the Jap culture, especially in the military. Ashes are sent home. I believe that looking for bones (on Butaritari) is a lost, useless cause."

It is quite possible that Jimmy Roosevelt came to this same conclusion when he returned to Butaritari Island in 1943. Hepburn, for example, believes that Roosevelt, for security reasons, may not have gone ashore, relying instead on information supplied by those who did. He may have been told there was no grave site and thus no bodies to recover. Bodies that had been cremated would certainly be "nonrecoverable."

If Roosevelt determined that the bodies were "nonrecoverable" because they had been burned, it would have been an extremely sensitive situation, one that would have certainly been classified as top secret. News of this nature would have certainly enraged the families of the victims. This might explain why there were no Raider bodies discovered in November of 1943.

If all this is true, however, it doesn't explain why Roosevelt, as late as the summer of 1987, told several Raider veterans at a speech before the Los Angeles Explorers Club that he stood ready to assist in any way he could to continue the search for the bodies of his comrades on Makin.

Three years after the war ended, a graves registration team went back to Makin to search for the graves of those Raiders allegedly buried there and found nothing. They spent about twenty-four hours on the island.

"They came one day and left the next. Some search. They must have pushed the 'who cares' button," said Don Harn, a former chairman of the Raiders' Fallen Comrades Committee.

The team allegedly dug several test holes near the southwest end of an airstrip, which was far removed from the battlefield. There was evidence that the area had been bulldozed in the construction of an airstrip. Therefore, it was assumed, had there been any Raider remains at the site, they would have been scattered and irretrievably lost.

In 1989, in answer to a query from the Marine Raider Association concerning the alleged burial site at Makin, a retired brigadier general, E. H. Simmons, then director of the Marine Corps history and museums division, said that his staff had "determined from an examination of operational reports and unit diaries that eighteen officer and enlisted marines were killed in action during the 17–18 August 1942 raid on Makin Island. These eighteen marines were all interred locally on Makin Island, and their bodies determined to be nonrecoverable by a field board after the war."

As to the disposition of the nine Raiders who were captured and transported to Kwajalein only to be executed, the report said:

> We have examined primary and secondary accounts of the Makin Island raid, including the 400-plus pages of the Record of Proceedings of the military commission convened at U.S. Pacific Fleet, Commander Marianas, Guam, in which three Japanese officers were charged in the execution of 9 American prisoners of war on Kwajalein Island on 16 October 1942. Testimony taken at the trial clearly established that the 9 Americans were Marines captured on Makin by Japanese forces several days after the 2d Marine Raider Battalion raid. There is, unfortunately, no clue in the court proceedings as to the specific identity of the nine Marines. Moreover, it was specifically stated in the specifications of the trial that the names were unknown.
>
> It should be noted as well that it cannot be determined from the operational reports of the Makin Island raid whether these nine Marines were actually left on the island, or made their way back to Makin after the foundering of one of the rubber boats which the Raiders were using to return to the submarines waiting to pick them up in a Makin Island lagoon. At least one native from the island reported after the war that the bodies of several drowned marines were found on the Makin beach. This appears to account for the total of 12 marines listed as missing in action, as only 9 were captured by the Japanese several days after the raid.
>
> I hope this information will prove useful in your efforts to honor the bravery of the Marine Raiders during World War II.

Appendices

APPENDIX ONE
Honor Roll of 2d Marine Raiders Who Did Not Return from the Makin Raid

In December of 1999 an investigative team from the U.S. Army's Central Identification Laboratory in Hawaii recovered twenty bodies from a mass grave on Butaritari Island. Eleven months later, the team determined through medical and DNA testing that nineteen of the bodies were former members of the 2d Marine Raider Battalion, which invaded the island in August of 1942.

The identities of those recovered are as follows:

Castle, Vernon L., FM1 (USMCR 307868), Stillwater, Oklahoma
Earles, I. B., Cpl. (USMC 293609), Tulare, California
Gallagher, William A., Pfc. (USMCR 307593), Wyandotte, Michigan
Gaston, Daniel A., Cpl. (USMC 340727), Galveston, Texas
Hicks, Ashley W., Pfc. (USMCR 345385), Waterford, California
Holtom, Gerald P., Capt. (USMCR 07549), Palo Alto, California
Johnson, Harris J., Cpl. (USMC 334067), Little Rock, Iowa
Kunkle, Kenneth K., Cpl. (USMC 268716), Mountain Home, Arkansas
Larson, Carlyle O., Pvt. (USMC 346391), Glenwood, Minnesota
Maciejewski, Edward, Cpl. (USMC 299149), Chicago, Illinois
Maulding, Robert B., Pvt. (USMC 337436), Vista, California
Montgomery, Kenneth M., Pfc. (USMCR 305326), Eden, Wisconsin
Mortensen, Norman W., Pfc. (USMC 326651), Camp Douglas, Wisconsin

Nodland, Franklin M., Pvt. (USMC 333878), Marshalltown, Iowa
Pearson, Robert B., Cpl. (USMC 275291), Lafayette, California
Selby, Charles A., Pfc. (USMC 326661), Ontonagon, Michigan
Thomason, Clyde, Sgt. (USMCR 246433), Atlanta, Georgia
Vandenberg, John E. Pvt. (USMCR 335768), Kenosha, Wisconsin
Yarbrough, Mason O., Cpl. (USMC 309064), Sikeston, Missouri

Believed Missing
Mattison, Alden C., Pvt. (USMCR 337253), Blair, Wisconsin
Smith, Cletus, Pvt. (USMCR 347545), Angleton, Texas

Believed Captured and Beheaded on Kwajalein
Allard, Robert V., Sgt. (USMCR 26220), Woodside, New York
Beecher, James W., Cpl. (USMC 299268), Baxley, Georgia
Cook, Dallas H., Sgt. (USMC 291466), Red Jacket, West Virginia
Davis, Richard E., Pfc. (USMC 334063), Minneapolis, Minnesota
Gifford, Joseph, Cpl. (USMC 213498), Cornville, Arizona
Kerns, John I., Pvt. (USMCR 348233), Houston, Texas
Olbert, Richard N., Pfc. (USMCR 349489), Durango, Colorado
Pallesen, William E., Pfc. (USMC 336074), Manila, Utah
Roberton, Donald R., Pvt. (USMC 348240), Franklin, Louisiana

APPENDIX TWO
Complete Roster of Those Who Sailed Aboard the USS *Argonaut*

Allen, Harold A., Pvt.
Angel, Elbert C., Cpl.
Baggs, Kelly, Pfc.
Barnes, Edwyn E., Cpl.
Bauml, Raymond C., Pvt.
Beecher, James W., Cpl.
Bevon, John A., Pfc.
Bibby, Joe R., Pfc.
Blain, Albert F., Pvt.
Book, Harold L., Pvt.
Bowcutt, Don R., Pvt.
Buchanan, James W., Pvt.
Burleson, Lester L., Pfc.
Calas, Jack H., Pfc.
Cantrall, Arthur, PhM2c
Carson, Benjamin F., Pvt.
Chapman, Donald L., Pvt.
Clark, George R., Pfc.
Clark, Richard V., Pvt.
Clymer, Elmer L., Jr., Pfc.
Coco, Lamar U., Pvt.
Cotten, Julius W., Cpl.
Craven, Howard R., Pvt.
Croft, Orin, Cpl.
Davis, James N. M., Capt.
Davis, Richard E., Pfc.
DeBosik, Stanley F., Cpl.
DeLuca, Elmer P., Pfc.
Dinges, Adam R., Pvt.
Does, William B., Sgt.
Earles, I. B., Cpl.
Eineichner, Albert F., Pvt.
Eirich, Robert W., Pvt.
Elliott, Ellsbury B., GySgt.
Elterman, Walter J., Jr., PhM2c
Evan, Philip F., Pvt.

Faulkner, James C. O., Sgt.
Gallagher, William A., Pvt.
Gaston, Daniel A., Cpl.
Glidewell, Richard N., Pfc.
Gollberg, Joseph E., Sgt.
Griffin, Joe B., 1st Lt.
Gurman, Howard, Cpl.
Halley, Joe, Pfc.
Haug, Harry J., Pvt.
Healy, Clarence P., Pvt.
Hedger, Reuben E., Pvt.
Helsley, Edwin, Pfc.
Herrero, Henry, Sgt.
Hicklin, Jack W., Pfc.
Hicks, Ashley W., Pfc.
Hoffmann, Erwin L. H., Pfc.
Jenkins, Charles, F., Pfc.
Jennings, Robert L., Pvt.
Johnson, Harris J., Cpl.
Jurgens, August G. Pfc.
Kemp, Fred E., Pfc.
Kilgore, Charles L., Pvt.
King, Carl D., Pfc.
King, John H., Jr., Pvt.
Klein, Harold G., Sgt.
Kunkle, Kenneth K., Cpl.
Kuzniewski, Sylvester, Pvt.
Lamb, Charles T., 2d Lt.
Larsen, Raymond H., Pvt.
Larson, Carlyle O., Pvt.
LeBlanc, Herbert A., Pfc.
LeFrancois, Wilfred S., 2d Lt.
Lenz, Norman J., Sgt.
Lincoln, Glen A., Pvt.
Locke, B. G., Pfc.
Maciejewski, Edward, Cpl.
MacPherson, Francis K., Cpl.
Maghakian, Victor, Sgt.
Malanowski, Henry E., 1st Sgt.

Matelski, Cyrill A., Pfc.
Mattison, Alden C., Pvt.
Maulding, Robert B., Pvt.
McCall, William, Pvt.
McCool, Leon, Pfc.
McNussen, Ned E., Sgt.
Metcalf, Frederick A., Pfc.
Milewski, Ted B., Pfc.
Miller, Edward H., Pfc.
Mitchell, Olan C., Pfc.
Mitchell, Vern B., Pfc.
Moore, Willie D., Pfc.
Mortensen, Norman W., Pfc.
Nelson, Jim L., Pfc.
Nix, John D., Pvt.
Nodland, Franklin M., Pvt.
Norman, Clyde H., Pfc.
Oberg, Richard A., Pvt.
Oliver, Herbert K., Pvt.
Orrick, William F., Pvt.
Parsons, Aubrey D., Pfc.
Pearson, Robert B., Cpl.
Pilch, Lawrence E., Pvt.
Piskor, Ladislaus A., Cpl.
Plumley, Merwyn C., 1st Lt.
Poarche, Robert E., Cpl.
Putnam, Lon M., Cpl.
Rawlins, Bernard, Pfc.
Richardson, Frederick T., Pfc.
Richardson, William H., Pvt.
Ricks, Laurence J., Cpl.
Roosevelt, James, Maj.
Russell, John F., Pvt.
Russell, William J., Pvt.
Ryan, Harold E., Pfc.
Salistean, Gates S., Pfc.
Sebock, Joseph, Pfc.
Sheely, Raymond W., Pfc.
Smith, Cletus, Pvt.

Smith, Fred E., Pvt.
Spath, Richie J., Pvt.
Spotts, Melvin J., Sgt.
Stephens, Ralph, Pfc.
Stidham, Howard E., Sgt.
Stigler, Stephen L., Lt.
Stockley, George W., Pfc.
Stotts, Louis M., Pfc.
Thomason, Clyde, Sgt.
Tillery, James H., Jr., Pfc.
Toon, John E., Pfc.
Turner, Keith H., Pvt.
Vandenberg, John E., Pfc.
Veverka, Simon W., Cpl.
Wangen, Orville E., Pvt.
Watkins, Evort J., Pvt.
Weimer, Alvin J., Cpl.
Wilson, Peter J., Pfc.
Wittenberg, Julius C., Cpl.
Young, Howard A., Cpl.

Complete Roster of Those Who Sailed Aboard the USS *Nautilus*
Allard, Robert V., Sgt.
Amburgey, Wilford G., Pfc.
Barber, James W., Pfc.
Benecki, Edward P., Sgt.
Bigelow, Floyd B., Pfc.
Brown, Dean T., Pvt.
Brown, Sam R., Cpl.
Cameron, William M., Jr., Pfc.
Carlson, Evans F., Lt. Col.
Carroll, Walter D., Sgt.
Casey, James H., PhM2c
Castle, Vernon L., FM1c
Chapman, Leon R., Cpl.
Childers, Ellis, Pfc.
Cone, Samuel C., GySgt.
Cook, Dallas H., Sgt.
Coyte, Ralph H., Capt.

Dale, Harry R., Pvt.
Daniels, Donald D., Pfc.
Dawson, Charles E., Cpl.
Donovan, Alexander J., Pfc.
Dowling, Otis D., Pvt.
Farrell, Thomas L., Cpl.
Faulstick, Vernon F., Pfc.
Fitzgerald, Charles L., Pvt.
Francis, Roger E., Pvt.
Franklin, George W., Cpl.
Gifford, Joseph, Cpl.
Golaczewski, Chester L., 1st Sgt.
Grant, Dell L., Pfc.
Green, James C., Pfc.
Hawkins, Jess, Pfc.
Helm, Frederick T., Pfc.
Holtom, Gerald P., Capt.
Hood, Ray E., Pfc.
Horton, Milton G., Pvt.
Hudman, Denton E., Pvt.
Inman, Calvin L., Pfc.
Jablonski, John L., Pfc.
Jacobson, James P., 2d Lt.
Jansen, Raymond D., Pvt.
Johnson, Herbert M., Sgt.
July, Ernest R., Pvt.
Kerns, John I., Pvt.
Koontz, Daniel V., Pvt.
Lang, Lawrence A., GySgt.
Lawson, Frank J., Sgt.
MacCracken, William B., Lt.
Marsen, Erling, Pvt.
Mazzei, Lamar W., Pvt.
McCoy, Wade C., Sgt.
McCullough, Kenneth L., Sgt.
Mead, William F., Pfc.
Merrill, Kenneth H., Pvt.
Midulla, Benjamin L., Cpl.
Milligan, Neal F., Pvt.

Montgomery, Kenneth M., Pfc.
Moore, Charles A., Pvt.
Needham, Thomas J., Pfc.
Nugent, William O., Pfc.
Olbert, Richard N., Pfc.
Pallesen, William E., Pvt.
Parr, Melvin J., Pvt.
Paulson, Duane D., Pfc.
Peatross, Oscar F., 1st Lt.
Perez, Manuel, Cpl.
Plumb, John H., Pfc.
Potter, John W., Jr., Cpl.
Quirk, Brian J., Pfc.
Roberton, Donald A., Pvt.
Roth, Gordon J., Pvt.
Scofield, Adrian E., Pfc.
Seaton, Kenneth J., Pfc.
Selby, Charles A., Pfc.
Smith, Harry S., Pfc.
Sparkman, Cullen R., PhM2c
Sypniewski, Walter H., Pvt.
Thomson, Howard S., Pfc.
Voight, Dean S., Pvt.
White, Harry E., Pfc.
Winters, Dean G., Pfc.
Woodford, Joseph J., Pvt.
Wygal, Edward R., Sgt.
Yarbrough, Mason G., Cpl.
Yount, William I., Sgt.

APPENDIX THREE
Awards and Decorations Earned on Makin Raid

Medal of Honor—1
Thomason, Clyde, Sgt. (posthumously)

Navy Crosses—23
Allard, Robert V., Sgt. (posthumously)
Carlson, Evans F., Lt. Col.
Cook, Dallas H., Sgt. (posthumously)
Coyte, Ralph H., Capt.
Craven (aka Murphree), Howard R., Pvt.
Elliott, Ellsbury B., GySgt.
Faulkner, James, Sgt.
Haines, John M., Commodore
Kerns, John I., Pvt. (posthumously)
Lamb, Charles T., 2d Lt.
Lang, Lawrence A., GySgt.
LeFrancois, Wilfred S., 2d Lt.
MacCracken, William B., Lt.
Maghakian, Victor, Sgt.
Olbert, Richard N., Pfc. (posthumously)
Peatross, Oscar F., 1st Lt.
Plumley, Merwyn C., 1st Lt.
Roberton, Donald R., Pvt. (posthumously)
Roosevelt, James, Maj.
Sebock, Joseph, Pfc.
Spotts, Melvin J., Sgt.
Stigler, Stephen L., Lt.
Wygal, Edward R., Cpl.

Medals Earned During the Long Patrol on Guadalcanal

Navy Crosses—5
Auman, Joe, Pvt. (posthumously)
Carlson, Evans F., Lt. Col.
Miller, Jack, 1st Lt. (posthumously)
Schwerin, William, Capt.
Yancey, John, Cpl.

Silver Stars—7
Carlson, Evans C., 1st Lt.
Croft, Orin, Cpl.
Early, Cleland E., 1st Lt.
Gary, Albert Von K., Capt.
Jacobson, James P., 1st Lt.
Maghakian, Victor, Sgt.
Washburn, Richard T., Capt.

APPENDIX FOUR
Carlson's Eulogy to the Thirty Men Who Did Not Return from the Makin Raid, Delivered August 26, 1942 at Camp Catlin, Hawaii

We are gathered here today to honor the memory of our Raiders who remain at Makin. We miss them. Each had his special place among us, and that place is imperishably his. Being human we mourn the loss of each. But I believe these gallant men who so eagerly, so willingly, went forth to meet the enemy would not have us weep and bemoan their passing. They loved each other, these comrades of ours. They were vital, eager, thoughtful, realistic. They had convictions even to the point of sacrificing their lives. They believed that if this country of ours is to be saved, the job of saving it belongs to those who enjoy the benefits of our institutions. They didn't ask someone else to perform the task for them. They went out to do it themselves to the supreme heights of human achievement. Rather than have us weep over this achievement, I believe they would have us rejoice with them at the example of courage, of fortitude, and of nobility of character they have set for us.

Moreover, they are still with us in spirit . . . will always be with us. . . . Allard with his boyish smile; Johnson with his strange scowl; Jerry Holtom with his lumbering stride and eager, half-embarrassed manner; the others, you know the characteristics of each as well as I. Who will say that the spirit of all these men does not remain with us?

It was not possible to render honors to these fallen comrades on the field of battle. I did what I could. I went to each as he lay with his face towards the enemy. I placed each on his back that he might rest more easily, and I said a silent prayer over each. With the native Gilbertese I arranged for each to be given a Christian burial. And so, they lie there today, in the soil of that delightful South Pacific isle, beneath the palms under which they won their victory.

It behooves us who remain to rededicate ourselves to the task that lies ahead. The convictions of these comrades are our convictions. . . . With the memory of their sacrifices in mind, let us dedicate ourselves to the task of bringing into reality the ideals for which they died . . . that their sacrifice will not have been in vain.

We salute you as comrades. We salute you as Raiders, as Marines, as Americans, as men. God Bless You!

APPENDIX FIVE

(The following is part of the text of Carlson's Memorial speech honoring sixteen of his Raiders who lost their lives during the 2d Battalion's thirty-day march (November 4–December 4, 1942) behind enemy lines on Guadalcanal. It was delivered in late December at Camp Gung Ho on Espíritu Santo and widely circulated by American newspapers. The Office of War Information broadcast it to the troops overseas in a recording done by actor Fredric March. Admiral Nimitz said at the time that it was the best sermon he had ever heard.)

It is not given to us to know the process by which certain of us are chosen for sacrifice while others remain. We can only rest our faith in the infinite wisdom of the Supreme Being who guides our destinies. As I ponder the names of those we honor, it seems to me as if the most worthy among us are selected for separation in this way. These comrades of ours also loved life. Only yesterday their voices were heard among us as they joined in our songs, rejoiced over letters from home. . . . They knew the nature of the risk they took. But they knew also that human progress inevitably entails human sacrifice.

What of the future for those of us who remain? The war is not yet won; the enemy is still strong; there are incontrovertible signs that he realizes he has met his match, but his power has still to be utterly crushed before we can count our job done and our institutions secure. Our course is clear. It is for us at this moment, with the memory of the sacrifices of our brothers still fresh, to dedicate again our hearts, our minds, and our bodies to the great task that lies ahead. The future of America—yes the future condition of all peoples—rests in our hands.

We must go further and dedicate ourselves also to the monumental task of assuring that the peace which follows this holocaust will be a just and equitable and conclusive peace. And beyond lies the mission of making certain that the social order which we bequeath to our sons and daughters is truly based on the four freedoms for which these men died. Any resolution less than this will spell betrayal of the faith which these staunch comrades reposed in us.

APPENDIX SIX

Citation of 2d Raider Battalion for outstanding service
First Marine Division
Fleet Marine Force
c/o Postmaster, San Francisco, California

7 December 1942

Division Circular Number 38a-42
From the operational records of this division it appears that the 2d Raider Battalion, while attached to this division, took the field against the enemy at Aola Bay on 5 November 1942.

For a period of thirty days this battalion, moving through difficult terrain, pursued, harried, and by repeated attacks destroyed an enemy force of equal or greater size and drove the remnants from the area of operations. During this period the battalion, as a whole or by detachments, attacked the enemy whenever and wherever he could be found in a repeated series of carefully planned and well-executed surprise attacks.

In the latter phase of these operations the battalion destroyed the remnant of enemy forces and bases on the upper Lunga River and secured valuable information of the terrain and the enemy line of operations.

In these battles the enemy suffered four hundred killed and the loss of his artillery, weapons, ammunition, and supplies whereas the battalion losses were limited to fifteen [actually sixteen] killed. For the consummate skill displayed in the conduct of operations, for the training, stamina, and fortitude displayed by all members of the battalion and for its commendably aggressive spirit and high morale the Commanding General cites to the 1st Marine Division the Commanding Officer, officers, and men of the 2d Raider Battalion.

/S/ A. A. Vandegrift
Major General, U.S. Marine Corps

APPENDIX SEVEN

(Letter written by Carlson to the Marine commandant, Gen. Archie Vandegrift, in late July 1945, seeking his advice should he run for the U.S. Senate from California.)

Dear General Vandegrift:

You have probably heard the rumors that have been circulating about the possibility that I may become a candidate for the United States Senate on the democratic ticket from California. Until now these have been purely rumors, instigated by third parties without being referred to me for confirmation or denial. However, yesterday I was asked specifically whether or not I would run, and whether, if elected, I would accept. I want you to know the facts of this matter first.

I have not sought the nomination for the Senate, nor would I seek appointment to any elective public office, because I believe that the initiative in such matters should rest with the people. I am a firm believer in the democratic process.

You are probably aware that for many years I have been deeply concerned with our national affairs. When, in 1939, I became convinced that I could be of greater assistance to the nation outside the Marine Corps, I resigned at considerable sacrifice to myself. During the period I was in civilian life I used my savings and the proceeds from lectures and writings to sustain myself, though it seemed to be the popular belief in the Marine Corps that I had a prearranged source of income. From 1937 until his death last April I performed many tasks for our late President, at his request, and without requesting or receiving special favors. This charge I regarded as a duty to the Commander-in-Chief, and I revealed it to no one until he himself revealed it.

I have now been presented with evidence that it is the will of a considerable number of citizens of California, representing all walks of life, that I run for the office of Senator. I have informed these people that I cannot engage in politics while serving as an officer of the Marine Corps on active duty, but that if it is their will that I run for the Senate in 1946 I will request return to the inactive list in time to do so, and that if elected I will serve. I feel that the Senate would provide a broader field of opportunity for service to the nation, especially in the postwar period.

Throughout the years of my identification with the Marine Corps I have been devoted to the Corps. I have, from time to time, made constructive criticisms, conducted experiments designed to improve technique and general efficiency, and suggested new methods for attaining our objectives—always with the object of improving the efficiency and welfare of the Corps. My interest in the welfare of the Corps will continue.

At present I am recuperating from a bone graft operation during which a piece of my shin was placed in my right arm to unite the ulna where it was shattered when I was hit at Saipan. Subsequently, another operation has to be performed on the elbow to repair damage done there too. The doctors estimate that about five months of hospitalization will be required. I am wondering whether you would prefer that I apply for inactive duty at the time my hospitalization is completed, or that I wait until immediately prior to the time of filing for the Senatorial nomination, which is in March 1946. Any comment you desire to make I would appreciate.

Selected Bibliography

Benford, Timothy. *The World War II Quiz & Fact Book,* Vol. II. New York: Harper & Row, 1984.

Berry, Henry. *Semper Fi, Mac.* New York: William Morrow & Co., 1982.

Blair, Clay, Jr. *Silent Victory: The U.S. Sub War Against Japan.* Philadelphia: J. B. Lippincott & Co., 1975.

Blankfort, Michael. *The Big Yankee.* Boston: Little Brown & Co., 1947.

Carlson, Evans F. *Diaries and Notebooks.* Fullerton: California State University Col., 1971.

———— *Twin Stars of China.* New York: Dodd, Mead & Co., 1940.

Frank, Richard B. *Guadalcanal.* New York: Penguin Books, 1990.

Glines, Carroll V. *Doolittle's Tokyo Raiders.* Princeton, N.J.: Van Nostrand, 1964.

———— *Four Came Home.* Princeton, N.J.: Van Nostrand, 1946.

Goodwin, Doris Kearns. *No Ordinary Time.* New York: Simon & Schuster, 1994.

Goralski, Robert. *World War II Almanac.* New York: Bonanza Books, 1981.

Griffin, W.E.B. *Call to Arms.* New York: Berkley Publishing Group, 1987.

Haugland, A. *The AAF Against Japan.* New York: Harper & Bros., 1948.

Hoehling, A. A. *Home Front, U.S.A.* New York: Thomas Y. Crowell Co., 1966.

Hoffman, Jon T. *Once a Legend.* Novato, Cal.: Presidio Press, 1994.

Hoyt, Edwin P. *How They Won the War in the Pacific.* New York: Weybright & Talley, 1970.

———— *Raider Battalion.* Los Angeles: Pinnacle Books, 1980.

Karig, Walter. *Battle Report: Pacific War, Middle Phase.* New York: Rinehart & Co., 1944.

———— *Battle Report: Pearl Harbor to Coral Sea.* New York: Rinehart & Co., 1944.

Kimmel, Husband E. *Admiral Kimmel's Story.* Chicago: Henry Regnery Co., 1955.

Klingamen, W. *1941: Our Lives in a World on the Edge.* New York: Harper & Row, 1988.

Layton, Edwin T. *And I Was There.* New York: William Morrow, 1985.

Mason, Theodore C. *Battleship Sailor.* Annapolis: Naval Institute Press, 1982.

Merillat, Herbert K. *The Island: A History of the First Marine Division on Guadalcanal.* Boston: Houghton Mifflin Co. 1944.

Miller, Russell. *The Commandos.* Alexandria, Va.: Time- Life Books, 1981.

Morison, S. E. *History of U.S. Naval Operations in WW II,* Vol. IV. Boston: Little Brown, 1949.

Morrison, Wilbur H. *Above and Beyond.* New York: St. Martin's Press, 1983.

Peatross, Oscar F. *Bless 'em All.* Irvine, California: ReView Publishing, 1995.

Perkins, Francis. *The Roosevelt I Knew.* New York: Viking Press, 1946.

Potter, E. B. *Nimitz.* Annapolis: U.S. Naval Institute, 1976.

———— *The Great Sea War.* Englewood Cliffs, N.J.: Prentice-Hall, 1960.

Roosevelt, Eleanor. *This I Remember.* New York: Harper & Brothers, 1949.

Roosevelt, James. *Affectionately, FDR.* New York: Harcourt, Brace & Co., 1959.

———— *My Parents: a Differing View.* New York: Playboy Press, 1976.

Roscoe, T. *U.S. Submarine Operations in WW II.* Naval Institute Press, 1949. Annapolis:

Rosenquist, R. G., Martin Sexton, and Robert Buerlein. *Our Kind of War.* Richmond: American Historical Foundation, 1990.

Russ, Martin. *Line of Departure: Tarawa.* Garden City, N.Y.: Doubleday & Co., 1975.

Smith, Bradley F. *The Shadow Warriors.* New York: Basic Books, 1983.

Smith, Holland M., and Percy Finch. *Coral and Brass.* New York: Charles Scribner's Sons, 1948.

Terkel, Studs. *The Good War.* New York: Pantheon Books, 1984.

Thorpe, Elliott R. *East Wind, Rain.* Boston: Gambit Inc., 1969.

Toland, John. *Infamy: Pearl Harbor and Its Aftermath.* Garden City, N.Y.: Doubleday, 1982.

Tully, Grace. *FDR, My Boss.* New York: Charles Scribner's Sons, 1949.

Urwin, Gregory. *Facing Fearful Odds.* Lincoln: University of Nebraska Press, 1997.
Van der Vat, Dan. *The Pacific Campaign.* New York: Simon & Schuster, 1991.
Wheeler, Keith. *War Under the Pacific.* Alexandria, Va.: Time-Life Books, 1980.

Index